BOB VILA'S
GUIDE
TO BUYING YOUR
DREAM HOUSE

BOB VILA'S GUIDE
TO BUYING YOUR
DREAM HOUSE

by Bob Vila

with Carl Oglesby

Research by Nena Groskind

LITTLE, BROWN AND COMPANY
BOSTON   TORONTO   LONDON

FIRST EDITION

Library of Congress Cataloging-in-Publication Data

Vila, Bob.
   [Guide to buying your dream house]
   Bob Vila's guide to buying your dream house/ by Bob Vila with
Carl Oglesby; research by Nena Groskind.
      p.   cm.
   Includes index.
   ISBN 0-316-90291-8
   1. House buying. I. Oglesby, Carl, 1935–   . II. Guide to
buying your dream house. III. Title.
HD1379.V55 1990
643'.12 — dc20   89-8348
                                             CIP

10 9 8 7 6 5 4 3 2 1

RRD-VA
*Published simultaneously in Canada
by Little, Brown & Company (Canada) Limited*

PRINTED IN THE UNITED STATES OF AMERICA

To Chris, Nica, and Zanna, and especially DBDB

Contents

Acknowledgments

The subject of this book was established over lunch with Russell Morash. We developed it together and collaborated on every step of the preparation of the manuscript. While we worked on it, our editor, William Phillips, graduated from mere Senior Editor to Editor in Chief, yet he gave us the benefit from his exalted new position of a close line-by-line edit.

I thank them both.

Carl Oglesby joined this book project (code name: "Dream House") as writer soon after we launched it in the summer of 1986. Quickly he read and interviewed himself into familiarity with real-estate practices and brought often complex material into clear step-by-step prose; and he drafted chapters and revised and polished them with true professionalism.

Nena Groskind joined the team later on when we needed help sorting out the more daunting legal and financial aspects of real-estate transactions, and she lent advice on content throughout the book. She was unflappable even when the schedule was stressful.

I salute them both.

An assortment of bankers, Realtors, attorneys, and homeowners read the manuscript in one draft or another and offered suggestions and corrections. I happily and gratefully acknowledge them here: Kate Armstrong, Glen Aspinwall, Mary Bablitch, Ellen Balber, Jack Callahan, Dan Collins, Ruth Daniels,

Norman Flynn, Anne Gallagher, Bob Katz, Joseph P. Klock, Philip S. Lapatin, Esq., Benny McMahan, Michael McNabb, Dawn Meredith, Esq., Alice Senturia, Jack Sharpe, Kathleen Silver, Robert Silver, Donald Tambini, John S. Thibadeau, Sr., Ed Tyler, and David Williams.

Additional thanks go to Jerome D. Groskind, an attorney, who answered hundreds of legal questions and kept a lawyer's eye on the content; William Sutton, a home inspector, who helped with many of the construction-related questions; and Garen Bresnick, executive vice president of the Home Builders Association of Massachusetts, who also provided a lot of nitty-gritty building details.

Introduction

My father hand-built the house our family lived in. He took care of it with a craftsman's devotion to detail, and I grew up watching him do it and then, later on, helping him out and learning something of his feel for materials and functions and the right way to do a job. Maybe it was inevitable that my search for a career would lead me, at age thirty, with an apprenticeship in journalism and a few years in the Peace Corps behind me, into the home-remodeling business.

I was newly married, and that's the traditional time for settling down. So my wife and I started house hunting, and soon we found ourselves standing on a small street in one of Boston's suburbs, staring at a house that we both knew immediately we had to own.

At that point I was already a housing professional and should have known better than to let my emotions lead me into an actual real-estate transaction. The fact is, though, as I reflect on it, my most exciting and successful housing ventures have involved love at first sight. And that was the case with that first house.

It was white with green trim and had probably been built around 1850, a faded but basically sound Victorian beauty on a full acre of land with a dilapidated carriage house in back. The ad said it needed "work," and that turned out to be rather expensively true. But the location was ideal. It was within walking distance of one of Greater Boston's best shopping areas, and it abutted scores of acres of state-owned woodland. And the asking price was $40,000, a great deal even in terms of the Boston market of 1975.

So, since my wife was equally sold on the house, we told the broker on the spot that we wanted it and wrote out a check for $200 to accompany the offer. Then we sailed off in search of a mortgage.

At first the lender didn't think we were serious. My remodeling business was new, and my wife wasn't working. Our earnings, to put it discreetly, were unimpressive. But my wife had some equity in a house she already owned, and the loan officer was familiar with a rehab project I had done. He liked my work and thought my prospects were OK. So within thirty days of our first look at the house, we signed the papers that made it ours.

I have no doubt whatsoever that if we were in the same relative position today, at the dawn of the 1990s, this little story wouldn't have such a happy ending. First, the $40,000 price tag would probably be closer to a quarter of a million, and the renovations and fix-ups that cost $80,000 in 1975 would add another $200,000 now.

And second, the attitude of the lenders has changed. The loan officer on my first mortgage was professionally skeptical, but he was also sympathetic and willing to push a bit to help us get the loan. If I walked into a bank today with a comparable financial background, I probably wouldn't even be asked to sit down. And if I *did* get to sit down, I'd probably be bewildered and demoralized by what I was shown. There would be sheaves of forms to fill out, many certified verifications to obtain, and a seemingly endless array of types of loans to choose from. Fifteen yeas ago it took me about three minutes to fill out the application for a mortgage; now it could take three days.

The home-buying process has changed a lot from the days when I bought that Victorian. In the old days it wouldn't have occurred to me to ask anyone how to go about buying a house, or to try to find a book of practical advice on the subject. There really wasn't all that much that you needed to know.

But today you need to know a great deal: how to shop for a

home, how to compare values, how to evaluate the physical condition of a house, how to look at condos and co-ops, how to work with real-estate brokers, and, perhaps especially, how to obtain a mortgage.

That's why I set out to write what I intend to be an A-to-Z manual on the art and craft of home buying in America. My aim is to set down in clear and accessible language everything the contemporary home buyer needs and wants to know about home ownership. The book starts with the decision to buy, helping you to determine whether buying a home is right for you. It ends with some basic advice for those who have never owned a home before and aren't sure what happens after they move in. In between, I've tried to anticipate and answer the major questions that today's buyer is likely to face.

The book is written primarily for the house hunter who has never gone through it before, but second- and third-time buyers will also find it useful as a reference. The path to home ownership today is full of twists and turns and obstacles that are much more intimidating than they used to be. Today's buyers can't do anything to make that pathway to ownership any smoother, but they can at least make sure they know where the most dangerous curves and the sharpest pitfalls may occur. That's the only way to find the best route around them to the door of one's dream house.

BOB VILA'S
GUIDE
TO BUYING YOUR
DREAM HOUSE

ONE

Do You Really
Want to Buy a House?

Home ownership is the heart of what we call the American Dream. It stands for many of the things we value about our way of life. It's one way we think about progress, and for a lot of us, it's one of the definitions of success.

And from the depths of the Great Depression of the 1930s right on up to 1980, the progress in this respect was steady. In 1935, home ownership was confined to less than 30 percent of the population. By 1980, very nearly two thirds of the American people (65.8 percent, to be exact) lived in their own home.

But then the steady growth stopped and started falling back. By 1987 the home-ownership rate had declined to 63.4 percent, 2.4 points below the 1980 high.

Why did this happen? The basic reason for the turnaround is simply that home ownership, which was never cheap to begin with, has gotten more and more expensive.

The following facts will bear this out, and I suggest that all prospective buyers think about them carefully. You may find them troubling, as do I. Some readers may even find this a perversely negative way to begin a book about buying a house, but my aim isn't to sell real estate; rather, it's to help prospective buyers find their way through what can seem to be an impenetrable maze of considerations and choices. And if there's one thing my experience in the industry has taught me, in a hundred different ways, it's that buying a house entails extensive and weighty obligations and is not a task for uninformed, unrealistic people. There's nothing to be gained by pretending not to notice the obstacles that many first-time buyers face as they struggle to enter the housing market, or the costs and burdens that go along with owning a home. If reading through this chapter or the book as a whole gives you second thoughts about whether you want to buy a home or whether you're in a position to do so, I'm sure you'll thank me for the time, energy, and money I've helped you save.

On the other hand, if you're a person or part of a couple for whom ownership now makes sense, then a rigorous self-evaluation will bear that out. Realism never hurts for long.

So here's what you've got to ponder as you face the housing market.

Ownership costs are increasing more rapidly than income. In 1970, the median family income in the United States was $9,700 a year, and the median price of a single-family dwelling was about $23,000.

By 1987, though the median family income had risen by almost 100 percent, to $18,934, the median housing price had risen by 366 percent, to $84,300. In some areas of the country the rate of increase has been even greater.

For the record, here's a list of the median prices for homes in the United States' top ten housing markets in 1987, as compiled by the National Association of Realtors. (For those who have been too long away from their arithmetic, the "median"-priced house costs more than one half of all houses sold and less than the other half.)

1.	New York City	$180,000
2.	Boston	$178,000
3.	San Francisco	$176,000
4.	Orange County, CA	$174,000
5.	Hartford	$163,000
6.	Los Angeles	$145,000
7.	San Diego	$131,000
8.	Providence	$127,000

9. Washington, D.C. $122,000
10. West Palm Beach $103,000

Even in the nation's least expensive major market, which in 1987 was Des Moines, Iowa, the median-priced home cost an impressive $52,000. In 1970 you might have bought that same house for about $13,000. Going on twenty years later, you'd have to bring in that whole amount on closing day for a down payment and closing costs.

Steadily larger cash down payments are being demanded. It was primarily high interest rates that kept prospective buyers out of the market in the early 1980s, but as the decade closes, mortgage rates, while still high, are well below the peak of 16 percent that they hit in December 1981. Now it's the size of the required down payment that blocks the path to home ownership for many would-be first-time buyers.

Ten years ago the standard (20 percent) down payment on an average house required about a third of the average annual family income. Today the down payment represents more than half of what the average family earns in a year. In the nation's highest-priced markets along the West and East coasts, that ratio can approach 75 percent.

Monthly Principal and Interest (P&I) payments have soared. In 1970 the monthly mortgage payment on the median-priced ($23,000) house, with 20 percent down, a thirty-year term, and an interest rate of 8.5 percent, would have been $141.49. If you had bought the median-priced house in 1987, again putting up 20 percent as a down payment, your monthly principal and interest payments for a thirty-year mortgage at 10 percent would have been $591.70. That's an increase of 318 percent!

The impact of these rising costs falls most heavily on younger buyers. In 1980, almost two thirds of Americans between the ages of twenty-five and thirty-four owned their own homes. That set a historical record. But by the end of 1987 this proportion had fallen from two thirds to little more than one half.

Mortgage foreclosures are increasing. The number of home-mortgage foreclosures has soared in recent years in some areas of the country, notably in the economically depressed Energy Belt. You read every day about people in Texas and Louisiana and some areas of the Midwest walking away from homes that they can no longer afford, homes that are now worth less than the amount outstanding on the mortgage. That prospect has to be a bit unnerving to anyone thinking about buying a home.

But don't let me discourage you! If I'm not selling real estate, I'm not warning against it, either. I'm simply saying that it's harder to buy a home than it used to be, not that it's impossible. If you're a first-time buyer today, you'll have to look harder, be more creative, and display a greater willingness to compromise than you would have had to twenty or so years ago. The house of your dreams may be beyond your reach, but the dream of home ownership doesn't have to be.

Consider:

Prices vary. Whatever the median prices may be nationally or in major metropolitan areas, and whatever the national press may say about the housing-affordability crisis, the fact remains that *prices vary significantly* from one region to another, from one part of a state to another, and even from one neighborhood to another in any market. So it's important that you look beyond the "average prices" and get to know your own particular market carefully and in detail. Don't be intimidated by the Big Picture. You don't have to live in the Big Picture, just in one particular house. The fact that you can't afford the average-priced house doesn't mean you won't be able to find one that you *can* afford.

It won't get any better. It's easy to understand why many people might be more unnerved than excited by this listing of comparative home prices and by the data on the increasing cost of home ownership, but those rising costs are as much an argument *for* buying a home as they are a reason *not* to.

The real-estate market moves in cycles. Sometimes prices increase sharply, as they have in many areas in the past three or four years. Sometimes the rate of increase is more moderate. Sometimes prices hold steady or even decline, as they have recently in Houston, where the median home price dropped from $78,600 in 1985 to $62,200 in 1987.

But in general, barring severe economic problems on a national scale, there's no reason to anticipate a widespread, dramatic decline in real-estate values. That means that (1) it's not going to be any easier to buy in the future, and (2) as soon as you *do* manage to climb on board the housing train, the tendency of property to appreciate in value will start working for you, helping you to build equity in the home you own.

Renting is no bargain. For every horror story I hear about the cost of buying, there's another about what's happened in the same period to the cost of renting. It's not as if the renter never sees a sudden increase in expenses.

In some markets the problems of renters have been compounded by the conversion of apartments for rent to condominiums for sale, which can make rental units both hard to find and expensive.

If you're trying to decide whether buying a home might be a good move for you, one of the first things you should do is calculate the relative cost to you of renting versus owning your own home. I've included table 1-1, designed by the National Association of Realtors, to help you do that arithmetic.

Table 1-1: Rent-versus-Buy Decision		
	BUY	RENT
Income	$35,000	$35,000
House price	$70,000	—
Down payment	$12,000	—
Mortgage	$58,000	—
Annual rent (excludes heat)	—	$ 5,400
Annual mortgage payments	$ 6,625	—
Annual interest on mortgage (approximately)	$ 6,300	—
Annual real estate taxes	$ 1,200	—
Annual cost before taxes	$ 7,825	$ 5,400
Tax deductions due to house	$ 7,500	—
Income tax (approximation based on tax tables)	$ 3,700	$ 5,665
Tax savings from owning ($5,665 − $3,700 + $100 savings on state taxes)	$ 2,065	—
Annual after-tax cost of housing	$ 5,760	$ 5,400
Additional annual cost to own	$ 360	—

I've also found some interesting data, compiled by Harvard University's Joint Center for Housing Studies, comparing renter's and homeowner's costs on a regional basis.

The national average annual after-tax cost of owning a home in 1986, including mortgage payments, maintenance, utilities, insurance, property taxes, and so on, was $7,720. The average after-tax cost of renting came in a little below that, at $7,449. In the Northeast, average home ownership costs were $10,233, compared to rental costs of $9,863. In the Midwest, the average homeowner paid $6,929 a year, while a renter paid $6,686. In the West, the average cost of home ownership was $8,680, and the cost of renting was $8,375. And in the South, the figures were $6,581 a year for home ownership and $6,350 for renting.

Currently renting seems to have the edge. But it's only a modest edge, and it doesn't exist at all times in all markets. There have been periods in the recent past when the financial incentives have pointed heavily toward ownership over renting.

Another point: this comparison of rental and home-owning costs reflects the impact of the federal tax deduction allowed for home-mortgage interest. But it's equally important to consider the fact that under the existing tax code, mortgage interest is just about the *only* deduction left for most consumers.

Also missing from this equation is the fact that a home has investment value. This is a point that I hesitate to emphasize, since I think there has been a tendency in recent years to concentrate only on the speed with which a home might appreciate and to lose sight of its primary value — not as an investment but as shelter.

While it's true that some home buyers who got into the boom market early saw the value of their homes increase several times over, today's buyers for the most part cannot count on a continuation of that trend. Economists are predicting that home prices will continue to rise, but at somewhere between 5 and 8 percent annually — not the 30 to 35 percent that we've seen in some markets.

A home is still a "good investment" on many levels. But it isn't the equivalent of stocks or bonds. Most people don't pocket the "profit" they realize when they sell a home; they usually need that money as a down payment on another, probably more expensive dwelling. It would be a serious mistake, I think, to buy a home today with the primary aim of selling it in a year or two and making a financial killing. On the other hand, there are few other investments that offer a reasonable assurance of increasing in value faster than the inflation rate — and almost none that provide you with a place to live at the same time. Home ownership makes an important contribution to financial stability. For many of us, the home we own is a big part of our retirement nest egg.

But in the end, the rent-versus-buy comparison can't really be reduced to dollars and cents. For those who want to be homeowners, the desire to own is strong and deep-seated. It motivates them to overcome what may be great financial difficulty in raising the down payment and persuades them to trade a modest rental payment for what can seem to be a gargantuan mortgage note.

If you're living at home with your parents or in a rent-controlled apartment that costs $200 or so a month, and you're investing your money wisely, the argument could be made that you'd be better off not buying a home. But that's not going to keep you out of the housing market if you decide you want to be a homeowner — and it shouldn't.

Conversely, the desire *not* to own a home can overcome equally strong financial incentives *to* buy. The well-paid single individual or the professional couple earning a hefty combined salary very possibly might be better off *financially* with the tax benefits of home ownership. But for either one, the *life-style* benefits of not being tied down to a particular property might simply outweigh the financial logic of ownership.

The message to the potential home buyer, therefore, is that the decision to buy or not to buy should be based on considerations of life-style as well as of finance. What you must ask yourself is not only "Can I afford a home?" but also "Do I really want to be an owner?"

But shouldn't your decision be based on market conditions? This question is particularly troublesome when the market is changing. For example, if home prices appear to be falling, doesn't it make sense to wait until that trend bottoms out so you can be sure of getting the best possible deal? Or does it make more sense to buy now, for fear that the favorable trend might reverse itself and move rapidly in the other direction before you've made your move? Should you buy now or buy later? Rush into the market or hang back? When is the right time to buy?

Stop torturing yourself. This isn't a game of Russian roulette — or at least it shouldn't be. The object, after all, is to buy a house, not to demonstrate to all your friends how perceptive you are about market trends. Most economists don't know where the market is going (they're much better at explaining where it's been), and you're not likely to do any better than them at anticipating the cycles. People who try to outsmart the market are more apt to end up in frustration than in their dream house.

The time to enter the housing market is when you decide you want to buy a home and when you determine you can afford the cost. When you feel drawn to make such a decision and to analyze your personal finances with a view to that end, it will probably be because your financial status is stable, you feel secure in your job, and you've discovered by observation and reflection that you want the style of life that ownership promises.

If interest rates or home prices rise after you buy, you can congratulate yourself on having been smart enough to buy when you did. If rates fall a little, what you would have saved on your monthly payments by waiting won't be enough to make you really regret it. If rates fall a lot, you can always refinance your existing mortgage. (If you have an adjustable-rate loan, your rates may decline automatically.) Whatever happens to interest rates in the future, you'll own your own home. And that's the goal you're trying to achieve.

The question you must face now (and the subject of the next chapter) is, can you afford the cost?

TWO

Prequalification:
How Much Can You Afford?

BASIC TERMS AND CONCEPTS

You bring two things to the market: your buying power and your borrowing power. Together they determine your ability to buy a house.

Your *buying power* is a measure of the maximum amount of money you can afford to pay for a house.

Your *borrowing power* is a measure of the maximum amount of money you can expect a home-mortgage lender to advance you.

The problem is that the amount you figure you can afford to pay for a mortgage may not coincide with the amount a lender will actually agree to lend you. That's because lenders use special rules, known as *underwriting guidelines*, to evaluate your ability to qualify for a mortgage. By "prequalifying" yourself using the same standards that lenders will apply, and then adding onto this the sum that you can put down, you can get a general idea of the price range you can consider before you begin looking at homes.

Before we start talking about *qualifying ratios* and other special concepts, let me explain briefly the key terms that we'll be working with here.

The *monthly mortgage payment* you must make will have four major elements. The lenders' shorthand for these elements is PITI, referring to

1. *Principal:* the money you borrow
2. *Interest:* what the lender charges you for the use of that money
3. *Taxes:* the property taxes you are liable for. These are often collected each month by the lender.
4. *Insurance:* the hazard insurance that lenders will require you to buy (and that you'll need in any case) to protect your property. This category also includes the mortgage insurance you must ordinarily buy if your down payment amounts to less than 20 percent of the home's purchase price.

If you purchase a condo, you must add a fifth category to PITI — namely, the monthly condominium maintenance fee, a portion of which may go toward insurance.* The lender will include the maintenance fee in calculating your monthly housing payment.

The term *secondary market* is important here and will come up again several times in the course of our house-buying narrative. Most lenders today don't hold on to the loans that they write for individuals; rather, they bundle them up and sell them in great lots to any number of institutions and individuals that make up this "secondary" market. The buyers of these great lots of mortgages include insurance companies and pension funds and individual investors and sometimes even other banks. By far the biggest loan purchasers are two quasi-governmental agencies — namely, the Federal National Mortgage Association, known as Fannie Mae, and the Federal Home Loan Mortgage Corporation, known as Freddie Mac. Because these two entities buy the majority of the loans that are sold on the secondary market, they have the most influence in determining the rates lenders charge and the rules they apply in evaluating borrowers.

Since so many lenders sell their loans on the nationwide sec-

---

* Condo policies and what they cover can vary tremendously. Some condo master policies may offer hazard insurance for both common areas and individual units; others will apply to the common areas only, leaving it to unit owners to be sure their own policies have a hazard component.

ondary market, you'll find that the qualifying process for mortgage-loan applicants is fairly standard across the country.

The purpose of the following calculations is to estimate the maximum amount that a lender *operating under secondary-market guidelines* will allow you to allocate for your monthly housing expenses. The method that we'll demonstrate in arriving at this figure conforms, step by step, to standard practice in the mortgage-loan industry.

THE PREQUALIFICATION PROCESS

Table 2-1 summarizes the steps detailed below.

First, total your income from all sources. Make sure you include investment income (from stocks and bonds and so on) as well as your salary. Also include nontaxable income (from any child-support payments you receive, for instance). For the purposes of this example, let's take a married couple with a combined annual income of $52,000. (Note: that figure indicates gross, or pretax, income.)

Table 2-1: Qualifying for a Loan	
1. Total monthly income from all taxable sources:	$4,340
2. Total monthly income from nontaxable sources multiplied by 1.2:	510
3. Total income available:	4,850
4. Maximum allowable for payment of monthly principal, interest, taxes, insurance, and/or condo fees:	1,358
5. Total income available (from line 3):	4,850
6. Maximum allowed for PITI plus condo fees, if applicable, plus all nonhousing monthly debt:	1,746
7. Nonhousing debt payments (e.g., car, credit card, other loans):	400
8. Line 6 minus line 7:	1,346
9. Maximum monthly payment lender will allow for PITI plus condo fees (the lesser of lines 4 and 8):	1,346
10. Estimated property taxes, insurance, and condo fees, if any:	300
11. Maximum allowable for principal and interest alone:	1,046

Dividing that figure by 52 gives us the weekly income, $1,000, and that figure multiplied by 4.34 (the average number of weeks in a month) produces an average monthly income of $4,340.

I'm also assuming that the wife in this couple receives $425 per month in nontaxable child-support payments. Because that money is not taxed, we multiply the amount by 1.2, producing $510 per month. This is added to the $4,340 monthly salary, producing a total monthly income from all sources of $4,850.

The rule of thumb followed by most lenders holds that your monthly housing expenses — that is, PITI plus, if applicable, a condo fee — should not exceed 28 percent of your gross monthly income (sometimes the figure is 25 percent). So if we multiply this couple's monthly income ($4,850) by 28 percent, we come up with $1,358, which is the maximum a lender would allow them to spend for monthly housing costs.

That's only the first of two calculations the lender will perform, however. The second rule of thumb holds that a borrower's monthly housing expenses plus all other regular debt payments — including student, auto, or personal loans with more than ten payments remaining, and revolving charge accounts — should not exceed 33 to 36 percent of gross monthly income (again, the limit can vary).

So we take the gross monthly income calculated above, $4,850, and multiply it by 36 percent to get $1,746. From that amount we subtract any nonhousing-related debt payments. In this example, I've used a figure of $400, but that's for illustration purposes only. That leaves $1,346 as the maximum allowed under the debt-to-income-ratio calculation.

The lender will take the smaller of these two numbers, so the maximum that this couple would be able to spend each month for PITI (principal, interest, taxes, and insurance) payments, plus any condo fee, would be $1,346.

We now want to translate this into a rough estimate of the maximum loan amount that the couple will be able to obtain. We'll have to subtract an estimate of the monthly amount required for hazard insurance, mortgage insurance (if there is any — again, this applies only when the down payment is less than 20 percent), property taxes, and condo fees, if applicable.

I've estimated a combined total of $300 for those payments. This is on the high side, but it's therefore probably safe for just about every market.

The result of this calculation is the maximum amount allowed each month for principal and interest payments only. That's the final calculation on the worksheet (lines 9 through 11), and it shows that the couple in our example will have a maximum of $1,046 a month to spend on principal and interest payments. That is the outside limit that the lender will approve.

Now turn to table 2-2, the amortization table, for the final step in this process, which is to figure out how large a mortgage that sum will buy. Select the appropriate interest rate (check your local newspaper or call a bank in your area to find out what the current rate is), then move your finger to the right until you come to the thirty-year column. (If you want a fifteen-year loan, stop at the fifteen-year column.) The number you see — in this case, 9.53, assuming an interest rate of 11 percent — is the monthly payment required per $1,000 borrowed on a thirty-year loan. Going back to our example, this couple knows it can pay up to $1,046 per month. If we divide that figure by 9.53, we get 109.76, which when multiplied by $1,000 gives a total of $109,760, representing the maximum mortgage amount this couple can afford at 11 percent.

So this couple could afford the principal and interest payments on a mortgage of up to approximately $110,000 at an interest rate no greater than 11 percent. If rates are significantly higher, the maximum loan amount will be lower; if rates are lower, this couple will be able to afford a larger loan.

Before we go any further, let me make a point about these ratios. While lenders do have some discretion in applying them, you'll find that in practice most institutions that sell their loans (or plan to sell them) on the secondary market — that is to say, the majority of lenders today — won't stray very far from these guidelines. So if your calculations suggest that the mortgage loan you need will saddle you with payments totaling 75 percent of your monthly income, you can probably safely conclude that your chances of obtaining that loan are slim to nonexistent. On the other hand, even if your income and debt ratios are well

Table 2-2: Amortization Table
Monthly Payments
on Principal Sum of $1,000

Interest Rate	Term (Years)							
	5	10	15	20	25	30	35	40
6	19.33	11.10	8.44	7.16	6.44	6.00	5.70	5.50
6¼	19.45	11.23	8.57	7.31	6.60	6.16	5.87	5.68
6½	19.57	11.35	8.71	7.46	6.75	6.32	6.04	5.85
6¾	19.68	11.48	8.85	7.60	6.91	6.49	6.21	6.03
7	19.80	11.61	8.99	7.75	7.07	6.65	6.39	6.21
7¼	19.92	11.74	9.13	7.90	7.23	6.82	6.56	6.40
7½	20.04	11.87	9.27	8.06	7.39	6.99	6.74	6.58
7¾	20.16	12.00	9.41	8.21	7.55	7.16	6.92	6.77
8	20.28	12.13	9.56	8.36	7.72	7.34	7.10	6.95
8¼	20.40	12.27	9.70	8.52	7.88	7.51	7.28	7.14
8½	20.52	12.40	9.85	8.68	8.06	7.69	7.47	7.34
8¾	20.64	12.54	10.00	8.84	8.23	7.87	7.66	7.53
9	20.76	12.67	10.15	9.00	8.40	8.05	7.84	7.72
9¼	20.88	12.81	10.30	9.16	8.57	8.23	8.03	7.91
9½	21.01	12.94	10.45	9.33	8.74	8.41	8.22	8.11
9¾	21.13	13.08	10.60	9.49	8.92	8.60	8.41	8.30
10	21.25	13.22	10.75	9.66	9.09	8.78	8.60	8.50
10¼	21.38	13.36	10.90	9.82	9.27	8.97	8.79	8.69
10½	21.50	13.50	11.06	9.99	9.45	9.15	8.99	8.89
10¾	21.62	13.64	11.21	10.16	9.63	9.34	9.18	9.09
11	21.75	13.78	11.37	10.33	9.81	9.53	9.37	9.29
11¼	21.87	13.92	11.53	10.50	9.99	9.72	9.57	9.49
11½	22.00	14.06	11.69	10.67	10.17	9.91	9.77	9.69
11¾	22.12	14.21	11.85	10.84	10.35	10.10	9.96	9.89
12	22.25	14.35	12.01	11.02	10.54	10.29	10.16	10.09
12¼	22.38	14.50	12.17	11.19	10.72	10.48	10.36	10.29
12½	22.50	14.64	12.33	11.37	10.91	10.68	10.56	10.49
12¾	22.63	14.79	12.49	11.54	11.10	10.87	10.76	10.70
13	22.76	14.94	12.66	11.72	11.28	11.07	10.96	10.90
13¼	22.89	15.08	12.82	11.90	11.47	11.26	11.16	11.10
13½	23.01	15.23	12.99	12.08	11.66	11.46	11.36	11.31
13¾	23.14	15.38	13.15	12.26	11.85	11.66	11.56	11.51
14	23.27	15.53	13.32	12.44	12.04	11.85	11.76	11.72
14¼	23.40	15.68	13.49	12.62	12.23	12.05	11.96	11.92
14½	23.53	15.83	13.66	12.80	12.43	12.25	12.17	12.13
14¾	23.66	15.99	13.83	12.99	12.62	12.45	12.37	12.33
15	23.79	16.14	14.00	13.17	12.81	12.65	12.57	12.54
15¼	23.93	16.29	14.17	13.36	13.01	12.85	12.78	12.74
15½	24.06	16.45	14.34	13.54	13.20	13.05	12.98	12.95
15¾	24.19	16.60	14.52	13.73	13.40	13.25	13.19	13.16

Interest Rate	Term (Years)							
	5	10	15	20	25	30	35	40
16	24.32	16.76	14.69	13.92	13.59	13.45	13.39	13.36
16¼	24.46	16.91	14.87	14.11	13.79	13.65	13.59	13.57
16½	24.59	17.07	15.04	14.29	13.99	13.86	13.80	13.77
16¾	24.72	17.23	15.22	14.48	14.18	14.06	14.00	13.98
17	24.86	17.38	15.40	14.67	14.38	14.26	14.21	14.19
17¼	24.99	17.54	15.57	14.86	14.58	14.46	14.42	14.40
17½	25.13	17.70	15.75	15.05	14.78	14.67	14.62	14.60
17¾	25.26	17.86	15.93	15.25	14.98	14.87	14.83	14.81
18	25.40	18.02	16.11	15.44	15.18	15.08	15.03	15.02
18¼	25.53	18.18	16.29	15.63	15.38	15.28	15.24	15.22
18½	25.67	18.35	16.47	15.82	15.58	15.48	15.45	15.43
18¾	25.81	18.51	16.65	16.02	15.78	15.69	15.65	15.64
19	25.95	18.67	16.83	16.21	15.98	15.89	15.86	15.85
19¼	26.08	18.84	17.02	16.41	16.18	16.10	16.07	16.05
19½	26.22	19.00	17.20	16.60	16.39	16.30	16.27	16.26
19¾	26.36	19.17	17.38	16.80	16.59	16.51	16.48	16.47
20	26.50	19.33	17.57	16.99	16.79	16.72	16.69	16.68

within the secondary-market limits, the approval of your loan is not necessarily guaranteed. A poor credit rating or a low property appraisal, for example, can still prevent you from obtaining a mortgage.

The best advice I can give you for going through this prequalification process is this: be realistic about what you can afford and what a lender is likely to approve, but don't give up too easily. If your calculations show that you're over the approvable limit, then maybe paying off some of your bills or increasing the size of your down payment will be enough to push you back into the lender's safety zone.

If these calculations seem too complicated or otherwise forbidding, you can, if you choose, fob them off on a real-estate broker, who will be glad to walk you through the process.

Often the lenders themselves will also be happy to assist you, especially when the market is slow. In fact, many are now offering "prequalification" programs to help you figure your mortgage limits. And some are even offering "preapproval" programs, in which they essentially preapprove a loan of a specified amount *before* you find the home you want to buy.

We'll talk in more detail later about these programs (see chapter 9). The point here is that there's plenty of help available if you need it for this all-important first step of figuring out how much of a house you can afford.

THE DOWN PAYMENT

We've determined that the buyers in our example, a couple, could qualify for a mortgage of $110,000. But in addition to the amount it will allow this couple to borrow, the lender will also require that they invest some money of their own toward the purchase. That amount is called the down payment. Typically it must be at least 5 percent of the purchase price, though many lenders insist on a minimum of 10 percent.

If our buyers add their maximum loan figure to the amount of money they have available for a down payment, they'll have an idea of how much they can afford to pay for a house.

How large a down payment should you make? The bigger your down payment, of course, the less money you have to borrow and the lower your monthly payments. That doesn't mean, however, that you'd necessarily want to pay cash for the house even if you could afford to. Another investment might make better use of your funds, and borrowers in higher tax brackets might find it beneficial to borrow more money rather than less because of the tax deduction allowed for mortgage-interest payments.

Although the average down payment made by home buyers in 1987 was 25 percent, almost one third of all buyers that year put down less than 20 percent. And most interesting, the National Association of Home Builders (which compiled these figures) says that the average down payment made by first-time buyers was closer to 10 percent!

Buyers who put down less than 20 percent, however, are generally required to pay for private mortgage insurance (PMI) — that is, insurance that protects the lender in the event that the borrower defaults on the loan. The added cost of mortgage insurance is another argument in favor of making a larger down payment if you can afford it. The cost varies, depending on the type of loan and the size of the down payment. In 1988, for a thirty-year fixed-rate mortgage with a down payment of between 5 and 10 percent, the Mortgage Guaranty Insurance Company (MGIC), the nation's largest mortgage insurer, required a payment at closing of 1 percent of the mortgage amount plus 0.5 percent of the outstanding balance annually. On a $110,000 loan, that would mean $1,100 paid in advance plus premiums of $550 annually, or about $46 per month.

On an adjustable-rate mortgage of the same amount ($110,000), with the same (5 to 10 percent) down payment, MGIC would require 1.2 percent, or $1,320, at closing, plus an annual premium of 0.55 percent of the outstanding balance — adding up to $605 annually, or $50.42 a month.

The mortgage insurance must remain in place until: (a) you have repaid enough of the principal to reduce the loan-to-value ratio to 80 percent or less; or (b) appreciation has boosted your equity to 20 percent or more of the property value. Some lenders will consider a request to eliminate PMI after a year, if an appraisal shows that the property has appreciated sufficiently and if your repayment record has been spotless. Other lenders won't accept appreciation as a basis for eliminating the mortgage insurance unless the loan has been in place for at least five years. If your lender falls into the latter category, the only way you can remove PMI is by either repaying a large chunk of the outstanding principal balance or making substantial improvements that significantly increase the property's value.

Clearly, the cost of mortgage insurance reduces the amount you'll have available for principal and interest payments. This in effect reduces the size of the loan you can qualify for.

When you're trying to decide how large a down payment you can reasonably make, bear in mind the grim and ugly fact that the mere process of getting your loan application approved will cost you something. These *closing costs*, which I will go into in detail in chapter 15, can easily amount to several thousands of dollars. In addition, most lenders will insist that you keep something in reserve — usually enough to cover at least two months' mortgage payments — after you close the loan. Don't make the mistaken assumption that you can put every penny in your bank account into your down payment.

Armed thus with a realistic idea of what you can afford to pay for a house, you're now ready to begin your search.

THREE

Study the Market

If you could live anywhere and were looking simply for the best house your money could buy, you'd face an embarrassment of riches. A recent article in *Life* magazine made this point very dramatically by supposing that a buyer had $100,000 to spend for a house and then going to different places in the country to see what that sum would buy.

There were, of course, many places where it wouldn't buy much at all, particularly if you wanted to live within almost any metropolitan center, or on the water. But if you could be happy living, for example, in the countryside near Lake Charles, Louisiana, your $100,000 could buy a fully restored 1899 Victorian with three bedrooms, two baths, and more than 2,600 square feet, beautifully placed under weeping willows on a large tract of prime bottomland.

For the same price in Akron, Ohio, you could get a beautifully landscaped thirty-year-old French Normandy house with four bedrooms and two and a half baths in one of the city's lovelier residential neighborhoods.

In St. Paul, on the street where F. Scott Fitzgerald once lived, your $100,000 would buy an 1897 Victorian with more than 3,100 square feet of living space, featuring four bedrooms and three and a half baths.

Or if you wouldn't mind living in your own 2.3-acre patch of Colorado mountain forest, you could move into a three-bedroom log cabin–style house, solidly built in 1926 and fully modernized inside, near the little town of Conifer.

But most of us can't live just anywhere. Among other things, we have to worry about getting to work and back. Some of us have to think about what the school situation is in one place compared to another.

So before you're ready to decide where you're going to buy, you have to make some pretty basic decisions about the kind of house you'd prefer and the kind of neighborhood and environment you want to live in.

GET BASIC

Start with the style of house you'd prefer to live in. Do your tastes run toward a Colonial, a Cape, a ranch, a split-level? Do you like modern architecture, or more classical designs? (See the appendix.) How many rooms do you think you need? What kinds of amenities do you want your house to include? You'll probably have to make some hard choices later, when you face the inevitable clash between what you want and what you can afford. But at this point you're simply making a list of the details that seem most important to you in a house.

One of the major questions you have to answer early on is whether you'd prefer an urban, suburban, or rural location. City life offers access to myriad cultural amenities as well as, in many cases, freedom from dependence on a car for transportation. On the other hand, few city dwellings have large yards (or any at all), and that could be a big problem for people with children or pets. Parking can also be a problem in many urban neighborhoods.

If you have children, how do you feel about raising them in an urban environment? Many people prefer the pace and the ambience of the city. They like the idea of having a child who is "streetwise" at an early age. Others feel children need the open spaces the suburbs and countryside can offer. It's much harder to tell a child to go outside and play if there's no yard, or if you're living on the thirtieth floor of a high-rise condo on a major thoroughfare.

What about schools? If the urban school system is good, or if you can afford (and are willing to consider) a private school, this won't be a concern. But if private school isn't an option, the quality of the public school system will be an important consideration for you in choosing the community you want to live in. And in most areas today, the desire for quality schools still prompts buyers to follow the path of prior generations of home buyers in moving from the city to the suburbs.

You may prefer the suburbs for other reasons: because you want a yard to putter around in; because you like mowing grass, shoveling snow, and enjoying other subtle pleasures of home ownership; because you want a bit more space between you and your neighbors. If you want to live in the suburbs but work somewhere else, you'll have to consider access to transportation. How will the working spouse or spouses or significant other(s) get to work? If you're planning to travel together, do your schedules make that feasible? If one party takes the car, where does that leave the other? Will one person be housebound all day? If so, are there stores and recreational activities nearby?

Whether you're leaning toward the city, the suburbs, or a more rural environment, it's important to consider the demographics of the neighborhood in which you're thinking of making your home. Are there a lot of people around with life-styles similar to yours? Are you going to be the only young working couple in a neighborhood of retirees? Are you going to be the only woman who stays at home with the kids in a neighborhood full of working singles or working couples without children?

People who have children, or are planning soon to have them, are usually happiest living in a neighborhood in which other residents have children too. In recent years some younger people with children who have bought into communities dominated by older residents have discovered that bond issues needed to fund their school systems are consistently voted down by those older residents, who no longer feel any obligation to support the schools.

There are a lot of factors to consider when evaluating what kind of neighborhood is best for you, and you should think carefully about your preferences. But you should also be aware that the primary factor dictating location for most people (at least the first time they buy a house) is cost. The house you can afford may not necessarily be in the town or the neighborhood you most want to live in.

Once you have a general idea of the kind of house you're looking for and the sort of neighborhood you want to live in, you're ready to start reading the classified ads in the major newspapers serving your area. You need to get a sense of which communities meet your geographical and other criteria and which ones have homes for sale at prices you can afford. The ads will also give you a sense of which real-estate brokers are active in the areas you're considering.

If you're happy commuting in a car, find a map and draw a circle with a radius of forty miles around the place where you work. If you're not a happy car commuter, define your area in terms of rail and bus lines. The cities and towns that lie within those boundaries of convenience represent your housing market. Once you know what your market is, you can concentrate your search for desirable and affordable possibilities.

SEE WHAT'S OUT THERE

Your goal isn't necessarily to see all or even most of the houses within your target area, but rather to make sure that you've looked closely at the best examples of your basic options. You don't want to be hit-or-miss about this. Buying a house is a big deal, and the best break you can give yourself is to try to do it right. The need to be careful and thorough may seem obvious, but this is a point that I sense too many first-time buyers ignore.

My strong impression is that most prospective buyers make up their minds too soon about where they're willing to look and what they're willing to consider. In fact, this is the biggest mistake first-time buyers are apt to make. The house they have in mind, their ideal, is often the one they grew up in. They tend to forget that this probably wasn't the house their parents started out in, either. Your dream house is something you work toward; it likely won't be the first house you buy.

It seems to me that the most important characteristic for successful first-time buyers to have is open-mindedness. Be open-minded about where you're willing to live and the kind of dwelling you're willing to live in. The home market isn't an easy place for buyers today. Affordable housing is in short supply; options for first-time buyers are limited, to say the least. So try to take a fresh look at familiar areas and a first look at areas that are altogether new to you. Look for new options in places that you may not have paid attention to before. You may have been living in the same place for a few years and grown accustomed to using certain routes through the city and the countryside. You may assume that you know what's happening in all those places that your routes never lead you to. Take the trouble to check them out.

As a person with a professional interest in houses, I always have an eye on property. Since I travel a lot, I see a broad national range and am aware of how quickly the character or spirit of an area or a neighborhood can change. And yet I'm constantly amazed to rediscover neighborhoods that have altered radically and often vastly for the better in a matter of two or three years. In real estate, your preconceptions can cost you money and happiness, so you should learn to be wary of them.

A certain amount of subjectivity is unavoidable. It's probably all right to eliminate an area because of an indefinable sense that its atmosphere is wrong for you. You're buying into other people when you buy a place to live, and into other vistas beyond your own front yard. You should want the place where you live to feel right in an overall way, not just in some nice particular.

Yet still fresh in my mind is the frustration of Alice, a young mother in northern Ohio, who told me, "My father offered me and Jack an acre of land he's been holding on to in a woods out in Ghent. And Jack says, 'We're not going there, I don't like the people in Ghent, they're too stuffy.' Now, do you know what an acre of land in Ghent is worth today?"

I can sympathize with Jack's need for a community to feel comfortable in, because that's the whole point of owning a home. And he may have had some legitimate feelings about living across the meadow from his in-laws. But this couple's struggle with the question of what felt right and what was acceptable kept them not only from that acre lot but also from two or three other chances that came along. And now the interest rate is less favorable than it was, prices are even higher, and Jack and Alice are having trouble finding anything at all in their price range.

I'm not saying you should take whatever comes your way; just make sure your information about places is current and sound. If you don't have a good reason for crossing a neighborhood off your list, then drive through it again and take a new look. You want to be able to choose from the widest possible selection of houses that you can afford.

Spend a few weekends driving through some of the areas that fall within your circle. Your goal is to form a general impression of the neighborhoods and communities mentioned in the ads and, at the same time, to begin pinpointing more definitely the kind of house you want and the compromises you're willing to make.

This is a good time to begin making a long list of everything that's important to you in a house. You'll need such a list, as well as a clear sense of your priorities, when your financial limitations ultimately force you to make hard choices about what's absolutely essential and what isn't.

It may be on these leisurely drives that you discover that the houses that you think are the most attractive are the ones your spouse wouldn't want if they were free. With luck you'll resolve such differences as you carry out your search, and at some point you'll see something that makes both of you want to stop the car, get out, walk around, and go inside.

While you continue a creative discussion with your spouse, your significant other, or your other self as to which communities and house styles are acceptable, you should also be absorbing information and impressions about the communities you're driving through. Notice the size of the lots and the distance between houses. Is there a downtown area? If so, how does it look? How well kept are the homes? Is there any sign of new construction? Are there kids around? If so, are they raking leaves or throwing stones at passing cars?

READ ALL ABOUT IT

You'll need to get more information than you can pick up just by driving through, of course. You're actually performing a small-scale private demographic study, and you need to do a certain amount of research.

For a general sense of the market, there's no more informative exercise than gathering up three or four months' worth of the Sunday real-estate section of the largest metropolitan daily newspaper in your area and going through all the ads at once. Later we'll consider the fine points of reading the classifieds, but at this point all you want to do is get a general sense of the condition of the market, locally and in the communities you've identified as worth checking out. Do there seem to be a lot of properties for sale? If so, what kinds of houses predominate? Mainly single-family homes, mainly condos, a mix? Do prices seem to be holding steady, or are they moving visibly up or down? Do the same ads appear again and again, or is there a quick turnover?

A good real-estate broker can provide or help you obtain much of the detailed information you'll need. But your search will go far more smoothly if you establish your preferences and priorities *before* you begin working with a broker or start actively looking at houses. A South Florida broker tells me that as few as 5 percent of his prospective buyers have taken any trouble at all to find out what the market is up to in the areas that are of interest to them. Make it your business to be among that 5 percent.

As you peruse the real-estate ads, you should be looking not only for specific information about home prices and sales activity, but also for more general information about economic conditions or development trends that might affect the real-estate market in the areas you're interested in. For example, let's say you see some attractively priced houses advertised, but they're in a neighborhood you wouldn't ordinarily consider because it's badly run down. In studying the real-estate pages, however, you learn that the noisy, ugly elevated tracks of the transit system are going to come down, or that the area has been targeted for a major redevelopment program, virtually assuring that this down-and-out neighborhood is on its way up. If you find out about these plans early enough, you may decide to get into that neighborhood before it's "discovered" and prices begin to soar. In order to get that kind of information, you may want to scan the smaller, community newspapers, since they're likely to cover such local development stories before the major metropolitan dailies do.

Many newspapers' real-estate pages offer regular feature articles profiling suburban towns, and these can also be important sources of basic information about the communities you're interested in. You may also want to establish a clipping file to organize this information and to keep track of the classified ads over a period of time. That's a good way to gauge how long properties are staying on the market and to see whether prices seem to be heading up or down.

Also, in your quest for information, you shouldn't ignore the shoppers — that is, the tabloid-format newspapers that circulate in a much smaller area and are typically distributed free in shopping centers. They can be incredibly valuable aids in your search process, often carrying pictures of the advertised properties, which the dailies don't do.

In addition, cable TV stations in many communities run "home shows" consisting of still shots of available properties along with basic specs. These shows are usually on at odd hours, don't even begin to show everything that's for sale, and don't give you an in-depth tour of the properties they do show. But even if you don't see a house you want to visit, you'll at least get a good glimpse of several homes in different areas and perhaps come up with some ideas about new places to consider.

DECODE THE CLASSIFIEDS

As you study the classified ads and real-estate columns for background information, you'll also be looking for houses that seem particularly interesting as actual prospects. You therefore need to know how to read the ads.

Ads will give you the basic information about a property — its location, its price, and, typically, the number of rooms it has. But the primary aim of any advertisement is to attract attention, not to tell the truth, the whole truth, and nothing but the truth.

I remember one impressive classified that read as follows:

Cape Cod, 2 BR, original, large lot, adjoins conservation land, Belmont, foot of Belmont Hill, $179,000.

It sounded like a great buy. Belmont Hill is one of Boston's more desirable suburban neighborhoods. I rushed right over to see it, and when I arrived there were already four other cars in the driveway. The ad had clearly done what it was supposed to do, which was to bring out the buyers.

And there wasn't a word in it that wasn't true. The ad didn't mention the fact that Belmont Hill has two sides, and that the side this house was on is a floodplain that goes underwater a few times a decade.* The ad also neglected to note that the house was sited on its spacious-sounding half acre in such a way that the front door was about twenty feet from one of Belmont's busiest and most dangerous roads.

I'm not advising that you ignore the classifieds, but you should certainly read them with a critical eye and an understanding of the special language they employ. The following is a guide to some of the most common real-estate code phrases.

convenient to transportation = commuter rail runs through the living room
cozy = very small to tiny
fixer-upper or *handyman's special* = run-down
must sell = Bring your checkbook but keep it in your pocket. Be prepared to ask if the owner is selling because he or she is being transferred or because the house is such a turkey that he or she would do anything to get rid of it.

---

* I must add, however, that it's a sign of the times in the real-estate business that people living in the flood-prone basin formed by the Passaic and Pompton rivers in New Jersey, where flooding did $330 million in damages in 1984, are generally refusing the state's offer to buy them out. According to a report in the *New York Times* of April 23, 1987, "Soaring real-estate prices in the New York metropolitan region have made even a chronically flooded area such as this one too attractive to abandon."

new to market = a new broker will give it a try

original = built a hundred years ago, and no one has done
   anything to repair or improve it since

southern exposure = requires year-round air-conditioning

21-acre paradise, $5,800 = located somewhere north of
   Caribou and accessible only by dogsled

What am I advising about the want ads? Don't jump to conclusions. Before you go racing off to see a home that sounds
perfect in the ad, make a phone call and ask a few more detailed
questions. If the ad says the house is large, your question is,
how large?

So at this point you've decided that you want to buy a house,
you've figured out how much you can pay, and you've defined
and surveyed the areas that are of interest to you.

Now you're ready to start thinking about a broker — most
specifically, do you want to use one?

FOUR

What Do You Want in a Broker?

WHAT A BROKER CAN DO

There are a good many arguments in favor of working with a broker, and very few against it. Buying a house is a lot like setting out on safari: you may be able to find your way through the jungle on your own, but the trip will be much easier if you're accompanied by a guide who's been there before.

A good broker can help you in four ways:

1. A broker can prequalify you and thus help you estimate the price range you can consider.

2. A broker with a thorough knowledge of the local market (and access to the Multiple Listing Service) can introduce you to a broad range of home prospects, allowing you to cover more ground more quickly than you could on your own.

3. A broker can explain financing alternatives and provide current information on interest rates and mortgage products.

4. Some brokers can provide detailed real-estate information on a variety of communities and neighborhoods.

So there's no question that a knowledgeable broker can be a valuable aid in your search for a home.

THE BROKER'S LEGAL ROLE

But there's one thing that buyers should never expect a broker to do for them, and that's represent them. Yes, there are business deals in which the buyer hires an agent; such arrangements are common, for instance, in commercial real-estate transactions. And *buyer's brokers,* who are hired by the buyer and represent the buyer alone, are seen more frequently than they used to be in residential sales. But in most parts of the country they're still the exception rather than the rule. Unless another arrangement is specified, the broker in a real-estate transaction is *legally* the agent of the seller and is *legally* obligated to act in the seller's best interests.

Relationships among the broker, the buyer, and the seller can grow complicated, and they're often misunderstood — by brokers as well as by buyers. So let's look at the broker's situation in some detail.

When a homeowner decides to put his or her home on the market and approaches a real-estate broker for help in selling it, that broker is known as the *listing broker,* and he or she typically assumes responsibility for advertising the house, attracting interested and qualified buyers, and seeing the transaction through.

A prospective home buyer may go to that same broker — the listing broker — to seek help in finding a home to buy. The broker shows the buyer the home he or she has listed, the buyer likes it, and the deal goes through. The agent clearly has performed a service for the buyer, but he or she is still the seller's agent and will receive a commission only from the seller. And this commission will usually depend on the purchase price. The more the buyer pays for the house, the bigger the broker's commission will be.

That situation, at least, is reasonably straightforward. The relationships become murkier when, as is often the case, two brokers are involved. This situation can arise, for example, in the following way. A buyer approaches a broker for help in finding a house. First the buyer is shown all the homes listed for sale by that broker and his or her firm. If the broker both lists and sells a house, he or she keeps the entire commission. But if one broker lists the house and another sells it, then the two of them share the commission, which is paid by the seller. Ob-

viously, brokers prefer to sell all the properties they list themselves, but that isn't always possible.

Let's say our buyer doesn't like or can't afford the homes the
broker has listed. The broker then turns to properties listed by
other brokers. If a deal is struck, the first broker, called the
selling broker in this instance, and the second one, called the
listing broker, share the commission between them.

The selling broker works closely with the buyer but has little
direct contact with the seller, so it's easy to see why many buyers
and even some brokers assume that the selling broker is working
for the buyer. That's not the case, however — at least, not unless
such an arrangement is specified from the outset. The selling
broker in this transaction is legally the subagent of the listing
broker. This makes the selling broker, too, beholden to the seller,
not to the buyer.

There's so much confusion surrounding the question of the
broker's relationship to the principals that nineteen states have
adopted "disclosure" regulations — that is, requirements that
brokers explicitly inform buyers, sometimes in writing, that they
are representing the sellers, not the buyers.*

The disclosure rules that are now in effect in those states vary
widely. The most restrictive standards appear to be those of
California, the only state in which disclosure is required by statute rather than by administrative regulations. Under California
law, a broker can operate as the agent of the buyer, the agent
of the seller, or the agent of both buyer and seller together, but
the type of relationship must be disclosed in writing to both the
buyer and the seller. In some states, including Hawaii, disclosure is required, but it doesn't have to be in writing. And while
Florida requires that the agency be disclosed, there's no requirement that it be explained.

---

* The states with some kind of agency-disclosure rule in effect are California, Colorado,
Florida, Georgia, Hawaii, Indiana, Maine, Massachusetts, Minnesota, Mississippi, Mis-
souri, Nebraska, New Hampshire, New York, Ohio, Pennsylvania, South Carolina, Ver-
mont, Utah, and Washington. Regulations are pending in another ten states — Alabama,
Delaware, Idaho, Iowa, North Dakota, Rhode Island, Texas, and Wisconsin. And "every
state is talking about it," according to Donald Harlan, a Realtor in Denver who chairs
the National Association of Realtors' Communications Committee.

Depending at least in part on the nature of the regulations that affect them, brokers in some states are scrupulous about disclosing their agency, while brokers elsewhere still resent and resist the idea of having to tell buyers outright that their loyalty lies with the seller. As I noted earlier, some areas have seen an increase in the number of buyer's brokers, as a way of addressing the ambiguity.

In fact, under rules adopted by California's Sonoma County Board of Realtors for its Multiple Listing Service, all selling agents represent the buyer and all listing agents represent the seller.

Some believe that this may be the wave of the future. My own feeling is that this trend is neither inevitable nor desirable. The buyer is already paying, at least indirectly, for the selling broker, since the commission is invariably reflected in the purchase price. The buyer also pays for his or her own attorney, if applicable, and typically for the lender's attorney as well. A buyer's broker in most cases would mean simply yet another fee that the poor buyer would have to pay. Housing costs are high enough; we shouldn't be looking for ways to increase them even more, especially if we're not doing anything to improve the process significantly.

The current system, in which brokers represent the seller even as they serve the buyer, works well for sellers and buyers alike. A problem exists only when a buyer or a seller fails to understand the broker's role, and that problem is easily addressed by requiring brokers to disclose their role in the transaction and their relationship to the buyer and the seller.

Buyer's brokers are usually merely unnecessary, but *dual agencies*, in which a broker represents both the buyer and the seller, are even worse. Dual agencies, if undisclosed, are illegal in most jurisdictions. But even if they *are* properly disclosed, I still think they're a bad idea, because the most competent broker with the best intentions in the world is going to be hard-pressed to adequately represent two parties whose interests are as contrary as those of the buyer and the seller of a piece of property. The traditional subagency arrangement can serve both buyers and sellers well, it seems to me, as long as it's fully disclosed and understood.

If the broker is representing the seller, as is still true in most situations, what should the buyer expect from him or her? One thing the buyer should certainly *not* expect is to see the broker negotiate a lower purchase price or anything else that would give the buyer an advantage over the seller.

The broker shouldn't tell you things like, "The buyer is asking two hundred thousand, but I'm sure he'll take less." To do so is to violate his or her fiduciary duty to the seller. Certainly you can benefit from the broker's knowledge of the market, but you should not rely on his or her opinion of a specific property's price. Objectivity is a lot to ask of someone whose commission will depend on what that price turns out to be.

Nor should you rely on the broker as a primary source of information about where to obtain a mortgage. The broker wants to see the deal consummated as quickly as possible, and the lender who will process your loan the fastest may not be the lender offering the lowest rates or the most favorable terms for you. This is not to suggest that brokers are in general incompetent or dishonest — it's just that their interests and your interests are not the same. The true professional will always make sure that the buyer understands that.

TYPES OF LISTING ARRANGEMENTS

In the course of dealing with various brokers and sellers, you may encounter several different kinds of listing agreements, so let me describe them for you now so you'll understand how they work.

The most common type of agreement between a seller and broker is known as the *exclusive right to sell*. The seller agrees to list the property with the broker for a specified period and to pay that broker, the "listing broker," a commission if the house is sold during that period (or within a certain length of time after it expires), no matter who actually makes the sale. That is, the listing broker gets a commission even if the owner ends up selling the home with no broker involvement at all. Most of the homes listed on the Realtors' Multiple Listing Service are under an exclusive right to sell.

In an *exclusive agency* — a listing agreement that is not terribly popular with most brokers — the seller again agrees that only the listing broker is entitled to a commission (which will still be split, of course, with any selling broker). But if the owner sells the home on his or her own while the agreement is in effect, he or she does *not* have to pay the commission.

Even less popular with brokers is the *open listing,* in which the owner lists the house with an unlimited number of brokers, agreeing to pay a commission only to the broker who actually makes the sale.

THE BROKER'S FEE

The broker's fee is typically paid by the seller from the proceeds of the sale. Contrary to popular opinion, the fee is not fixed, either by law or by industry practice. It is subject to negotiation by the broker and the seller. As a practical matter, however, you'll find that the majority of brokers in most areas charge a fee of about 6 to 7 percent. A broker's willingness to negotiate the amount will vary, of course, depending on the area and on market conditions. The tighter the market, the more flexibility brokers will show.

Although the fee is paid by the seller, most sellers start with a bottom-line idea of how much they want to make on their house and then add in the broker's fee on top. This is why many buyers rightly assume that it is they who are actually paying the fee. When market conditions are difficult and home sales particularly slow, though, some brokers will waive a portion of their fee in order to help bring a buyer and a seller together and close a deal that might otherwise fall apart.

FOR SALE BY OWNER

What about buying a home directly from a seller, with no broker (and consequently no brokerage fee) involved?

Certainly it's possible to do that, and there's no reason not to explore "For-Sale-By-Owner" properties (or FSBO's, referred to in the trade as *fizz-bow*'s). The primary advantage is that a seller who doesn't have to pay a brokerage fee will typically reduce the price of his or her home — maybe not by the entire 6 or 7 percent that most brokers seem to charge, but often by enough to make it worth your interest.

So by all means watch out for FSBO opportunities, but don't let that prevent you from working with a broker. If you stumble across a FSBO on your own, you're free to pursue it without any obligation to the broker, regardless of how many homes he or she has shown you or how much time you've spent together.

NO END RUNS

One thing you should *not* do is cooperate with a seller who has listed his or her home with a broker but now wants to deal directly with you in order to avoid paying the broker's fee. It sometimes happens: the broker shows you a house, you express an interest in it, and then the owner takes you aside or contacts you later and suggests that you wait a while, then make the deal on your own, cutting out the broker and the broker's commission. And sometimes buyers themselves seize upon the temptations of the end run and propose it to sellers.

Either way, it's not a good idea. For one thing, a court might view it as an attempt to defraud the broker. For another thing, you'll find that most listing agreements between brokers and sellers specify that the commission is due in any case if the home is sold within a specified period after the listing has expired — no matter *who* sells it — if the buyer saw the property during the listing period. So even if the ethics don't bother you, the legal implications should.

HOW BROKERS ARE LICENSED

If you do decide to use a broker, the next big question is, how do you find someone who is knowledgeable, reputable, and compatible?

The first thing you should know is that real-estate brokers and salespeople (who typically have less experience than brokers and must be supervised by them) are licensed by the state in which they operate. Licensing requirements vary dramatically from one jurisdiction to another, however. One of the more demanding states is Delaware, which requires salespeople to have a minimum of ninety-three hours of course work in order to obtain a license; to get a broker's license there, one must have five years of experience as a sales agent and at least thirty home sales. In Arizona, sales agents must complete forty-five hours of course work in real-estate principles; brokers there need an additional ninety hours in specialized real-estate courses and must have three years of experience. Louisiana demands ninety hours of course work for a sales license and 150 hours plus two years of experience for a broker's license.

At the other extreme are states such as California, which requires only three real-estate courses of its sales agents. California brokers must be licensed agents who have acquired at least two years of sales experience within the previous five years. New Hampshire has no educational requirements at all for salespeople and demands only one year of real-estate sales experience for brokers. Rhode Island likewise has no requirements for sales agents, but brokers there must complete ninety hours of course work in real-estate subjects or have one year of experience as sales agents before obtaining a license. In addition to the licensing prerequisites that are in place in most states, thirty-five states require continuing education for salespeople, brokers, or both.

Clearly a license means different things in different jurisdictions. All it really tells you is that the agent has completed whatever educational requirements that particular state imposes before granting a license. It tells you nothing about the agent's knowledge of the market or his or her competence or reliability. To get a sense of that, you really have to ask around. There's no substitute for someone's firsthand experience, so you should just start asking people whether they know any brokers and, if they do, what they know about them. If you want to check out a particular agent more rigorously, you can contact the state

licensing agency and the local Better Business Bureau to find
out whether or not he or she has a record of consumer complaints.

BROKERS AND REALTORS

As you begin your search, you should be aware of the difference
between brokers and Realtors (with a capital *R* or with the Realtor trademark). The Realtor appellation tells you that the broker
is a member of the National Association of Realtors, the major
professional trade association for the real-estate industry. That
affiliation implies at least some degree of professional commitment and suggests that the broker has access to the educational
programs, information, and support services that the trade association supplies in abundance.

One major advantage of dealing with a broker who is a Realtor
as opposed to one who isn't is that Realtors have access to the
Multiple Listing Service offered by their local real-estate board.
The MLS is a bulletin board (computerized, in many areas) of
home sales, through which member brokers cooperate in order
to provide sellers with the widest possible exposure of their property and to give buyers the broadest possible selection of homes
for sale. (In some areas the Multiple Listing Service is owned
privately and is open to non-Realtor members.) According to the
NAR, approximately 70 percent of all home sales nationally are
displayed through the MLS. (In some markets, such as Greater
Boston, that percentage is far lower; in others, such as Dallas,
close to 90 percent of the homes sold go through the MLS.)

As a condition of membership in the NAR, Realtors must
subscribe to the Realtor Code of Ethics, which requires, among
other things, that they treat buyers and sellers fairly. The Realtor
affiliation does not guarantee fair or professional treatment, but
I think it does at least improve the odds.

SHOPPING FOR A BROKER

The only way to find a good broker is to shop for one. You don't
want to hitch your house-hunting wagon to the broker who just

happens to answer the phone the morning you call to ask about an ad. So get referrals from friends, use the classifieds to identify brokers who seem to be active in the areas you're interested in, and then take an afternoon to interview two or three or four who pass your initial screening — that is, who come highly recommended and/or have no history that you can discover of being in trouble.

DETAILS TO BE CONCERNED ABOUT

When you talk to a broker, try to find out the following:

1. How long has he or she been in business?

2. Is the firm well established in the markets you've identified as being of interest to you?

3. Does the firm have a number of listings in your price range?

4. How professional does the broker appear to be? Does he or she ask intelligent questions and really listen to your answers?

5. Can the broker answer basic questions about the tax rates, development trends, school systems, and municipal services in the markets you're considering?

6. Does the broker seem willing to help you find the house you want, or does he or she seem more interested in pushing whatever listings happen to be on hand?

7. Is the broker available during the times that are most convenient for you to look at homes?

8. Does the broker have "exclusive listings" that can be seen by the buyers working with him or her before they are advertised more widely? That is, will using this or that broker give you any particular advantage?

HOW MANY BROKERS SHOULD YOU WORK WITH?

That depends. Unlike the seller, who is often locked into listing the house with just one broker at a time, a buyer is free to approach as many brokers as he or she wants. Certainly, if you're interested in communities that are located a considerable distance from each other, it may make sense for you to rely on a different broker in each of those areas. And if you see a property advertised that the broker you're using hasn't shown you, you should by all means feel free to follow up.

But in most cases I think you'll find that getting involved with more than one broker creates an unnecessary and confusing duplication of effort. Chances are that all the brokers you select will be plugged into the same Multiple Listing Service and so will be trying to show you the same properties. If you find a broker you like who seems to be doing a good job of covering the areas you want to see, there's probably no need to look further.

On the other hand, if you've been driving around with the same broker for three weeks and still haven't seen anything you like, it's probably time to find another agent, one who either has a better selection of homes or is more attuned to your needs.

THE SIZE OF THE BROKER'S FIRM

This really isn't critical. Nor does it matter, usually, whether you deal with an independent agency, one that's affiliated with a national company (such as Coldwell Banker or Merrill Lynch), or a franchise of a national chain (such as Century 21, Realty World, or ERA).

A large firm or a franchise affiliate may be able to offer a broader array of services — access to a mortgage banking subsidiary, for example — but a small firm may know more about the specific community you're interested in. Far more important than the size of the firm, in my view, is whether you're comfortable with and have confidence in the broker you're working with.

WHAT TO AVOID

At their best, good brokers can function a lot like analysts, helping you to read your own mind. As one broker told me, "If I see that the buyers are close to 'yes' but faltering, I'll just ask some questions to zero in on what the problem is. Once that gets to be clear, then maybe I can suggest other ways around it. Is the house too small? Well, how about building a new room over the garage? Is it too dark? How about a skylight?"

That kind of feedback from the broker can be positive and can help you sort through your preferences, set your priorities, and identify the home you want.

There are some brokers, however, who cross the line between guiding you toward a decision that you want to make and pressuring you into a decision that you're not sure of. These are the brokers, naturally, that you want to avoid at all costs.

Steer clear of brokers who:

1. pressure you to buy a property "before someone else grabs it"
2. purport to represent you in the transaction
3. advise you not to consult an attorney
4. are evasive or ignorant when asked to provide detailed information about the property

Remember that *Realtors are required to disclose adverse information on properties they represent.* This is established by the Realtor Code of Ethics and in most areas by state law. How far the broker has to go to discover that adverse information is something of a gray area of the law. But as a general rule, brokers are not permitted to misrepresent the condition of a property or to withhold any vital information they know about it. If a hazardous-waste dump has been discovered in the backyard, for instance, or if the basement becomes an indoor swimming pool whenever it rains, the broker is obligated to tell you.

This doesn't mean that all brokers will be completely forthcoming about problems such as these, but it does mean that you'll usually have some recourse against those who aren't.

IF YOU HAVE A BROKER PROBLEM

In most states you'll find three major avenues open to you if you find yourself at odds with the broker involved in a home sale.

One is to file suit to recover whatever damages you've incurred.

Another is to file a complaint with the state licensing body, which generally has the authority to impose fines and suspend or revoke the agent's license.

The third option is available only if you're dealing with a Realtor, in which case you can complain to the local real-estate board. The board's interdisciplinary committee can't suspend the broker's license, but it can suspend or terminate his or her membership in the Realtor organization. Realtors are required to submit for arbitration by the committee any complaint filed by another broker or by a client — generally speaking, a seller. While arbitration is allowed for buyer complaints, it's not required, except in buyer's-broker situations, where the broker actually represents the buyer.

THE MOST COMMON DISPUTES WITH BROKERS

Most often these center on the return of, or the failure to return, the buyer's deposit when the purchase does not go through. Not far behind on the list of buyer complaints are allegations that the broker misrepresented the property in some fashion, either by lying outright about its condition or by withholding vital information. As I noted earlier, there are ways of pursuing complaints against brokers who are less than honest. The best strategy, though, is to protect yourself from the outset. That means understanding that the broker does not represent you, and behaving accordingly. The broker is required to provide honest information about the property, but you should also make an effort to obtain information on your own. Don't wait for the broker or seller to tell you about problems; ask specifically whether they exist. Have a professional home inspection done (more about that later, in chapter 11). Make your own assessment of market conditions and comparative values — don't rely on the broker's judgment alone.

NEED FOR A LAWYER

Above all, be sure you're represented by an attorney. A home is probably the most important and certainly the most expensive purchase most of us will ever make. There are many opportunities to make mistakes, and some of those mistakes can be costly.

It's silly not to spend the relatively small amount of additional money needed to hire a lawyer when that's the only way to minimize the chances of something going wrong on your end of the deal.

It's true that you may be working with a knowledgeable broker. But as I've pointed out already, the broker in most cases represents the seller. It's also true that you'll be required to pay the fee for the lender's attorney, if there is one. But that attorney will represent the lender's interests, and the lender's interests won't always be the same as yours. Unless you're represented by an attorney of your own, there won't be anyone else involved in this process whose sole responsibility is ensuring that your interests are protected.

Why do you need an attorney if everything is going smoothly? Because a good real-estate attorney should be able to anticipate problems and keep them from developing. It always costs less to avoid trouble than to get out of it.

When should you bring an attorney in? The best time is at the beginning of your negotiations with the seller, before you've signed anything that commits you in any way to the transaction.

The documents you sign and what they mean will be our subject later, in chapter 11. But first, at this point, you're ready to start looking for a house to buy.

FIVE

Narrowing the Search

Everything is subject to change, as you've noticed. Your life changes and so does your dream, and with it your dream house. What you need and desire will be different tomorrow than it is today, and different again the day or the year or the decade after that.

The truth of the matter is that the dream house hardly exists anymore, if by dream house we mean the one most suitable house that you would want to own and live in your whole life long.

Even if you do have a clear and unchanging idea of what your dream house should be like, the chances are good these days that you can't afford it, at least not the first time you buy a house. The trick is to incorporate as many of your priorities as you can afford in this house and then count on appreciation in home values over time to increase your equity and boost you up the housing ladder.

How does this work? Suppose our hypothetical buyers, a couple, start with a sum of $5,000 that they can pay down on a home. Suppose further that they qualify for a mortgage loan of $45,000. This combination of down payment and credit enables them to buy a $50,000 house. After living in this house for five years, they still owe a balance of $42,000 to the lender, but the market value of the house has risen to $92,000. So if they sell it for that amount and pay off their mortgage, they'll have

$50,000 to put down on the next house, which is ten times what they started with five years earlier. If their economic and financial circumstances have improved sufficiently in these five years to support a mortgage loan of $175,000, they can use the $50,000 as a 20 percent down payment and move up to a $225,000 home, or perhaps a $150,000 home with a mortgage of $100,000.

DEFINE YOUR ESSENTIALS

The best way to look at a house you might buy is with a divided mind. With one part, think of everything you want and need. With the other part, be realistic and look for alternatives to the ideal.

There will always be some points on which compromise is either impossible or too painful to be worthwhile. One such point might be the number of bedrooms you require. Another might be a work area, especially if you work at home. You might know that you wouldn't put your family in a condo, and might instead require a detached single-family dwelling. In contrast, you could probably get by without the greenhouse.

So right at the beginning (though obviously you may continue to refine this) you need to make two lists. One is the list of dreams; the other is the list of needs. You'll review each list with every house you see.

DOES STYLE MATTER TO YOU?

You're in better shape, of course, if style doesn't matter to you, since that opens you up to all the possibilities.

But if you know you can't stand Victorian architecture, then clearly you'd be wasting your time by looking at Victorians. If a redbrick row house is your dream, and if the possibility of losing a few weeks to a futile quest doesn't intimidate you, then go ahead and tell the broker, "Redbrick row houses only, please." It doesn't hurt to take a shot at finding the kind of house you really want, but you should probably give yourself a certain time limit and then broaden the search. Compromise may turn out to be essential.

In any event, an awareness of styles is the beginning of an awareness of homes as fabricated objects in natural settings, something you'll need when you get closer to making an offer. So, yes, pause at the outset, even if you might not otherwise have been so inclined, and ask yourself what styles you *like* in houses. To refresh your memory, I've included an appendix of drawings of the most important and common house styles in the United States.

NEW OR OLD?

One of the most significant questions you'll have to address is whether you'd prefer to buy a newer structure or an older one. There are up and down sides to each.

Older homes can offer charming architectural detail and often larger rooms than you'll find in more contemporary styles. On the other hand, those big rooms with high ceilings can cost a lot more to heat. Newer homes are likely to be better insulated and more energy-efficient.

Newer homes also offer the promise — but not the guarantee — of having fewer structural problems in the early years. A newer heating system, at least in theory, is less likely to break down than an older one. A four-year-old roof should last longer and be less prone to leaks than a roof that hasn't been touched in twenty years. On the other hand, a new house is apt to cost more than an older one to begin with; with the savings, you might be able to fix the roof *and* put in the greenhouse. These kinds of trade-offs have to be made in terms of particular houses.

DO YOU HAVE THE SOUL OF A REHABBER?

An older home that is located in an exclusive neighborhood and has been completely renovated is a very different proposition from the "handyman's special" in a marginal part of town.

That handyman's special can have considerable appeal to buyers for whom financing is going to be tight. But for some buyers the promise of affordability may be outweighed by the prospect of endless evenings and weekends devoted to making a ramshackle structure livable. With my background as a renovator, I'm not one to knock the idea of fixing up an old house. But since I do know how much effort can be involved in even simple-seeming repairs, my advice has to contain a note of caution here.

Try to be coldly realistic about what you can do yourself and what you can live with having done by someone else. If you don't know which end of a hammer to prop open a window with, or if sawdust makes you sneeze, or if it would seriously bother you to cook for three weeks off a hot plate set up in "what will one day be the dining room," then you should probably avoid buying a house that requires anything remotely resembling major renovations.

On the other hand, if you're having trouble finding a house you can afford, if you're handy and/or confident of your ability to coexist with carpenters, and if you're more excited by the idea of remaking a house according to your image of it than you are distressed by the idea of actually doing it, then the handyman's special may be just the ticket for you, and you should tell the broker that.

If you take this step, even if the work you're contemplating seems minimal, promise yourself to be as clear as you can about what you're getting into *before* you get into it. This means knowing what work has to be done and having a sound if general idea of what it's going to cost you. Unless you yourself are a professional in the construction business, you should hire a few hours' worth of the services of someone who *is* a pro to come look at your dream house–to–be and estimate how much time and money will be required to make it a reality. You may also need to verify that any changes or additions you're considering are allowed under zoning regulations and other local restrictions. The time to discover that you can't add another story to that two-story house is *before* you buy it.

Being realistic about living with work in progress is important. So is being prepared to have that work take longer, be messier, and cost more than you'd anticipated. Tales abound of two-week renovation projects that remained far from complete two or three or more months after they were begun. The husband and wife who set out, full of enthusiasm and comradeship, to remake the kitchen and add a bath are sometimes barely speaking to each other by the time the rooms are ready to be photographed for *House Beautiful.*

Some friends of mine, for example, bought a great old home and decided to modernize and expand it. They knew in advance that the required work would be extensive, but they had no idea that half a year later they'd still be sleeping in a tent, showering at a nearby athletic club, and using the toilet at a local burger joint. So again, be careful when you consider significant renovations.

TO BUILD OR NOT TO BUILD

In the course of evaluating your options, some of you may find yourselves in a position to consider whether to buy an existing home or to build a new one.

The appeal of building your dream home can be hard to resist. The paint is fresh, the systems are unused and probably covered by warranties, and, most important, *you* decide on the materials to be used, the layout of the rooms, and the size of the closets.

From a cost-efficiency standpoint, however, you stand to get significantly more house for your money by buying a previously owned and occupied house.

These are the key points:

1. Square foot for square foot, an existing house is cheaper than a freshly built new home. In 1987 the median price of new homes nationally was approximately $105,000, while the median price of existing homes was about $87,000.

2. An existing home has the additional advantage of being something of a known quantity. You don't have to guess what the utility costs will be, because the people who are already living there can tell you. If there are structural problems in an occupied house — a leaky roof or a damp basement, for example — you can find out about them before making the deal and moving in. As the first occupant of a new home, you'll be the one to discover all its hidden flaws.

3. Building generally requires undeveloped land, which is

scarce almost everywhere and virtually nonexistent in some of the major markets.

4. Financing a land purchase can be a problem, since in many areas lenders prefer not to get involved in land deals. You may have to buy the lot outright.

5. Managing any kind of building project is a headache. No matter what the project — whether it's rehabbing a kitchen or building a new home from scratch — there always seems to be a force at work that causes every job to take three times as long and to cost twice as much as planned. Finding reliable workers who do quality work can prove to be a challenge, and scheduling and supervising their work even more so. You can hire a general contractor to ride herd, which is expensive, or you can do the supervising yourself, which is vexatious, time-consuming, and usually more difficult than people who aren't in the business typically assume.

6. A house isn't going to be perfect just because it's new. A shoddily built home will mean an endless stream of problems large and small, from a leaky roof to a heating system that breaks down to a stairway that sways. Even in well-constructed homes, settling can cause walls to crack. New systems often have to be debugged, and even small problems can seem worse because you were expecting perfection.

7. Scheduling occupancy is more likely to be a problem with a newly built house than with an existing one. The pressure can get intense when you know you have to be out of your current apartment by an impending date and the contractors are still putting up staging and waiting for materials.

Building a new home can also be a brilliant solution. You may have a special shot at a choice piece of land. You may be living in a region where builders are desperate for work. You may be in a position in which financial factors are not constraining. If so, good luck and God speed.

But if you're among the almost 90 percent of new homeowners who buy existing homes, then let's move on to the business of sizing up houses that are already standing.

FROM THE OUTSIDE IN

Begin with the home's *surroundings*. You're not just buying the house, you're also buying into a *community and a neighborhood*. What's around the house can be as important as what's inside it. Consider the street on which the home is located, as well as the other streets within six blocks or so on all sides. Do the homes and yards appear to be well cared for? The condition of nearby properties will affect the value of the house you buy. If the houses around yours are in poor repair, you should be concerned about what's happening in the neighborhood. Maybe it's a down-and-out area that's on its way back up; on the other hand, it may be heading down. Make sure you know which way the trends are moving.

What kind of area is it in? Is it exclusively residential, or are there commercial uses as well? How much space is there between houses? What amenities — shopping, movies, transportation, parks, schools, churches, and so on — are close by? Are there any other developments planned for the area? If one of the things you like is the open space nearby, see if you can find out who owns the land and whether it's likely to stay open. This is the time to discover that a developer plans to build a 200-home subdivision across the road, or that the state has selected the nice field at the foot of the hill as the site of its new waste-treatment facility.

All of these questions about the neighborhood are of concern to you not only as a prospective buyer, which you are today, but as a prospective seller, which you may be in the future. Don't say about potential problems, "I guess we could live with them," without also asking, "But what about other people — the ones we might want to sell to later on?"

So if you're interested in a neighborhood, find out as much as you can about it. A real-estate broker should be able to provide basic information about market trends, development plans, and the like. But count on doing some research on your own. Now's a good time to start reading the community newspapers — the supermarket "throwaways" as well as the wider-circulation dailies and weeklies. Grab anything you can find that might give you a better idea of what it would be like to live in the area. This is how you might discover, for example, that a regional shopping center is in the works nearby or, in a less positive vein, that the local schools have lost their accreditation or that local property taxes are going to be revalued for the first time in twenty years (which means they're likely to jump).

Make sure your research on the neighborhood includes the other people living there. Is the area full of two-career families, leaving it practically deserted during the day? That might be a drawback to a new mother who's going to be at home with her child. Families with children typically like to live in areas where there are other children living nearby. It's true that you can't really know how you're going to like a neighborhood until you live there, but you can ask other people how *they* like living there. One very good question to ask some of your prospective neighbors is simply, "If you had it to do over again, would you still buy a house in this area?"

LOOKING AND SEEING

If you're satisfied with what you see in the neighborhood, it's time to look more carefully at the house, starting with the view from outside.

What do you see? A few scrawny bushes in a lawn full of weeds? Or a nicely kept lot around a house framed with flower beds and shrubs? Attractive landscaping always enhances the appeal and the value of a home, but of course no landscaping, regardless of how beautiful, can compensate for very long for a house that's too small or structurally flawed.

The home's site is important, however. One of the first things you should notice is the size of the lot. Do you have a large yard? And do you *want* one? It's nice to have a good deal of space, but remember, the grass has to be mowed, the shrubs have to be clipped, and the trees have to be pruned.

And what about the location of the house? Is it sitting on top of a hill? That may afford a lovely view and a lot of privacy, but it may also make winter driving a bit of a challenge.

Does the house have a driveway or a garage? If not, how do you feel about parking your car on the street?

Privacy is an important consideration in your evaluation of the site of a house. Clearly you should have different expectations for a house in the suburbs or the country than for a town house in the city. But whatever the context, you want the site to provide the sense of privacy and protection that's a part of what makes a house a home.

ORIENTATION OF HOUSE ON PLOT

You're not looking for glaring errors or strokes of genius here. Particularly in urban areas, as you'll find, a house will essentially fill up its lot. But you do want to know whether the bedroom is filled with the glare of headlights from cars turning off an intersecting street. Will traffic noise be a serious problem? It could be in rooms facing a busy thoroughfare. I've already mentioned (in chapter 3) the house that sounded so great in the ad but turned out to be situated on a floodplain, only about twenty feet from heavy traffic. If you moved that same house to a different spot with a curving wall and a line of trees around it, you'd double its value without touching a shingle.

It's important to visit a house you're considering at different times of day to find out which areas are sunny and which are always or much of the time in the shade. It's also not a bad idea to get a feel for the neighborhood at different times, too. Dropping by after eight in the evening may show you a peaceful, well-lit street, or one controlled by neighborhood toughs hanging out on the corner.

VISTAS

Houses are not only for looking at but for watching from. The appealing house is laid out and landscaped to present the inhabitant with attractive views and to minimize eyesores. Many vista problems that might be tiresome to live with can be remedied with relative ease. Fences, walls, hedges, trees, bushes, and artificial hillocks can produce dramatic improvements in the feel of a house and in how it presents itself, but if those are features you're thinking about adding to a house that currently lacks them, naturally you should consider their cost and feasibility.

QUALITY OF SOIL AND VEGETATION

Maybe you'd like to raise a few tomatoes or plant a rosebush in that corner at the far end of the yard. Before you allow yourself to be transported by visions of bright flowers or bountiful harvests, take a look at what, if anything, is growing in that area now. What is the quality of the soil? Is it sandy or rocky, or does it seem rich and fertile? Is the corner you have in mind bathed in sunlight or hidden in the shadows for most of the day?

Ask also how well the grounds suit your life-style. Is the yard large enough for the play area you want for your children? Is it small enough to permit easy maintenance? The flower beds around the house are beautiful, but do you know what it takes to keep them up? Are you ready for that?

The smaller questions such as these will finally bring you closer to the big question, which is, do you like this house enough to offer to buy it? So take careful note of what you like and don't like about the houses you see. You probably won't find a house that has everything you've always wanted, but you *will* find the one house, among all those you see, that comes closest to that ideal.

Be careful about how much weight you attach to any particular fault. If the community and the neighborhood are right, it would be frivolous to reject a house whose chief drawback is that it has only a carport and not the garage that you want. When you walk away from a prospect, it should be because of a critical defect in the house itself.

And the house itself will be our subject in the next three chapters.

SIX

Recognizing the Dream, Part I: The Outside

In this chapter I'll go through a checklist of considerations that I suggest you bear in mind as you evaluate the physical qualities of a house.

This isn't intended as a substitute for the professional home inspection that you should absolutely have performed before you commit yourself to buy (we'll return to the question of professional inspection later, in chapter 12), but you don't have to be or become a construction expert to look at houses with a more educated eye and tell which ones are worth getting serious about and which don't deserve a second glance. At a minimum, you should be able to recognize the difference between a major structural concern and a minor cosmetic problem.

As you look at a house, you should be thinking both of things you'll want to do with it and of things you'll have to do. You should keep that list of additions and repairs clearly in view as you consider what the seller is asking for the house and what you're willing to pay for it.

A house is a big, somewhat complex thing and must be looked at in several ways from several angles. In this chapter we'll basically be looking at the house from the outside. Our considerations will be style, overall impression, the roof, the gutters, the siding, the foundation, structural soundness, and what to look for in houses that have been altered. In chapters 7 and 8 we'll continue the evaluation from inside the house.

STYLE

The first thing to notice about any house you're considering is its style. Is it a Victorian or a contemporary? Is it on one level, or does it have two or more floors?

To me the only really important question you ask yourself about style is whether you like the way the house looks in its particular setting. If only to be able to read the listings, though, you should have a working knowledge of the principal styles you might come across during a typical home search. You'll find the most common types illustrated in the appendix.

The architectural style of a house, however, is no indicator of its material qualities. So if a particular house looks all right to you and suits your basic needs in terms of location, size, and price, it's time to get beyond style and consider a few much more important questions: Is the house structurally sound? Are the systems in good working order? Will the house work for you?

OVERALL IMPRESSION

No advice to the *seller* on *selling* fails to point out that a spruced-up house is easier to sell. Buyers, naturally, overhear this, and some of them therefore grow cynical about appearances.

Don't let yourself be one of these, though, because that's a false sophistication. Give the property a chance to show its best face. You'll look into everything more carefully before making up your mind, so don't resist being impressed by a well-cared-for house or put off by a neglected one. Houses need to be cared for. If an owner loses interest, the house will suffer, and this will turn up as trouble for whoever owns it next.

Walk all around the house and look it up and down. Try to get a sense of its bones and some idea of how its past and present owners have treated it. Ask the broker (if there is one; otherwise, ask the seller directly) about every physical detail that catches your eye, no matter how slight. You want to know when the roof was seen to last, how old the current paint job is, when the chimney last had a sweep. If there's any evidence of alterations, repairs, or additions, determine when and why the work was done. If the work was major, ask whether it was done by professionals. Take a medical history of the house. How long have the present owners had it? What, if anything, have they fixed or added or taken away during that time, and how much money have they spent? Why are they putting it up for sale?

And pay a lot of attention to details. Note the condition of porches, walkways, and stairs. If you're looking at a brick exterior, is the masonry in good condition, or is it in serious need of repair? Repointing bricks is labor-intensive and costly. If the exterior is painted or stained, how does it look? Is the paint faded and peeling? A new paint job can cost several thousands of dollars. New siding can cost around $5,000 if you use aluminum or vinyl, and up to $15,000 if you want cedar shingles or clapboards. You can generally assume an average life of at least fifty years for shingles and clapboards (ten or fifteen years longer if they've been painted or stained). Vinyl and aluminum siding can last well over thirty years.

THE ROOF

Problems with a roof are likely to be among the most disturbing you'll encounter in your search for a house. This is because they can be so expensive to repair. They're not necessarily deal-breakers, but they're almost always serious enough to need the attention of experts.

One home inspector I know tells me that 40 percent of the homes he inspects either need a new roof or will need one within the next year or two. That means that the people who buy those homes are facing bills of at least $3,000 apiece.

How do you know what's up there? You're not going to crawl around on the roof yourself, and chances are you wouldn't be able to tell much even if you did. But you can and should ask the seller and/or the broker some questions. How old is the roof? What is it made of? The material used will give you some idea of the roof's condition. For example, the experts say that asphalt shingles have a life expectancy of fifteen to twenty years, and up to thirty years if they're of double thickness or more. Clay or cement tiles will last for twenty years or longer. Slate shingles will last anywhere from thirty to a hundred years, depending on the quality of the slate. Red cedar shingles are good for about twenty-five years.

Another obvious but important question to ask about the roof is whether it has ever leaked. Has it been repaired? If so, when? What was the problem, and how was it corrected?

Generally you can expect to have more problems with a flat roof than with one that has an adequate slope, or "pitch," simply because water runs off a flat roof less efficiently. As a result, drains are more likely to clog and the roof itself is more apt to suffer from bubbles and ripples. It's very difficult to fabricate a waterproof roof where the pitch is gentle, let alone where it's "flat." Today such roofs are covered with rubberized membranes held down with modern adhesives. They can fail after several years and will need to be replaced periodically. Thin sheets of copper cladding fused with lead solder will do the job, but the roof will still need to be replaced every generation or so. Both alternatives are expensive. In no event can shingles be used on roofs with little or no pitch; they will always result in leaks. Check out all flat roofs to discover problems — you may be surprised at the misery they can cause.

You should be concerned if you find out that an old roof has been maintained by adding more than two successive layers of shingles over the original. Local building codes typically limit the number of layers allowed, so if there is layering, you should be sure it complies with the existing code. One concern about multiple layers is the weight they add; it can be enough to cause structural problems. Covering an existing roof is less expensive than replacing it, but according to the American Society of Home Inspectors (ASHI), a covered roof will last only 65 to 75 percent as long as a replaced roof.

The most obvious symptom of a leaky roof will be water stains on inside walls and ceilings. Anticipate problems — both financial and structural — if you find such signs. In the first place, it's often difficult to pinpoint the source of the leak. And then the repair almost invariably involves more than simply taking off the old shingles and installing new ones; to get an acceptable result, you'll probably have to strip the roof down to its boards.

Finally, the boards themselves are often found to be rotten and in need of replacement.

If there are no water stains on the ceilings inside, by the way, don't assume that the roof must therefore be tight. A brand-new coat of paint could be concealing stains, and a minimum-effort patch-up job may have stopped a problem leak temporarily.

VENTILATING THE ROOF

One way to help protect a roof from structural damage is to make sure that attics or crawl spaces are ventilated properly. An easy way to check the ventilation is simply to put a thermometer in the attic on a warm day when there isn't much wind. If the reading is ten or fifteen degrees higher than the outside temperature, then the air flow isn't all it should be. Improper ventilation is a problem not only because of the excess heat in the summer, which can reduce the life of some roofing materials, but also because of trapped condensation in the winter, which leads to wooden rafters or roof sheathing rotting. Moisture can also decrease the effectiveness of insulation and make roof shingles buckle and blister.

GUTTERS

On older houses, it's not uncommon to find gutters fashioned of wood. If they were correctly installed in the beginning and are adequately maintained every season through the removal of leaves and other blown debris, they should remain perfectly serviceable. But if they aren't cleaned and oiled, they'll clog up and won't be able to carry the water away. The runoff will therefore back up and spill over, leading to a watery basement, and it will also stand in the gutter, causing it to rot. Our "This Old House" team once renovated a magnificent historic house in Newton, Massachusetts, designed by H. H. Richardson, the nineteenth-century architect who designed Boston's well-known Trinity Church. A great architect and a great house, but in the original design the gutters were too small to handle the runoff from the extremely steep roof, and when it rained hard, water would pour over the edge of the roof like a waterfall. Pretty soon the water overwhelmed the porous rubblework foundation, and eventually it did major damage to the sills.

If the gutters seem to be split or if a section of gutter is falling away or missing, then there's a possibility of an ice-dam problem. This is a serious defect and probably means ruined ceilings, walls, and floors. Ice dams are caused when warm air from the building melts the ice that has formed in the clogged gutters. The melted ice soon refreezes, and over time this process can built up a sheet of ice that is several inches thick and extends up the roof from the gutter. As it freezes and melts over and over again, the water can actually infiltrate the roof behind the dam, and the ice can become heavy enough to pull the gutters down. For a typical house at 1990 prices, it can cost from $1,500 to $2,500 to have the gutters replaced.

Heated cables are not the cure for ice dams, and if you find them being used to deal with an icing problem, your antennae for a repair problem in the making should tingle. The best way to control ice dams, I've observed, is to keep the gutters, down-spouts, and underground drains clean.

Worn-out or incorrectly hung gutters can also contribute to roof-leak problems. So can improper or deteriorated "flashing" or sealant around plumbing stacks, chimneys, skylights, dormers, and anything else that projects through the roof.

THE FOUNDATION

WETNESS

A house becomes a part of its world, but if it is to be an effective house, providing shelter on livable terms, then it has to be as much as possible sealed off from the world, especially from that part of the world which is wet. The earth shares in the general wetness of things, so anything resting on the earth will get wet. Anything porous will get wet inside. And wherever water goes, and especially where water and air meet, tiny living things that eat, excrete, die, and rot also go, producing in those processes the kinds of chemicals that break up the fibers that give wood its toughness. This is why the wooden-framed house has to be lifted up from the earth.

The earliest houses in America were built on heavy logs that rested directly on the earth. No doubt these logs served well enough for the immediate purpose of giving the builder a stable base upon which to construct the frame, but such buildings did not age well. These sills soon rotted away, and then all sorts of terminal problems arose. The floorboards bent and warped, the sides buckled, the bugs and the wet got in, and the house was done for.

You might think that this lesson, once learned, wouldn't have to be learned again. But what often happens is that a porch or a deck gets added to a building sometime in its lifetime, and then a later owner needs the porch for year-round living space and quickly converts it by putting up walls without doing anything to improve the simple foundation. So in time the new room settles, and when it does, it springs leaks, just like the early American house set on logs. With the leaks come water and the outside world, and soon the unhappy owner begins looking for another place to live.

This should be an old-fashioned problem gradually fading away along with the older houses themselves, but the advent of so-called pressure-treated lumber has tended to encourage people to once again take a chance with building on a foundation of wood alone. Pressure treatment essentially involves the use of high pressure to permeate a piece of lumber with water-repellent chemicals. The wood is thus protected against both rot and dry rot for a period of thirty to forty years. This technique has provided an effective means of dealing with some basic problems in house carpentry, but it was never intended to eliminate the need for proper stone or concrete foundations. So be suspicious and cautious when you see a part of the house resting directly on the earth. It may not be a deal-breaker, but you had better count on correcting the condition sooner or later. If there is wood-to-earth construction, at the very least you want to see that the interface area (the point where house and ground meet) is well drained and that the lumber has been pressure-treated.

Certain kinds of structures can be quite desirable and can at the same time cry out for extremely close examination. Homes that have been fashioned out of old barns, for example, can offer both great attractions and great problems. One gentleman farmer I know in Ohio very cleverly converted a former 200-square-foot chicken coop into a most comfortable year-round writer's lodge (as he calls it) with full facilities, but he was able to accomplish this only because it had been built well to begin with, on a solid, well-drained foundation, and the basic structure was sound and in good physical shape.

You see similar cases in formerly quaint but today sorely overcrowded island and coastal communities in the East. On Nantucket Island, for example, where a friend of mine lives, residents have hastened spring along every year for generations by setting out in dozens of little boats at low tide, during late winter, to work the bottom in search of the delicious bivalves known locally as bay scallops. Shucking these creatures is a messy business, so local families copied one another in building, out in back of the main house, simple shacks made of whatever pieces were to hand. Generally painted all white inside and in-variably clad in used eastern white cedar shingles, the shacks each contained one bare hanging light bulb and a hose for wash-ing the place down.

Never did their builders imagine that their shucking shacks would later be given adornment and put up not only for rent but, where the size of the plot permitted, for sale as a place to own and live in. It is possible, as I have seen many times, to live quite comfortably and well in a small, unlikely space, and I am as susceptible as the next person to the charms of houses that seem not so much constructed as organically created. I have even seen one of these Nantucket sheds finished out with a soaking tub and gold-plated fixtures.

But these are also apt to be the most difficult kinds of houses you'll encounter, and they can be too appealing for your own good. They might come with a great piece of land; just remember to make sure that the magical barn or country cottage on that land has a solid foundation underneath it, one capable of keeping the wooden parts dry and relatively motionless.

Today's houses are usually built on reinforced concrete, one of the strongest and most stable materials known. If they are properly installed on the right kind of footings, concrete cellar walls will last forever.

You rarely see this type of construction before 1950, however. Much more common in homes built in the first half of the century are concrete-block foundations. They're not as strong as reinforced concrete, and not nearly so impervious to water. Furthermore, the joints between the blocks are made of mortar, a lime-based material that is prone to leaking. Because of this, a concrete-block wall needs good drainage on the outside of the building in order to carry away the groundwater. Otherwise, leaky cellar walls can become an insuperable problem.

Another common building material used for foundations in older homes is simply fieldstone set in mortar. "Field" means just that, rocks collected from nearby fields or perhaps from the building excavation itself while the house was being built. These stones were never meant to be quarried or cut into uniform building blocks. A mason simply lays the irregular shapes as best he can, filling the joints with gobs of lime mortar. Often such foundations, called rubblestone by some, age badly. They tend to leak and weep through the mortar and cannot be waterproofed. Even good ones will always be a little damp on the inside. Additionally, stone foundations are prone to shifting and settling since there is so little "glue" to hold the pile of rocks together. When water damage or structural failure has occured, most contractors will simply remove the rubblestone walls altogether and replace them with concrete.

Wet basements are bad news and all too common. Home inspectors estimate that at least 70 percent of the homes they see have had water problems of some degree of severity at one time or another.

At any home show, you'll see on display many products dedicated to the wet-basement problem, too many of them intended for application to the inside of the offending wall. Everyone I know who has worked with such products has wound up unhappy with them. The laws of physics do not allow you to hold back hydrostatic pressure amounting to hundreds of pounds per square inch with something you apply with a brush to the inside of the walls or floor. To make the water in a cellar go away, you must correct the basic problem. *You must divert the water away from the foundation.*

One way to do that — and it can seem the easiest — is simply to install a sump pump. You go ahead and let the water in, but then you pump it out. The basement might flood, but then it will dry out again. The problem is that pumps run on electricity, and the same conditions that can flood your basement can also knock out your power supply, as a friend of mine found to his displeasure and considerable expense. After the failed pump had done its damage, he dealt with the problem at its root by digging a trench that started at the lowest point on the perimeter wall, went down a foot deeper than the wall itself, and then led downhill away from the wall. In this drainage trench he installed a line of six-inch tile drainage pipes, then filled it in. Now he has a dry basement. Don't fight water — drain it away. And if you don't feel you have the heart or the resources to do it right the first time, go on to the next house.

CRACKS

Unsettling though they may look, cracks in the foundation are commonplace and need not indicate a serious problem or indeed any problem at all.

Vertical and diagonal cracks are generally innocuous. They are a natural and inevitable result of settling and of the shrinkage of concrete. Cracks of this kind that are no more than a quarter of an inch wide are probably nothing to worry about.

Bigger cracks, of course, may indicate a bigger problem, especially if the house is less than ten years old. If you see such cracks in the foundation of a newer house, be sure to call them to the attention of the professional home inspector and ask if you have cause for concern.

Horizontal cracks indicate a potentially more serious problem. Regard them as a red flag. They could indicate negative grading (i.e., the ground around a house slopes toward it instead of away from it) or poor drainage. Horizontal cracking of the basement wall is something the inspector ought to notice and explain. In bad cases, problems of this kind can require substantial rebuilding of the whole foundation. That's not common, but it happens, and you'd rather it didn't happen to you.

SLABS

Slab foundations are level pads of concrete that are poured on top of the ground underneath the floor of the house. This method is seen from time to time in the Northeast, where it was favored in the post–World War II building boom because it was fast and cheap. It is more common in the South and California, and it is seen everywhere in Florida, where the groundwater is only a few inches below the grass. If there's no frost to worry about, why *not* use a slab? If there's no need for oil storage, no need for a place to put the heater, and no need for occasional plumbing and wiring changes, a slab is all right.

I really wonder about slabs for main house living, though. For one thing, they can crack. For another, many people find them cold and hard to walk on, even though judicious use of carpeting and tile can moderate the problem somewhat. If they're not well insulated, they add to your heating costs and make plumbing additions very difficult. To add a new bathroom off the family room, you have to put a jackhammer to the slab. If you find yourself with a termite problem, it's almost impossible to cure.

CRAWL SPACES

This term indicates a method of building on a concrete foundation that goes into the ground only slightly below the frost line.

The frost line is a point in the ground below which the ground never freezes. As you might guess, the depth of the frost line depends on many variables besides degree of northern latitude, such as groundwater, shade conditions, and composition of the subsoil (e.g., sand never freezes). In the coldest parts of the United States, the frost line is a maximum of about four feet down. Most people excavate at least that deeply to be sure of avoiding the frost heaves that can ruin a house's frame.

The walls of a proper crawl space extend below the local frost line and protrude at least eight inches above the ground line (or mean grade) at its highest point. This is to insure that the wood of the frame and the siding never comes into contact with the ground.

The floor of the crawl space should be covered with a layer of sand for comfort and dryness. The space should be well ventilated; otherwise, airborne moisture from the crawl space will invade the living space above. A polyethylene sheet should be laid across the entire earthen floor of the basement, to absolutely prevent groundwater from seeping in and, incidentally, to make the space bearable to crawl around in.

Whenever you come across any crawl-space type of construction, whether it's under the frame of the house itself or supporting a deck that's external to the house's main structure, you have to take a close look at the footings.

Footings are relatively large, solid concrete pads that bear the weight of the foundation wall proper, which is the wall of concrete or concrete blocks that in turn supports the wooden frame of the house.

At least get a flashlight on them, so that you'll understand where they are relative to interior walls and be able to see how the house works as a structure.

Many foundations constructed since 1950 will rest upon footings, though not all building codes required them.

OVERALL STRUCTURAL SOUNDNESS

It's a mistake to assume that an older house, just because it *is* older, is somehow sturdier than a newer house. True, they don't build them like they used to, but that can mean many things, not all of them negative for the newer structures. Today's home-engineering technology can fulfill a dream of domestic comfort that the greatest builders of the past could hardly imagine. On the other hand, some modern contractors may be more willing to use lesser-quality materials and to take unsound shortcuts with their work than were their Victorian counterparts. The point is that you have to make judgments about soundness on a house-by-house basis.

So what should you look for?

STRUCTURE

Stand outside by each corner of the house in turn and sight down the line where the framework meets the foundation to see if it's straight. If it's an older house that has already seen weather and has had a few years to settle, and there's no apparent sign of structural deformation, then that's a good sign. Foundation problems are hard to conceal, simply because they affect the very shape of the house itself.

Every house has a frame. The frame is usually made of large timbers that support the building and that the foundation, siding, roofing, and sheathing are attached to. Some of the earliest American houses were framed with the post (vertical member) and beam (horizontal member) construction favored for centuries by barn builders.

An alternative method introduced late in the last century is called balloon frame because carpenters who were accustomed to post and beam construction thought of houses built in this way as being held up by nothing but air. A friend of mine lived happily for years in such a house, however, and thousands of balloon-frame houses are still standing despite the fact that they often have insufficient timbering to meet today's building codes.

This method may have achieved its considerable popularity because it enabled carpenters to build a house with less wood than was required for a post and beam frame, and thus to save on construction costs. But there was precious little science to house carpentry when this technique was introduced. If a building stood the test of time, the construction technique was considered proven. Nobody had to worry back then about heavy hot tubs, waterbeds, and the like, and nobody would have thought of removing interior walls from such structures without adding additional support. In any case, many balloon-frame buildings today show signs of insufficient structural support.

How do you tell if your prospective dream house is in this

category? A building with too little wood in it will have bouncy foors. Go to the middle of the room and jump up and down. If the floor moves appreciably, chances are that either a wall is missing underneath it or the joists are undersized.

Another tip-off will be window and door openings that are out of square; if the building is sagging, windows and doors won't close properly. The most obvious symptom of weak structure is often the ridge of the roof. It should be perfectly straight; if it isn't, make sure to have the inspector (see chapter 11) find the cause.

A third construction method is the platform or "Western frame" method, in which a deck is built and rests on the foundation. From there up to the second floor, stud walls are built, then another deck is added for the second floor. Another stud wall carries to the roof level, and then the roof rafters are added. Most homes built today use this method, which results in a good strong frame. Houses built this way are also the easiest to modify after the fact.

What do you do if a house you're interested in shows signs of structural weakness? Don't walk away from it. You may be surprised to learn that structural problems can often be corrected in straightforward, effective, and relatively inexpensive ways. Often the problem can be fixed by simply placing floor jacks where the added support is needed. Bouncy second-story floors are harder to deal with because no one wants floor jacks in their living room, so the added strength has to come by adding thicker and wider timbers alongside the originals. This "sistering" technique works fine as long as there is enough space for the new lumber. Our "This Old House" team once took the roof off a nicely built ranch-style house, added hefty timbers where the old ceiling joists used to be, built a platform or deck structure on those timbers, put stud walls on top, put in a system of trusses to carry the weight of a new roof, and thus successfully transformed a simple ranch into a two-story garrison colonial.

Another common solution for structural weakness, or for those occasions when renovations call for expanded openings in the frame, is to use steel or glue-laminated I-beams. Old-time carpenters employed very little steel in residential building, but its use today is widespread because it makes possible easy solutions for otherwise quite impossible problems.

SILLS

These are the wooden members attached directly to the foundation walls upon which the rest of the building sits.

The sills of today's homes are nearly always built with pressure-treated lumber — that is, lumber treated chemically to repel moisture. This keeps the sills nice and dry, unaffected by the moisture that inevitably migrates up the concrete foundation. But pressure-treated lumber has come into general use only in the last fifteen years, so if you're looking at a house older than that, you should pay special attention to the sills.

The problem is that if sills are too close to the ground or exposed to frequent drenching by improperly installed rain gutters or clogged drainage pipes, they rot. When they rot, they lose their load-bearing ability, compress under the weight of the house, and cause many problems.

The list of symptoms of rotted sills is as long as your arm: sagging floors, windows that won't open or close smoothly because their frames are out of square, porches that have slipped away from horizontal. Carpenters generally love the problems posed by rotted sills and are astonishingly skillful at fixing even the most hopeless-seeming cases, but it's major surgery. Normally the exterior siding will have to be removed and replaced because it too has rotted. Then the sheathing will also need to be removed, exposing the studs. If the damage isn't too severe, the studs can be saved and nailed back to the new sill, but occasionally the rot is so extensive that the studs themselves have to be cut back and bolted to new stud ends.

Besides removing the rot and replacing the sills, studs, sheathing, and siding, the carpenter must also, of course, diagnose and correct the cause of the problem. Was it a leaking roof? Was it the grade around the house? It doesn't make much sense to go to the expense of repairing the sill problem if you're not going to take steps to prevent a recurrence.

THE ALTERED HOUSE

I have learned the hard way to go very slowly in making irreversible decisions about modifying the original materials in houses, or the spaces themselves. It used to be that whenever you bought an old house, the first thing you did was tear down as many interior walls as possible and paint the whole space flat white. But then the energy crisis made heating such spaces more expensive — and perhaps, too, people began to miss the privacy and isolation that are so difficult to find in most settings today.

The trend seems to be changing back to having more rooms with specific purposes. Not long ago, for example, you would have had trouble finding a separate dining room; today's buyers, however, consider it important. Yesterday the home office was a corner of the kitchen or dining room; today, like the day *before* yesterday, it is once again a distinct, dedicated space.

Apart from design considerations, substantial alterations in a house also raise the question of craftsmanship. The important question for you is not whether the remodeler should have done what he did, but whether he did the job well. Did he even know *how* to do it well? Remodelers whose trails I have come across have too often cut short the steps that can't be seen — as though that made them less important.

I remember one house I saw that had been remodeled several different times; someone had even torn out the front yard to make a parking space. One owner was a mason who knew a lot about bricks. He had built a huge hearth in a tiny kitchen and set a lovely wood stove on it. His problem was that he hadn't bothered to leave enough room between the stove and the door, so that while the stove was cranking, the door was blistering. It appeared to have been the same do-it-yourselfer who put a bathroom in off the kitchen without bothering to install a plumbing vent — the safety valve that carries away sewer gases.

Another owner destroyed his perfectly reasonable dining room by covering its walls and ceiling with an imitation stucco product that was wholly at odds with the atmosphere of the home. It was like iron to take off. Another owner-artisan decided that the upstairs screened-in porch would make a swell bedroom, so he closed it in without bothering to notice that the room hung on simple posts resting on stone piers. Within two years it had slipped away from the house, and major work was needed to make it right.

Beware the house that has had too much creativity lavished upon it, and not enough consideration and craftsmanship. If you have the soul of a remodeler yourself, hold out for an original.

SEVEN

Recognizing the Dream, Part II: The Inside

In this chapter we'll scrutinize the candidate dream house from the inside, evaluating its floor plan, its kitchen and bathrooms, its walls, ceilings, and floors, and a handful of especially significant details.

THE FLOOR PLAN

The first thing to consider when you move inside the house is the number of rooms it has, and whether they are adequate for your needs. Are there enough bedrooms and baths? How are the rooms laid out? Will you be happy if you have to walk through the master bedroom to get to the kitchen? If it's a two-story house, what's upstairs and what's downstairs? Don't underestimate the inconvenience of a two-story house that doesn't have even a half-bathroom downstairs.

Pay careful attention to the size of the rooms, and don't just rely on your general impression of how large they are. Get out your tape measure and write down the actual numbers. This is the time to figure out whether your grand piano will fit in the living room, not when the movers are glaring at you with the thing on their backs.

Also, try to imagine these rooms filled with your furniture, not with that of the people living there. Your Salvation Army surplus may not set off the fireplace and bay window quite as nicely as does the current residents' Danish Modern living-room set.

Another general point about the floor plan: as you go through a house, develop an overall impression of whether its rooms tend to be bright or dark. Bright, airy rooms with lots of windows can be a definite plus, especially if you envision filling them with plants. Darker rooms offer other possibilities — a cozy study, for example, or a well-lit work area. Consider every detail of the house in terms of your life-style and your family's needs for space, privacy, and an appropriate layout.

If the existing space does not seem adequate, then your next question is whether the house has expansion possibilities. An unfinished basement or an attic could become that additional room you have to have. A large lot may give you room to expand to the side or the rear.

If you are considering an unfinished basement or an attic for extra living space, make sure it's dry. That's something you have to ascertain in any case, whether you intend to use it for conversion to a new room or for storage.

Be honest with yourself about the extent to which you can bend your needs to fit the limitations of the house. The house may be charming and well located but wrong for you. If it has only one bedroom and you need two, you cannot learn to be happy with it. Be realistic about what you need, what you can concede, and what you can afford to do. Adding two bathrooms, raising the roof, and digging out the basement might make the house "perfect," but you might be better off waiting for a house that comes closer to meeting your needs without all that work.

If you decide that expanding an existing structure (by building up or out) would be essential before you could live in it, and if you are certain that you can afford the needed renovations, wait one more minute before you sign the contract to buy it. Check the local zoning and building codes to be sure you won't run afoul of *setback requirements* — the distances that must be maintained between your house and the street and your house and those next to it. Would you need a "variance" from those rules in order to build an addition? If so, are you positive you could get it? It's not always obvious what changes to your own property you have to get other people's permission for. In many areas neighbors are given a legal right to object to any request for a variance. If you need to do something to the house that might raise a zoning-related issue, you should discuss your plans with your potential new neighbors to see how they'll react. A zoning dispute is not the best way to meet your neighbors.

BATHROOMS AND KITCHENS

The most important rooms in any house, as most people come to agree, are the kitchen and the bathrooms. Studies have shown that for most people, a well-designed kitchen with plenty of cabinets and counter space and a bathroom with luxurious appointments can compensate for a great many shortcomings in other departments. Even if you now tend to think of a kitchen as an unnecessary waste of space that might better go toward a studio, look carefully at what it offers. Is it large enough to put in a table with a few chairs? Is there good work space that's conveniently located relative to the stove, the refrigerator, the pantry?

What about the appliances, built in or otherwise? How old are they? Do they work? Are any of them still under warranty? Is the owner planning to take any of them out? Is the lighting what you need?

Check the bathrooms with equal care. Are the fixtures in good condition? Are there showers and bathtubs, or only showers? Does it matter to you?

The source of heat in the bathroom is not a trivial matter. Some people may like the idea of stepping out of a hot shower into a cold bathroom in the dead of winter, but if you're like me, you'll want to find out how well heated the bathroom is.

Never fail to check the water pressure at every tap. If this is a house you're beginning to think seriously about, turn on all the taps, upstairs and downstairs, and let them all run at once. Make sure the pressure remains strong at each of them. Check under the sinks in the bath and kitchen for leaks and for water stains, evidence of past leakage.

WALLS, CEILINGS, AND FLOORS

In your tour of each dwelling, you'll look at a lot of broad, flat surfaces. You're looking for cracks, stains (an indicator of leaks), and peeling paint.

If you have small children, peeling paint is of medical as well as aesthetic concern because of the danger of lead poisoning (see the final section in this chapter, "Toxic Environments").

If there's wallpaper, is it in good condition? Is it a color and style you can live with, or will you want to get it off the walls as soon as you take possession?

If there's wall-to-wall carpeting, can you stand it? Will it last a while, or does it really need immediate replacing?

If there are area rugs, look under them to check the condition of the floors. Look behind paintings as well, to see if they're covering holes or water stains. I know that doesn't seem terribly polite, but you're not trying to win a popularity contest; you're trying to find out as much as possible about the home you're considering investing a lot of money in. You should be a lot more concerned about avoiding a costly mistake than about offending the seller. Of course, before yanking back the throw rug, you might first ask, "Do you mind?"

DOORS

Nothing in a house gets more action than the windows and doors. If they don't fit exactly as they should, then they'll catch on the jamb or threshold and suffer the consequences. And windows and doors that are made of wood are always changing their shape slightly, getting bigger in the summer and smaller (because drier) in the winter. Carpenters account for this variation in standard construction technique, but if the house has gone out of square, or if the hinges and related hardware are not in good order, then the built-in tolerances won't be adequate.

Unfortunately, most older houses' doors show their age. They're either too drafty or too tight. They typically display the ravages of several attempts to get them to lock better with a variety of bolts, latches, slides, chains, and the like.

One of the worst old front doors I ever saw was on a farmhouse that our "This Old House" team once renovated. The door had nearly lost its threshold through wear. The sidelights, which had once been a nicely multipaned decoration, had been stuffed with cardboard and covered with Plexiglas in a struggle against the oil cartel. The door's glass panels were cracked. The knob hung loosely from the broken lockset. The jamb was splintered. The leavings of several failed attempts to weather-strip the door were evident.

I knew we were in for trouble with this one. You can't just replace what's missing or broken; you often have to restore it, not just for aesthetic reasons but to make the door work right. When a pair of hundred-year-old sidelights has to be replaced, you go to a mill with your specs, prepared to wait a long time and pay a big price.

We sent the door itself off to the stripper, who for a hundred dollars removed all of its many layers of paint. The stripping process is very hard on doors. The whole door is dipped into a solution of caustic chemicals, which is terrific for getting rid of the paint but also makes the door's various joints swell up. Then, after the door is rinsed in another solution and dried under heat, it shrinks, and this causes the joints to separate. Fixing the resulting mess requires glue and clamps.

Once the door is back on its hinges, the next step is to "dutch-man" its holes and splits — the wounds left by previous owners in their various attempts to install locks and chains. To dutch-man is to insert pieces of wood to fill in the voids, the objective being to make the repair invisible once a new coat of paint is applied over the patch. It should be done only by those who understand chisels, knives, and other woodworking tools.

After a great many man-hours, our old door was working just fine, with a new lock, new weather stripping, a new storm door, and, of course, new sidelights. With a new oak threshold and some new molding, the door looked as if had been there forever. And the whole job cost about $1,500.

Moral: entrance doors that don't work cost lots to fix, and there's no walking away from a door that doesn't work.

Patio doors. These have been causing problems since they

were introduced at least fifty years ago. The earliest versions were constructed of aluminum frame and "thermal" glass — that is, two pieces of single-thickness tempered glass, or "lights," with an air space between them. This air space creates a measure of insulation, but the seal can break. When that happens, moisture gets into the air space and condenses, causing streaks that cannot be removed. Another problem is that the aluminum frame is an excellent conductor of cold. Such doors are cold to the touch and can actually frost up on cold nights. Newer patio doors use wooden frames to overcome that problem, as well as an improved glass sandwich to keep out the heat in the summer and the cold in the winter. The down side is that installing such doors is not cheap.

WINDOWS

Windows also get a lot of action. And now more than ever, people care about how well the windows keep out the cold. In most old houses, alas, the windows don't work well at all.

In the old days you kept a window up with a stick or some other prop. This serviceable but primitive method gave way in time to the use of weighted sash cords, which generally worked pretty well (aside from needing to be replaced occasionally). But the cord-and-pulley system requires side pockets or slots in the window frame, and these let the cold air in. If you buy a house with sash cords, you're buying one part of an energy hog. You can find replacement devices for the sash cords, but our experience is that such gadgets cannot hold up the heavy sashes found in many old houses. Probably a better approach from an energy-conservation standpoint is to cover them with aluminum storm and screen windows. This is expensive, and sometimes the aluminum storms look out of place on an older home, but on balance this is usually the best approach to the problem of leaky windows.

Steel casement windows. These are not terribly common, but when they do show up, they're murder. They conduct the cold, condense moisture, rarely close tightly, and are difficult to get replacement parts for. Finding them in a house shouldn't make you turn it down, but they're not an asset, and they'll give you trouble until you finally replace them.

SIGNIFICANT DETAILS

There are many significant details to notice when you go through a house. The following are the basic ones.

Electrical outlets. Note their number and location. Think about where you might need them. Is there an outlet on the wall where you want to put the TV and the stereo? Are there fixtures in place for lighting? Are they adequate? Will you need new lamps?

Closets and storage space. No one ever has enough. If you have to bring in a freestanding closet, it can cost you ten square feet of floor space.

Skylights. These do wonders for the decor and provide a tremendous amount of light. But the sun that streams in will also create heat. This is fine in the winter but can be a disadvantage in the summer. Also, cheap skylights — that is, ones made without insulating glass — tend to leak, not just through faulty sealing or bad casework, which can be remedied fairly easily, but through natural condensation, which cannot. I understand the appeal and the purpose of skylights, but in my experience they're almost always trouble. If a house you're looking at has one, or if you're thinking of installing one, make sure that the skylight unit itself is top-of-the-line equipment.

Fireplaces and heating stoves. These can have a certain charm, but they can also be hazardous. Find out when the chimney was last swept and consider having it inspected to be sure that there are no cracks through which flames might reach a flammable surface. If a stove that burns coal or wood is plugged into the chimney, make sure the connections comply with the local fire-safety code.

Bulkheads and cellar entrances. It can be a real convenience to have access to the cellar from the yard, but exterior cellar doors can cause a lot of problems, too. In older houses they are generally made of wood, so they are heavy to lift and doomed to inevitable rot. Replacement units are available, but in our security-conscious age they are made of steel (and therefore costly), and it's just a matter of luck as to whether one of the standard sizes will fit your door. You might have to replace the cheek walls, too. And in the case of a bulkhead that has been leaking for many years, the water will undoubtedly have penetrated to the stairs below, causing them to rot as well. Finally, because it is nearly impossible to get a good seal between the cellar walls and the bulkhead opening, you had better plan on springing for some kind of field-designed-and-built doorway and door to shut out the cold from the bulkhead.

TOXIC ENVIRONMENTS

Apart from the unique horrors of a Love Canal, there are three particular toxic situations that you must be aware of, two of them involving insulation materials (urea formaldehyde and asbestos) and the third a naturally occurring radioactive gas (radon).

UFFI

Urea formaldehyde, commonly referred to as UFFI and pronounced "*YU*-fee," is one of the most effective insulations available and was widely popular until about ten years ago. Then it was found to be a source of serious respiratory disease and other medical problems in homes in which it had been improperly installed.

For about three years the installation of UFFI was banned by several states and by the Environmental Protection Agency. Then it became clear through evidence that the health threat was posed only by UFFI that had been improperly installed, and the ban was lifted in all states except Massachusetts, where it is still in effect.

Those who have properly installed UFFI insulation say that it has been problem-free. But UFFI's reputation has taken a heavy beating, and that might be of concern to prospective buyers even if the medical question is not. Ban or no ban, the fact is that the presence of UFFI is considered by many consumers to be a serious drawback. Even if you decide you can live with it, you have to consider the impression it may make on some future potential buyer.

My advice is to steer clear of UFFI-insulated houses. You may have no doubt that it was properly installed, that it never caused any problems for the sellers, and that it won't cause any problems for you. But try selling this to a worried prospect five years from now when you're in a hurry to sell this house and buy the next one, the one with the pool room and the den. This is why I suggest that you avoid it altogether.

If you find yourself in a situation where you can't avoid it — if pickings are slim, for instance, or if the house is otherwise perfect — then you should plan to have the UFFI removed and negotiate the purchase price accordingly. UFFI removal is difficult and messy and, according to industry experts, can cost upwards of $20,000.

ASBESTOS

This is another once-popular insulation material now out of favor because of its toxicity. It was used not for wall insulation but to insulate pipes. It is most likely to be found today in houses that are more than forty years old. Intact asbestos is not a hazard, but if it deteriorates, asbestos particles become airborne. Inhaled, they pose a serious threat of lung cancer.

Removing the asbestos is not always the best solution. Sometimes it is less risky and less expensive simply to encase it.

A competent home inspector will usually be able to tell you if asbestos is present, though sometimes it's hidden, and sometimes inspectors are sleepy. An asbestos-removal contractor can tell you whether removal or encasement is your best approach.

If you have an asbestos problem, be sure to contact a reputable and experienced removal company. A bad removal job can create a more serious health risk to occupants than just leaving the stuff alone.

RADON

Odorless, colorless, and radioactive, radon is a gas that is released naturally wherever uranium is present in the soil. The existence of radon itself is not a problem. Normally it is released into the air, where it dissipates without causing harm.

But when radon gets trapped inside dwellings, it becomes a potentially grave threat to health. In extreme cases of radon buildup, exposure can be as dangerous as smoking four packs of cigarettes a day.

High levels of radon were detected about five years ago in houses in New Jersey, Pennsylvania, and New York. More recent testing has revealed high radon concentrations in about twenty other states, indicating that the problem is more serious and more widespread than officials had initially thought. The results of the most recent testing prompted the Environmental Protection Agency to recommend that every house in the country be tested.

The tricky thing about radon is that there is no way to predict from one neighborhood to another, or even from one house to another, where it will be present in unacceptably high concentrations. Publicity about the problem has attracted the attention of homeowners, many of whom are having their homes tested. An increasing number of buyers, meanwhile, are demanding radon tests before they will commit to a purchase. Some real- estate experts predict that the radon test will become as common as the home inspection. My advice is, by all means have the house tested for radon, but don't panic if you find it. Of all the problems you might uncover in a house, the presence of radon is certainly one of the easiest and least expensive to fix.

Initial screening for radon can be accomplished quickly and inexpensively for less than $50 through use of an activated-charcoal radon detector, now commonly available at hardware stores. The canister is hung in the basement, close to the floor, where radon is most likely to enter the house. After an exposure of from three to seven days, the canister is closed up and sent off to a lab for analysis. You should get the results within a couple of weeks, depending on the lab and how busy it is.

If the test shows a radon concentration greater than 20 picocuries per liter, the Environmental Protection Agency recommends that you run a follow-up test to confirm the results and take immediate steps to reduce the concentration.

You need to treat a high radon reading very seriously, but you don't need to run from it. Usually all you need to do to solve the problem completely is improve your ventilation. Sometimes opening a window or two is enough; sometimes a vent and fan must be installed. Your inspector may recommend that you seal any cracks in the basement floor and walls, which can be accomplished for less than $500. A radon expert in Connecticut tells me that it cost less than $2,500 to correct the highest radon level recorded in any house to date.

LEAD PAINT

Any house built before 1940 is a very good bet to contain lead paint. In houses built between 1940 and 1955, the danger is less, though it still exists. After 1955, paint manufacturers finally stopped using a lead base, though the use of lead wasn't actually banned until 1970.

Removal of lead paint is costly. To delead and repaint surfaces accessible to small children in a medium-sized house can cost as much as $6,000. And there is really no alternative to removal, since lead poisoning can devastate a child. Some jurisdictions now require the removal of lead paint from dwellings occupied by children under the age of six.

But you should be concerned about the presence of lead paint even if you don't have young kids, simply because it could become an obstacle when and if you decide to sell.

EIGHT

Recognizing the Dream, Part III: The Major Systems

Now that you've completed your thorough survey of the outside and the inside, it's time to get to the bottom of the house: to the basement, or wherever the working parts of its vital systems are to be found. If you've got an idea that you might find a particular house livable, now you have to determine how well it functions. We're talking about the *infrastucture* of the house — the systems that heat it, cool it, and supply it with water and power.

HEATING AND COOLING SYSTEMS

At a minimum, you want to know what kind of system is in place, how old it is, what condition it's in, and how much it'll cost to operate. Typically, you're not going to select or reject a house because of the type of heating system it has or doesn't have, or because of the size of its hot-water heater. On the other hand, if you're buying this house on a shoestring and would have to declare bankruptcy if you had to replace so much as a fuse within the first six months, then the house with the newer heating system will obviously be more appealing than the house with the furnace that will have to be replaced before next winter.

Generalizations about comparative energy costs and the relative merits of different systems and energy sources are problematic, since so much depends on the climate and the cost of energy where you happen to live. The type of dwelling, the age and kind of the system, and your life-style also have a lot to do with how high or low your energy costs will be. But with those limitations in mind, you can use the following considerations as a guide in weighing the pros and cons of the various systems you may see.

COMPARING SYSTEMS

The first thing you want to know is what kind of heating or cooling system is in place. The ones you are most likely to encounter are the following:

Hydronic heating systems. These transmit heat through hot water or steam. They require a boiler, which can be powered by electricity, natural or propane gas, or oil. The boiler heats the water, which is circulated by a pump via pipes to the radiators or baseboards, through which the heat is distributed to the room. Forced hot water is preferable to steam. Steam systems are not as comfortable to live with. Their heat cannot be zoned, and yet it tends to be uneven throughout a house. They dry the air. They are slow to respond. They are noisy. They are inherently less efficient than systems based on hot-water circulation. You won't find steam heat in many newer homes, but it's still in place in many older dwellings.

Warm-air systems. These can use electricity, gas, or oil as their primary fuel source. The most common type is forced air, which requires either fans or blowers to circulate the warmed air from the furnace throughout the house. Gravity systems, which rely on the tendency of warm air to rise, are also still in use, primarily in older homes. They are far less popular than forced-hot-air systems, however, because they require huge furnaces (which must be located in the middle of the basement) and extensive duct-work and are notoriously inefficient to operate. Another disadvantage of gravity systems is that you cannot operate central air-conditioning through them. Because of all these drawbacks the experts I talk to say that if you have a gravity-hot-air system, you should plan to replace it as soon as possible.

In a *natural-gas* heating system, a heat exchanger transmits heat from the combustion area (the furnace) to the distribution system. A standard warm-air furnace powered by natural gas has an efficiency rating of about 65 to 70 percent. Newer gas furnaces have an efficiency rating of around 78 percent.

(The standard for measuring energy efficiency is called the Annual Fuel Utility Efficiency Rating. It indicates how much heat you receive for every dollar you spend. The other energy measure you should look for on newer equipment is the bright yellow "Energy Guide" that is now required by law, where manufacturers indicate the estimated annual cost of operating the unit.)

Furnaces powered by *oil* are similar to gas furnaces, except that the fuel is delivered by truck, as opposed to being piped automatically into your house from an outside gas line. Oil also doesn't burn as cleanly as gas, and as a result, oil furnaces have to be cleaned regularly to operate at peak efficiency.

Unlike gas and oil systems, *electric* systems involve no combustion and therefore produce no exhaust. But in most areas, electricity is the most costly energy alternative.

You may encounter an electrically powered heat pump, which can provide both heat and air-conditioning. In cold weather, the pump heats the outdoor air and pumps it through the house. In hot weather, it cools the indoor air and moves it outside. The disadvantage of heat pumps — and the reason you will find them primarily in warmer climates — is that at colder temperatures, below 25 to 30 degrees Fahrenheit, the system can't draw enough heat from the outdoor air to provide sufficient heat indoors. Consequently a backup heating system is usually needed.

COMPARING COSTS

The costs of controlling your indoor air temperature by heating and/or cooling should be a major factor in your assessment of a prospective home. After housing payments and food, energy costs are the largest single expense item in most households, absorbing up to 10 percent of the family budget. You want your dream house and its heating system to be as energy-efficient as possible, of course, but you need to know the truth about the prospect before you. It's one of the most important questions you can ask about a house: how much does it cost to operate?

You should request to see the utility bills for at least the two previous years. This is the only way to get a good idea of what the energy costs of a particular house are likely to be.

Utility companies in most areas will provide energy audits at little or no cost, and you might consider obtaining one (or asking the current owner to do so) before you buy.

An energy audit will also suggest improvements that would cut down on energy costs, such as insulating the hot-water pipes or replacing the furnace.

What should you expect to pay for heating and cooling? National generalizations suggest a gross range, but beyond that they are meaningless, if only because the figures cover so many different climates and there can be such wide variation even from house to house in the same neighborhood. But the following stats (compiled by the Energy Information Institute) will give you a sense of what's common across the country and in selected states.

Average annual energy costs per person:
- Highest: $3,362 a year (Alaska)
- Lowest: $1,449 a year (New York)
- National average: $1,847

Average heating-oil prices (in terms of millions of BTU's — British thermal units — delivered):
- Highest: $8.55 (Vermont)
- Lowest: $6.55 (Louisiana)
- National average: $7.56

Average natural-gas prices (per million BTU's):
- Highest: $7.41 (Maine)
- Lowest: $1.19 (Alaska)
- National average: $4.60

Average electricity prices (per million BTU's):
- Highest: $30.96 (Hawaii)
- Lowest: $9.54 (Washington State)
- National average: $19.85

It's also interesting to stack the same sort of data a different way to compare the costs of different heating and cooling systems in different regions. To illustrate the range in a few key markets:

New Mexico (1985 figures, per million BTU's delivered)
- Gas heat: $4.64
- Oil heat: $7.71
- Electric heat: $22.42

Louisiana (1985 figures, per million BTU's delivered)
- Gas heat: $3.08
- Oil heat: $6.55
- Electric: $18.52

Or, to shift to to average yearly costs per household:

Northeast (1984 figures):
- Gas heat: $588
- Oil heat: $734
- Electric heat: $1,443

South (1984 figures)
- Gas heat: $466
- Oil heat: $285
- Electric heat: $1,055

National (1984 figures):
- Gas heat: $537
- Oil heat: $550
- Electric heat: $1,123

Nationally (as of 1984), 55.4 percent of households in the US used natural gas, compared to 16.8 percent using electricity, 14.1 percent using kerosene or fuel oil, and 13.75 percent using other forms of energy. In the Northeast, only 7.5 percent heat with electricity, compared to 44.7 percent using oil or kerosene and 39.2 percent using natural gas. In the North-Central region, natural gas is the choice of 75.8 percent. In the South, 28.7 percent use electricity to heat their homes, and 44.7 use natural gas; only 8.1 percent use oil or kerosene. In the West, 65.3 percent use natural gas, 19.8 percent use electricity, and only 2.7 percent use oil or kerosene. All of which shows you what to expect and proves that you might run into anything.

REPLACEMENT

While you are carefully analyzing how much your energy costs are likely to be, don't forget to ask the most basic question of all about any temperature-control system — namely, does it work? If it's 40 degrees Fahrenheit in the living room when you look at the house in January, it's easy to tell that something is wrong. But in the middle of July, in most places in the United States, a heating problem would not be readily apparent.

The home inspector should test the heating system to be sure it fires up, and should let it run for several hours (even longer on a warm day) to be sure it's operating properly. This is a routine part of the inspection and will probably be conducted as a matter of course by a professional inspector, but it can't hurt you to know that it has to be done. If you don't find a reference to the heating-system test in the inspector's report, ask for an explanation.

Unfortunately, you can't run the same kind of out-of-season test on an air-conditioning system without risking serious damage. If the system can't be tested because you're buying the house in the middle of winter, I'd recommend putting some portion of the purchase money — at least $2,500 — into an escrow account to cover repairs should you discover problems later.

Bear in mind that with heating and cooling systems, bigger is not necessarily better. A system that's too large for the living space it's serving will be inefficient and costly. Find out as much as you can about the age of the system and its maintenance history. An older system that has been well maintained is less of a worry than a newer one that has not been touched since it was installed. But if maintenance is equal, newer systems are generally more efficient, more trouble-free, and more likely still to be covered by warranties.

Don't jump to conclusions about what needs to be replaced and what can be fixed up or lived with. A furnace that doesn't work clearly will have to go, but replacing a less efficient unit with a more efficient one may or may not be something to put at the top of your list of priorities. You'll have to consider the savings you would realize in energy costs, the one-time cost of the change, and how long it would take you to recover your investment.

For example, if you calculate that spending $10,000 on a new heating plant will save you $500 a year, as it well might, consider that it will take twenty years to recover the cost of your initial investment. Especially if you plan to live in the house for only a few years, that may be an unattractive concept. Before considering a massive overhaul of any existing system, make sure first that you have exhausted all the less dramatic remedies and have priced out the options carefully. Adding insulation and practicing good conservation measures require a relatively small investment and can produce huge savings immediately.

INSULATION

Insulation is one of the first things you want to find out about with any house that is exposed to what humans judge to be extremes of heat and cold.

Start by asking, "Is the house insulated?" The answer should be yes. Then the question is, what kind of insulation does the house have, how much, and where is it located — just in the roof or attic, or in the sidewalls as well?

Fiberglass is one of the best kinds of insulation on the market, but others, such as cellulose or foam of various kinds (rigid foam, foam board, and poured-in foam) are all certainly effective.

As I noted in chapter 5, you do *not* want to hear, however, that the house has been insulated with urea formaldehyde (UFFI) or that there is asbestos insulation wrapped around the hot-water pipes. While they are not necessarily deal-breakers, they do represent situations that you'll have to address in your negotiations with the seller.

THE HOT-WATER HEATER

Every home needs one of these, and you want to be sure that yours is large enough to supply your needs. The system should not be overwhelmed if you want to run the dishwasher and take a shower at the same time.

The key is recovery time rather than sheer holding capacity: how long does it take the unit to reheat the water if it starts from empty?

Oil-fired and gas-fired water heaters are quite efficient, and reheat quickly. A thirty-gallon holding tank is therefore usually adequate. An electric heater takes longer to reheat, so it's usually paired with a sixty-gallon tank. If you have a family of twelve, or one teenager, your household needs may exceed the norm.

WATER SERVICE AND SUPPLY

One of the first questions you want to ask about any house is where its water comes from. Is it hooked up to a municipal water and sewer system? Or does it have its own well?

Urban dwellers might have been able to assume, until a few years ago, that any water delivered by the municipal water system was above reproach. This is still largely a valid assumption, but there have been so many alarming instances of serious pollution of the public drinking water in the past several years that it has to be a checklist item for anyone buying a home. It may indeed be a growing problem. It's definitely something you have to look into when you're considering a move to any community.

Ask two additional questions about any house served by a municipal supply: (1) Have there been any recent problems with water quality or supply? And (2) how much do residents pay for water and sewer service? Those costs used to be so small as to be insignificant, but as water-supply systems age and begin to require upgrading and replacement, water and sewer charges in many areas have become an important household expense.

As I write this I'm involved with a project to dig a new well, so water is on my mind these days. In our research we discovered, to our surprise, that more than 50 percent of all homes in America depend on wells for their water. If a house you're looking at is one of these, then you should ask if and when its well has ever run dry, and whether the water has been tested recently for potability. If you're interested enough to consider making an offer, you should have the water tested by a lab to be sure it's safe to drink. A lab test will determine the chemical content of the water, telling you not only whether it's safe but also whether it tends to be hard or soft.

If the house has a well, you'll also want to ascertain whether a lot of salt is used on the street or road in the winter. If it is, then you want to see where the drains are in relation to the water source, in order to make sure that the well isn't likely to become contaminated.

Find out where the septic field is located in relation to the well. What about the locations of any septic fields serving nearby lots? It's absolutely essential that your well not lie in the path of other people's contaminants. That's a particular concern in older subdivisions or areas that were once sparsely developed but have become more crowded in recent years.

For homes built around lakes, you want to be sure the drinking water doesn't come from the lake itself. I know of many lakeside communities that have been coping with serious drinking-water problems in recent years.

Another potential concern with well water, unheard of until recent years but now a full-sized headache for many communities, is the disintegration of old gasoline-storage tanks. This process releases toxic amounts of petroleum products into the watershed and thus into the well water; even a well several hundred yards away from the storage tank can be contaminated. You might want to learn, if you can, whether any areas near your potential dream house were occupied by service stations in years past.

Still another basic fact to determine about a well is its capacity. How much water does it dispense? How quickly? How quickly does it refill? Does its supply vary with the season? The answers will in part depend on the depth of the well and on the size of the reserve tank, as well as on your demand. The experts say that if the well can't supply enough water for two simultaneous showers over a period of fifteen to thirty minutes, or if your demand is likely to exceed that level, then you should probably consider shelling out $200 to $300 for a larger reserve tank. Some home inspectors and water-testing labs can run this water-capacity test for you; otherwise, before you make a final commitment to buy, hire a contractor who specializes in water and septic systems. Make sure your Purchase and Sale agreement specifies that the purchase is contingent upon a satisfactory test of the water supply.

If the house is served by a *septic system* (rather than being connected to the municipal sewage system), then that will also have to be carefully checked. Ask the seller about the age of the septic system. Ask if there have been any problems with it. Before you make a commitment to buy, and regardless of how glowingly the owner describes the system's condition, you should have it checked out by an independent septic contractor, preferably someone recommended by a friend or your attorney rather than by the broker or the seller. Typically, the contractor will pump the system out to see how much waste it contains (if it's full of solid waste, that indicates there may be a problem with the leaching field) and will run a dye test to be sure the system is flowing properly.

You should also ask the seller how frequently the system has been pumped out. Systems vary, but the rule of thumb is that most should be tested every two to five years. Less frequent maintenance leads to a buildup of waste, but more frequent pumping can deplete or destroy the bacteria needed to keep the system running cleanly.

Older houses may have a cesspool and no leaching field, which means the systems will have to be pumped more often. If the cesspool is very old — that is, older than twenty-five or thirty years — it may have to replaced with a new septic system in the not-too-distant future. That operation can cost from $3,000 to $5,000.

Whether your potential dream house is hooked up to the municipal system or to a well and septic system of its own, you want to get a good idea of the condition of the plumbing in the house — how old the pipes are, what they're made of, and whether they comply with current code requirements.

Older pipes in some areas of the country are lined with lead — a potential health concern. Pipes laid many years ago also tend to be narrower, which can be a source of water-pressure problems in the house.

ELECTRICAL SERVICE

In addition to the number and location of the electrical outlets in the house, you also have to check the adequacy of the service. The amount of electricity you'll need will depend largely on the number and type of electrical appliances you have. The standard service in most homes today is 150 amps. Older homes may have only 60 amps or less, and may also have to be rewired. All-electric dwellings, on the other hand, may need 300-amp service to ensure adequate capacity. If a house you're considering looks like a strong candidate for rewiring, don't let it scare you too much. It's an important expense, but not necessarily a huge one — generally less than $2,000. Houses owned by do-it-yourselfers may already have been rewired, in some fashion, in the past.

Your home inspector will tell you if the building fails to meet code requirements or is in any way unsafe. The inspector can also tell you the age of the wiring and its general condition. You should remember to ask questions about it.

The state of the wiring — does it meet code requirements? and above all, is it safe? — should be evaluated carefully as you try to determine what this house is worth to you.

Does the wiring system use old-fashioned fuses or new-fangled circuit-breakers? There's nothing wrong with fuses, but the circuit-breaker system is easier to manage. It's the difference between flipping a switch back to *on* and walking through a blizzard to find the drugstore fresh out of fuses and the hardware store closed for a long weekend. Some people, of course, are smart enough to keep some fuses handy in an easy-to-get-at place, with a flashlight nearby. If you're among them, don't worry about which system the house uses. If you're not, think twice about that fusebox.

NINE

The Condo
and Co-op Alternatives

The idea of home ownership in America traditionally conjures up an image of a single-family home on a nice lot surrounded by trees and flowers and a white picket fence. But an increasing number of people have found that because of their financial limitations or their life-style needs, the traditional single-family detached house doesn't work very well for them. When these buyers sing "There's no place like home," what they have in mind is a condominium or a cooperative, typically an apartment unit that they own rather than rent.

There are a lot of good reasons to own a condominium or a cooperative. There are also a lot of good reasons not to. If you're considering these options, there are many things to think about. Before we get into the pros, the cons, and the cautions, we need to review a few basics. What are condominiums and cooperatives, precisely? How do they differ from each other as well as from regular ownership?

CONDOS AND CO-OPS DEFINED

Mention a condominium to most people, and they immediately think of a high-rise apartment building. But contrary to that widespread misconception, condos and co-ops are not types of buildings. The terms refer, rather, to a form of collective or joint ownership. Almost any structure can be organized as a condo or a co-op — a high-rise apartment building, a garden apartment, a triple-decker. Even boat slips and parking spaces are often owned as condos now.

With both condos and co-ops, ownership of a particular structure is subdivided among two or more parties. Each party owns part of the structure separately and part of it in common. The primary difference between condos and co-ops is the way the ownership interests are structured.

In a condo, each unit is owned individually in the same way a detached single-family house would be owned. The common areas of a condo building (the lobby, halls, grounds, laundry room, garage, tennis court, and so on) are owned jointly by all the unit owners, and each owner is required to pay a monthly condo fee, which represents his or her proportionate share of the cost of maintaining the common areas.

In a co-op, the common-area ownership arrangement is similar to that of a condo, but co-op owners do not actually own the individual units they live in. Instead, they own shares in the cooperative corporation that owns the building. Those shares, together with a "leasehold interest" in the living unit, give the co-op owner the equivalent of a lifetime lease. This leasehold, however, is not the same as the ownership enjoyed by condo owners. In New York City, where co-ops have been established for a long time, this distinction makes no difference. Almost everywhere else, however, it's harder to obtain financing for co-op units than for condo units.

To explain it further: the condo owner obtains a mortgage on his or her individual unit, just as would the owner of a single-family home. We'll look below at some factors that *do* set condo ownership apart from detached-home ownership, but for the most part the fact is that lenders treat condo buyers pretty much that same way they treat buyers of detached single-family houses. That is, they use the condo itself as security for the mortgage, the same way they would use a single-family house.

The co-op owner, however, owns shares in a corporation rather than the real estate itself. As a result, most lenders view loans for cooperative units as personal loans rather than real-estate mortgages.

In practical terms, and in most cases — and again, outside New York City only — this means three things for the buyer of a co-op as compared to the buyer of a condo or a house: (1) finding a loan is more difficult, and (2) when a loan *is* found, the interest rate is higher and (3) a relatively larger down payment is required.

The difference arises in part from the fact that on a nationwide basis, lenders tend to be unfamiliar with cooperatives. Outside New York it's a fairly exotic form of ownership. This unfamiliarity alone makes lenders reluctant to finance coops. This may explain why, in the United States today, there are ten condo units for every co-op unit.

There are a few details worth knowing about co-ops. First, cooperative owners must generally make two mortgage payments, rather than the single mortgage payment the condo owner faces. Unless the unit is bought for cash outright, the buyer has to obtain a loan (known as a cooperative-share loan) in order to finance the difference between the down payment and the purchase price. In addition to paying that share loan, the co-op owner is responsible for paying a proportionate share of the "blanket mortgage" outstanding on the cooperative building as a whole.

For a typical case, consider an apartment building that is being converted into a cooperative. Suppose the owner of the apartment building is still repaying the original mortgage. At the time of the conversion, the outstanding mortgage might be taken over by the new cooperative association, made up of the people who purchase the co-ops in the building. The co-op owners would then be jointly responsible for the monthly payments on the blanket mortgage.

Under certain circumstances, this can be advantageous. If the blanket mortgage has been in place for a long time, for instance, the chances are good that it was written at a relatively low interest rate. Therefore the unit owner's share of the blanket mortgage payment, combined with the payment on the individual share loan, might be lower than the single mortgage payment that would be required for a condominium in a comparable building.

(Figuring the value of a cooperative relative to a condo or another cooperative can be a bit tricky, however. Take as an example a co-op in a building with a hundred units, with a blanket mortgage of $10 million. The co-op share may cost $70,000, but the buyer must also assume the liability for a share — $100,000 worth — of the blanket mortgage, and that has to be factored into the value of the unit. So this unit really costs $170,000, not $70,000.)

A second possible advantage of a co-op over a condo lies in the fact that the co-op as a whole typically is taxed as a single apartment building, whereas with condominiums, each unit is taxed separately. The result is that the property-tax bill may be lower for the co-op owner than for the owner of a comparable condo.

Yet another possible tax advantage of co-ops over condos stems from the fact that condo owners cannot deduct any part of their monthly condo fees. They can deduct their mortgage-interest charges and their property-tax payments, of course, along with single-family and co-op owners, but the government regards the condo fee itself as a nondeductible cost. The monthly fee paid by co-op owners, on the other hand, includes their share of the interest on the blanket mortgage, and that portion is therefore deductible.

A fourth and somewhat more ambiguous advantage of a co-op over a condo is that co-op owners often (though not always) exert more control over who can and cannot buy into their building. A condo owner buys directly from the seller or the developer; in most cases, the other unit owners are not even aware that the unit is changing hands. A co-op buyer, in contrast, usually has to appear before the cooperative association's board of directors and answer detailed questions about his or her financial condition and life-style, among other matters, before any offer to purchase can be approved.

The rationale behind this is that there is a higher level of economic interdependence among co-op owners than among condo owners. If a condo owner doesn't make his mortgage payment, for example, that's between the owner and the lender holding the mortgage. If a co-op owner fails to pay his share of the blanket mortgage, however, the other owners must make up the difference or face the risk of having the lender foreclose on the building. Citing as justification their interest in insuring the financial stability of buyers, many cooperative boards have established rules limiting the portion of the purchase price that can be financed with a loan.

Discrimination based on race, sex, handicap, marital status, religion, or national origin is illegal, as is discrimination against families with children, but co-op boards often use their power to screen prospective buyers as a means of discriminating against those they would consider to be "undesirable" as neighbors. The classic examples are the buildings that refused to accept Richard Nixon because he was a politician and Barbra Streisand because she was a celebrity, the co-op boards regarding politicians and celebrities as being destructive to the atmosphere they wanted to maintain.

THE GOOD THINGS ABOUT CONDOS

The big question for prospective home buyers is, why would anyone want to own an apartment rather than a detached single-family home? One answer is that not everyone has a choice. With the median price nationally of an existing home today rising above $80,000, affordability is a serious problem for many first-time buyers. A condominium, on the other hand, can cost $50,000 or less in some markets and may be the logical way for some buyers to crack the affordability barrier. In fact, it's said that condominiums have become the "starter" home for the current generation of buyers, much as the simple ranch home was for their parents.

But even some buyers for whom affordability is not a limiting factor opt for condominiums because they like the idea of having someone else to do the chores, or the sense of security that comes from always having other people around or perhaps a doorman or guard on twenty-four-hour duty. This last can be an especially important consideration for people who travel frequently.

Many buyers are attracted to condominiums because of the amenities they offer. People who can't afford to buy a home with a pool or tennis courts attached may be able to manage a condominium in which the cost of those amenities is shared with a lot of other owners.

Condo owners enjoy the benefits of home ownership (their property taxes and mortgage interest payments are deductible) without the responsiblities that can make ownership less of a pleasure than some unwary buyers expect. Like the tenants in an apartment building, many condo owners can expect someone else to take care of the lawn and shovel the snow, but unlike apartment renters, condo owners can build equity in their units over time. And they don't have to worry about being hassled by an unreasonable landlord or being evicted if their apartment is converted to a condominium and sold out from under them.

THE NEGATIVES

There is a down side to condo living, however, and it should not be underestimated.

It's true, for starters, that condo dwellers own the units they occupy, but these units are still, typically, apartments, and the fact that they are owned rather than rented does not finally make them less so. Nor does it reduce the annoyances that can characterize apartment living. Many of those apartment-life annoyances, such as the young marrieds who shout at each other on the other side of your bedroom wall, or the cook down the hall who's so fond of garlic, may become less tolerable when you're paying a hefty mortgage note every month instead of writing out a rent check. The fact is, simply put, if you don't like living in an apartment as a tenant, chances are you aren't going to like it any better as a condo owner.

Another factor to keep in mind with condos is that you're not just acquiring a place to live. You're also going to become a voting member in a self-governing community. A condominium, in a very real way, is democracy in action, with all the good — and difficult — things this implies.

On the positive side, as an owner rather than a tenant, you will actually have something to say about the issues that affect your environment. You will have a voice in the building's management, its maintenance, its repair, and its improvement.

Your voice will be, at the same time, one among several or many. You and your fellow owners may not always share views. Spending eight hours listening to condo owners debating about whether the lobby should be painted white or beige has caused more than one condo owner to question the wisdom of his or her purchase. What they say about never watching sausage or laws being made applies even more, I'm told, to the deliberations of most condo associations.

Although you'll have more control as a unit owner than you would as a tenant, you'll have less control than the owner of a detached single-family home. If the single-family's roof is leaking, the owner simply has it repaired. The condo owner, however, may have to convince a dozen other owners that the repair is (a) necessary and (b) an expense that should be apportioned among all unit owners. That may not be a problem if everyone's roof is leaking, but it could be a challenge if the leak is confined to your unit alone.

One of the biggest mistakes many condo buyers make is to assume that living in a condo will be just like living in an apartment, except that they'll own their space instead of renting it. That's not entirely the case. One of the advantages of being a tenant is that if the sink gets clogged or the wiring has to be replaced, it's the landlord's problem and the landlord's expense. For a condo owner, if something goes wrong, there's no landlord to pester. You have to take care of it yourself. And if there's a problem in the common areas, you and your fellow owners have to worry about it until it's taken care of. There may be a management company in place, responsible for keeping things running smoothly, but the management company works for the unit owners. I don't want to exaggerate the extent to which condo owners must be involved in the hands-on management of their buildings, but the fact is, you own this property, and you have a vested interest in seeing that it's well maintained and well run. You may have fewer headaches than the owner of a single-family home, but condominium living doesn't offer the totally carefree existence that many developments advertise and that many purchasers expect.

HOW TO LOOK AT A CONDO

If you've weighed all the pros and cons and decided that a condo may be right for you, it's time to think about evaluating the units you're going to see.

Most of the factors I discussed in relation to single-family homes (see chapters 6 to 8) apply to condos as well. The community in which the home is located, the surrounding neighborhood, the distance from your work — all of these considerations are as important to someone buying a 1,000-square-foot condo as they are to someone buying a 3,000-square-foot Colonial.

Buying a condo, however, is more complicated.

There are more documents to read, more questions to ask, and more details to consider. There are whole books on buying condos and co-ops, and all of them together won't tell you everything you might ever need to know about the process.

I'm going to cover some of the basics. But again, these are just the *major* issues — not the only ones — that condo owners should consider.

THE UNIT ITSELF

Start with the physical basics. Is the unit large enough to meet your needs? Is there adequate storage? Is there additional storage available in the basement or elsewhere in the building? Is it an added cost or is it included in the purchase price? Is the room layout acceptable? Is it even livable?

What about the soundproofing in the walls? There's nothing you can do about the fact that other people are living in the building, but if you sneeze and the occupant four stories up says "Bless you," you may want to reconsider.

Remember my advice in chapter 8 about getting copies of

back utility bills from the seller of a single-family home? The same thing applies to condos. You want to estimate as carefully as you can how much it will cost you to occupy the unit. If it's a new development, you'll have to rely on the developer's estimate of what those costs are likely to be, but you can check by looking at the costs for comparable units in comparable buildings. One important question to ask the broker or the developer is whether there are individual meters — or even separate systems — for electricity, heat, and water, which means you pay for what you use, or central meters for the entire building, which means you subsidize owners who are less conservation-minded than you.

In looking at the cost of any condominium, don't forget to factor in the monthly maintenance fee, sometimes known as the common-area charge or condo fee. (Bear in mind that lenders will add that fee to your monthly PITI calculation in their assessment of your ability to qualify for a mortgage. Also remember that your monthly fee in a condo is not a tax-deductible expense.) You'll want to know not only how large that fee is but precisely what it covers. Is access to the pool and exercise room included, or is there an extra charge for that? Is parking included in the fee?

Speaking of parking, are the spaces "deeded"? That is, do the unit owners buy their parking spaces too, as part of the condo purchase, or are the spaces sold separately to those owners who want them? Are there enough spaces to go around, or will the scramble for scarce spots trigger daily melodramas in the parking lot?

You should ask similar questions about any amenities offered with a condo. The first question is, do you want or need the amenities you'll be paying for? If you're not going to swim, you might be better off with a lower-priced unit in a development that doesn't have a swimming pool. On the other hand, if it's the availability of the swimming pool and tennis courts that most appeals to you, take a good look at those facilities in relation to the number of people likely to be using them. How much of an attraction can those two tennis courts be for you if there are always thirty people waiting to use them?

As you explore different condos, remember that in addition to buying a unit, you'll also be acquiring an interest in the common areas as well. Pay as much attention to the areas outside of your unit as you do to the unit itself. If you're looking at a newly constructed condominium or a newly renovated one, pay particular attention to the quality of the workmanship and the quality of the construction details. That will give you some idea of the care — or lack of care — that the developer has put into the project. But don't be so snowed by the brass doorknobs on the entryway or the Jacuzzi in the bathroom that you overlook the things that really matter — the condition of the heating and cooling systems, for example, or the age of the building's roof.

The condition of the building's infrastructure is important to you, and you'll definitely want to hire a qualified home inspector or structural engineer to inspect the building before you buy it. You'll want him to look at the common areas as well as at your individual unit. If the roof is going to have to be replaced or if the heating system is on its last legs, it's better to find that out *before* you decide to buy rather than a month after you move in.

If you're looking at a recently renovated building, make sure to find out exactly what was done to it. Did the developer gut the building and start over, or did he simply slap on a new coat of paint, polish the doorknobs, and change the building's name from 274 Refuse Way to One Condominium Place?

If you're considering new construction, find out how much of what the developer is planning has been completed and how much remains to be done. That new clubhouse with the indoor swimming pool and tennis courts may look great in the drawings, but what happens if that phase is never completed? Will your unit still be worth what you're about to pay for it if those amenities aren't part of the package? You should also find out precisely how many units are planned for this unfinished development. Will you still be happy with your purchase if the developer builds two high-rise buildings and a waste-treatment plant in the meadow behind your unit?

Developers will sometimes offer price concessions to purchasers at the beginning of a new construction or conversion, and it *is* possible to save a lot of money by getting in on the ground floor. But there are some definite risks involved. For one thing, you only have the developer's word (and his drawings) as to what the finished building will look like. Also, as one of the first buyers rather than one of the last, you have no way of knowing how popular these units are going to be, or how quickly they're going to sell. They may move very quickly, but sales may also be slow, either because the units themselves aren't well received or because the market takes a turn for the worse. In either event, you may find yourself as one of only a few owners in a mostly vacant development, or one occupied mainly by tenants, to whom the developer was forced to rent the units that he couldn't sell.

For several reasons, that's a situation you want to avoid. For one thing, because of secondary-market regulations (more about those below, under "Financing"), an excess of tenants in a condominium will make it difficult for buyers to obtain financing to purchase the units. Also, experience suggests that tenants are often less conscientious about maintenance than owners, who have a vested interest in the value of the property. Even more of a concern is the fact that absentee owners aren't always as committed to upkeep as those who are actually living in a development. As a result, owner-occupants in buildings dominated by absentee owners sometimes have a hard time mustering the votes needed to approve major repairs.

Another possible issue for anyone buying into an unfinished development, or one that's going to be built in phases, is the question of who pays the maintenance fee for the new units between the time they're completed and the time they're sold. Make sure it's the developer who assumes that obligation, not the owners of the other units.

If you're looking at a recent conversion or new construction, find out whatever you can about the developer's track record. Has he done other condominium projects? Were the owners there satisfied with his work? Or have they filed suit?

The major concern for people buying into a newly constructed condo development is whether it will be finished as promised and on schedule. The major concern for people buying into recently converted buildings, on the other hand, is whether they'll be able to occupy the units they purchase. This is because many communities have adopted laws designed to protect tenants from being displaced by the conversion of their apartment units into condos. These laws run a long gamut. Some require advance notice of any upcoming conversion and give tenants the right of first refusal on the purchase of their units. Some, such as the law enacted in Cambridge, Massachusetts, permit buyers to purchase converted rental units but require that they be maintained *as* rental units. That is, you can buy a unit in a converted building in Cambridge, but — except under certain conditions — you can't occupy it. That's clearly something you'd want to know all about before you signed on the bottom line, and it's exactly the sort of thing you should ask the broker and the seller. So if you're contemplating a condo purchase, make sure you find out if there are any state or local requirements in effect that might limit your ability to occupy it.

CHECKING IT OUT

Talking to other owners in an existing condominium is always a good idea, for the same reasons that it makes sense to talk to the other residents of any neighborhood you're considering for your future home. Ask if the other unit owners like living there. Ask what they don't like. Does the condo association operate effectively? Do the residents tend to get along reasonably well, or did the last meeting end with a shoot-out in the front hall?

You also want to get some sense of whether the development is well managed and well maintained. Is there a professional management firm on retainer? If the building has more than twenty or twenty-five units, there probably should be, since it's unlikely that association members would be able to devote the time required to keep up with all the management details. One fairly good indicator of how effectively a condominium is being run, I've found, is whether or not the common areas are clean and in good repair.

THE DOCUMENTS

Before you purchase any condo unit, you'll need to review — and more importantly, have an attorney scrutinize — the condominium documents. Reams of paper are involved in the purchase of a condo. From that imposing stack of documents, the four that will be of greatest concern to you are the condominium master deed, the bylaws of the owners' association, the rules and regulations, and the condo budget.

THE MASTER DEED

The master deed is the basic document that establishes the condominium and explains who owns what within it. It should describe in precise detail the boundaries of all buildings and of the individual units. It should specify what is included in the common areas. It should also specify what rights, if any, the developer retains in any undeveloped land on which the condominium and its attached facilities (clubhouse, swimming pool, and so on) are located. If the developer plans to build additional units in the future, for example, the master deed will assert his continued control over the undeveloped part of the property. If the master deed shows that the developer retains control over surrounding property, find out if the unit owners have anything to say about what gets built there.

Watch out for provisions indicating that the developer will continue to own or control the recreational facilities and lease them back to the condo owners. I'm much more comfortable with situations where the unit owners control the recreational facilities, because that avoids the risk that the developer may decide at some point to triple the fees or sell memberships to nonresidents. Also, you may find it more difficult to obtain financing for a condo unit if the recreational facilities are leased rather than owned outright by the condo association. If there is a lease involved, however, be sure (a) that the anticipated fees are reasonable, with explicit limits on how much and how often the charges can be increased, and (b) that there are no provisions permitting the developer to open the facilities to people outside the condo.

At the very least, you want to avoid what happened to a friend of mine who bought a unit in a handsome new condo development with a swimming pool, tennis courts, the works. It was a great deal until the developer put up another 150-unit complex nearby and gave those new owners rights of access to the facilities of the original complex. A swimming pool that could comfortably accommodate 150 units was overloaded by 300, and a dream condo became a bit of a nightmare. Had my friend read the master deed beforehand, he might have become aware of this danger before signing the contract. The fine print is important. Read it. Better still, hire an attorney to read it for you and tell you exactly what everything means.

Another important detail that you'll find in the master deed is an explanation of the owner's percentage interest in the common areas attributable to each of the individual condo units. Your percentage interest is important. It defines your proportionate vote in the condo association, and it determines the amount of your monthly maintenance fee. In some condos the percentage interest is based on the size of the unit, representing its square footage as a percentage of the total square footage in the whole complex. In others, the owner's percentage interest is a function of the value of the unit as a percentage of the aggregate value of all the condo units together, as calculated at the time the condo was established.

Practices may vary, but the most common approach by far is to base the owner's percentage interest primarily on the value of the unit. Size is a major factor in determining value, but it's not the only one. In any case, one method of calculating the percentage interests is probably as good as another as long as the results are fair, and they're fair as long as the percentage interests of comparable units are essentially the same. The more valuable the unit, the larger that owner's percentage interest is likely to be. The owner of the penthouse in a high-rise condo, for example, will have a larger percentage interest than the owner of the studio in the basement next to the boiler. On the other hand, the owners of two identical penthouse units or two identical basement units should have the same percentage interest in the common areas.

The important point here is not so much how the interests of the owners are calculated; rather, it's that you should be aware of what those arrangements are before you buy, and you should be comfortable with them, because it's virtually impossible to change them after the fact. Changing the percentage interests typically requires not only the unanimous agreement of all the unit owners but also the consent of all the lenders holding mortgages on the individual units. So if you don't like the way the interests are apportioned, don't buy the condo.

The master deed must also explain how its terms can be amended; as a rule, you want it to be reasonably difficult to make changes. The deed should describe any limitations on the resale of units. If the condo association has the right of first refusal — that is, the right to offer to buy any unit in the complex before it's sold — that must be spelled out in the master deed. This is important because it adds a step to the home-sale process, and you'll have to factor the extra time required into your schedule when you decide to sell. Such a provision may also affect the availability of financing, both for you and for subsequent purchasers.

If there are any limits on how the units can be used, they must be spelled out in the master deed as well. For example, some master deeds prohibit the rental of the unit; some prohibit use of the unit for business operations.

Restrictions of this kind may be included in the condo's rules and regulations instead of in the master deed, so both documents should be studied carefully from this standpoint before you decide to buy. In fact, it is unrealistic *not* to have an attorney read the documents before you make the offer. If you wait, you could wind up committed to buy a condo unit that you cannot use as you had planned. If it's not possible to have an attorney check the documents before you sign the offer, then make the offer contingent on an attorney's review of the documents.

BYLAWS

The condo's bylaws are its constitution. They establish the ground rules according to which this quasi-democracy is governed. The bylaws set up the structure of the condominium's board of directors, specifying (among other things) the number of directors and the length of their term in office, and they detail the board's responsibilities and its powers. Those powers typically include the right to collect the maintenance fee, the right to impose penalties if the fee is late, and the right to levy a lien on units whose owners fail to pay their fees. In some condos, the unit owners collectively have the right to veto any decisions made by the board. In others, the only way to overturn a decision you don't like is to vote the offending directors out of office.

One thing to look for as you read the bylaws is any evidence of undue control by the developer. As a general rule, the sooner the developer is out of the picture and the unit owners are in control, the better. In a new condominium, the developer typically retains a fair amount of control until all or at least most of the units have been sold. But some state laws set a time limit beyond which the developer has no choice but to turn over control of the condo association to the unit owners, even if a large number of units remain unsold at that time. I think that's a good idea. It's language I'd want to see in the bylaws of any newly constructed or newly renovated condo I was considering buying.

Watch out also for situations in which the developer retains the right to select the management company that handles the maintenance and general day-to-day operations of the condo. Not all condos have management companies, but many of them do, and probably more of them should. It's entirely possible that the developer or his brother-in-law can do a great job of managing the complex, but it's equally possible that some other company can do the job better and cheaper. I'm not saying you should walk away from a condo in which the developer has taken on the management role, but you should look carefully at the terms of the management contract. Do the costs seem to be in line with the management costs at other comparable developments? What about the term? A one- or two-year contract is one thing; but if the developer has written himself a ten-year contract with a no-severance clause, you'd be wise to start looking for something else.

RULES AND REGULATIONS

As owner of a detached single-family home, you're the king or queen of your castle. As the owner of a condo unit, you still have your crown, but then so do all the other owners. Even royalty, when pressed into coexistence, must acknowledge some restrictions as to what can and cannot be done with the condo unit itself, as well as with those areas that are owned in common with other kings and queens. So you can arrange your furniture however you please and use any wallpaper you like in your living room, but you may not be able to paint the outside of your windows the color of your choice. When you buy into a condo community, you also buy into its rules and regulations, so it's a good idea to find out what they are before you commit yourself to buying.

Many condominiums prohibit pets. Some, as noted before, won't allow owners to rent their units, even for short periods of time. Some even limit the amount of time visitors (including relatives) can stay. Still others have detailed rules governing what an owner can and cannot do to the outside of his or her condo.

So if you're planning to run a mail-order business from the spare bedroom, or see psychiatric patients in the study, you'd better make sure there aren't any rules prohibiting nonresidential uses of the unit. And you'd better be sure that the owner of the unit you're planning to buy hasn't made any unauthorized changes — installing windows different from those in place elsewhere in the building, for example. If such changes have been made without the board's permission and have not been corrected by the time you buy, you could get stuck with the cost of undoing the previous owner's damage.

BUDGET

A big question to ask about any condominium is, are its finances in good order? And one way to answer this question is to look at the condo's budget.

You don't have to be a financial expert; all you're looking for is evidence that the condo association collects its fees, pays its bills, and regularly sets aside funds for reserves to cover unforeseeable common-area expenses. If it's a new development, you'll have to rely on the developer's estimates for maintenance costs and other common-area expenses. But you can compare these estimates with the costs you see in other, similar condos to ascertain whether they appear reasonable.

Look with particular interest at the monthly maintenance figure. Some developers establish the base fee far below what it should be in order to attract buyers. Once they've bought in, the new owners are faced almost immediately with the need to increase the fee to a more realistic level. Be wary if the developer quotes a monthly fee that seems too good to be true; it probably is. The range of variance is wide, so once again, the best advice on condo fees is to look at the fees charged for comparable developments in the same market area.

If you're looking at an existing condo, you'll want to find out how frequently the condo fee has been raised in the past. If it's gone up 50 percent a year for the past five years, that's a bad sign. On the other hand, if the fee has never been raised, that could be an even worse sign, since it may indicate that the necessary maintenance is not being done and that a huge increase in the fee, or a special assessment to cover emergency renovations, is likely in the near future.

One indication of how well or how badly a condo is being managed is the size of its reserve fund. The monthly maintenance fee covers regular maintenance and operations; the purpose of the reserves is to finance major capital expenditures — replacing a roof, for example, or paying for common-area damages that aren't entirely covered by insurance. Every condominium should have a regular program through which owners contribute to its reserve fund, but the Community Associations Institute estimates that 10 percent of the condos in the country don't have any reserves at all, and that another 30 percent have reserve programs on paper but don't follow through on them every year.

Why should you be concerned about the reserves? Because if the roof caves in or the heating plant has to be replaced, the unit owners are going to have to cover the costs. Such special assessments can amount to several thousand dollars per owner. It's far better to be in a condo that saves for rainy days than in one that has to soak the owners when the inevitable crisis occurs.

One final point about reserve funds: secondary-market regulations require that condos have "adequate" reserves in place. What constitutes "adequate" is left undefined, but attorneys I know who handle real-estate transactions say they base their assessment on the individual condo. An older condo, where more things are more likely to go wrong, needs a larger reserve fund than a newer one, which in theory should face fewer problems involving expensive replacement and renovation.

In any case, if the reserve fund seems low, find out why. It might be because the condo association has not made a contribution to it in five years. This would be a bad sign. It also might be because the association just drew on the fund to finance a needed repair. This would be a sign that the condo is being responsibly managed.

INSURANCE

A condo is insured differently from a single-family detached dwelling. If you're insuring a single-family home, you buy a policy that covers the structure as well as its contents. In a condo, you need two separate policies — one to cover your unit and its contents (known in many areas as an H.O.-6 policy) and another, the master policy, to cover the condo's common areas.

The most important thing for prospective unit buyers to find out is exactly what is covered by the master policy and what is not. You want above all to avoid a situation in which the master policy coverage and your unit policy coverage fail to come together, leaving you potentially vulnerable to serious damage claims. The nature and extent of the condo insurance already in place are two of the things your attorney should be able to tell you after reviewing the condo documents.

Some condos have what is known as a "bare-walls" master policy. It covers only the building's shell and the common areas — the lobby, the grounds, the pipes, the roof, the electrical wiring, and so on. Unit owners have to buy coverage for structural elements within their units (bathroom fixtures, built-in cabinets, etc.) as well as for their personal property. If a condo you're considering has bare-walls coverage, then be sure to determine precisely where the master policy ends and where the unit owner's policy must begin. One way to avoid any question about whether or not something is insured is to obtain your unit policy from the same firm that issues the master policy.

Some condos have opted for what is known as "single-entity" coverage. This covers essentially everything that's a fixed part of the building, regardless of whether it is in the common areas or inside the units themselves. With this approach, the walls, cabinets, fixtures, and so on inside individual units are covered by the master policy. Unit owners need only insure their personal property.

If you encounter single-entity insurance in a condo you're interested in, be sure to find out what happens if individual owners make improvements to their units. These improvements raise the value of the whole complex and thus increase its insurance costs. You want to make sure that this increase will be paid by the particular owners responsible for it. It's not an expense that should be shared.

These are the most basic issues you have to consider under the heading of condo insurance, but there are many other aspects that vary with local conditions and state law. Because it's so important to be adequately insured, and because the whole area of condo insurance is so complicated, you shouldn't buy a condo without the advice of a competent and trustworthy insurance agent.

FINANCING

Financing a condo is similar in most respects to financing a detached single-family home, but it's more complicated. The secondary-market requirements for condominiums fill several volumes. I can't go into all those requirements here, but I can tell you that with the number of *i*'s that have to be dotted and *t*'s that have to be crossed, you shouldn't attempt a condo purchase without hiring an attorney to represent you.

The most basic question to ask about any condo you're considering buying is whether it has obtained the approval of either Fannie Mae or Freddie Mac, or is capable of being approved. As you saw in chapter 2, Fannie Mae and Freddie Mac are the two key entities of the secondary market. They purchase many of the mortgages that local lenders originate. Condo developers will often obtain Fannie Mae or Freddie Mac approval before they begin marketing their dwellings. Some existing condos already have the approval; some have not received formal approval but meet all the requirements needed to do so.

If a condo hasn't been and is not capable of being approved, you may have a hard time finding a lender willing to finance it. And even if you obtain a mortgage now, financing could be a problem for any subsequent buyers you might want to sell to in the future. All in all, it's easier to buy and sell a unit that meets secondary-market requirements than one that doesn't.

Among the hundreds of secondary-market requirements that condos have to meet, there are two that are especially critical and that buyers can check out on their own before getting too deeply into the purchase process.

First is the number of units that have been sold in a new development. Typically lenders won't approve a mortgage on a unit unless at least 25 to 30 percent of the other units in the complex have been presold. That's an obvious problem in a new development in which sales have just begun. So what often happens is that the lender providing the funds for the construction or the renovation will also agree to issue mortgages to the buyers of individual units. That ensures the availability of financing for early buyers, though those buyers may find the rate available from this lender to be a bit higher than prevailing mortgage rates in the market area.

The second secondary-market rule you should be aware of is that at least 70 percent of the units must be owner-occupied. A development in which more than 30 percent of the units are owned by investors who rent them out to tenants is not likely to pass muster with most secondary-market lenders.

DETERMINING VALUE

Once you've decided that everything else about the condo is to your liking, how do you decide whether it's worth what the seller or the developer is asking for it? As with any kind of real estate, the "fair market value" of a condo is whatever a willing buyer will pay a willing seller. But before you open your wallet, remember that there are some objective ways of measuring value.

First, look at the prices of comparable units in the same building and in the same and similar neighborhoods. There are publications in some areas that report real-estate transactions on a regular basis, and these are good sources of information on comparable values. You can also obtain such information from the registry of deeds or the town clerk's office, where all real-estate transactions are recorded. If the seller is asking $100,000 for the unit you're considering and an identical unit across the hall sold the previous month for $80,000, then you have a serious problem with the price. A look at recent selling prices of comparable units will give you at least a general sense of the market and a basis for deciding whether the price being asked for the unit you're interested in is reasonable.

One way to compare the price of different condos is to look at the cost per square foot. Just take the selling price and divide it by the total number of square feet in the unit. But make sure you use only the figure for livable square feet, which is not nesessarily the same as the total number of square feet. A 1,500-square-foot unit is not as spacious as it sounds if that area includes a 500-square-foot hallway. When you're looking at condos, it's not a bad idea to have a tape measure with you, since developers are sometimes imprecise about such distinctions. Suppose you're looking at two comparably priced condos. Each has 2,000 square feet, but condo A has a 200-square-foot hallway and condo B doesn't, so you're getting more living space for your money with condo B. At $100 per square foot, you're paying $20,000 for that hallway. You have to ask yourself whether it's worth it.

You also have to consider that size is not the only determinant of value. A 3,000-square-foot unit will not usually cost twice as much as a 1,500-square-foot unit in the same building. This is because some basic costs (the building infrastructure, for example) will be the same for both units. On the other hand, a 1,500-square-foot luxury unit with a water view will undoubtedly cost more than a 3,000-square-foot unit in a renovated warehouse on the wrong side of town.

When you're comparing one unit with another, you're obviously going to have to consider factors other than simply the cost per square foot. Don't mix apples and oranges when weighting the footage values of the dwellings you consider.

If you're buying a unit in an existing building, you're also going to want to have some idea of what the resale experience has been for other units in that complex. How rapidly have prices increased? When units go on the market, how quickly do they sell? Remember, you may want to sell your unit one day, so you'll want to be sure that the appreciation rate for condos in this building has been in line with the general appreciation rate for condos in your market. You can check on recent sales by doing some research at the appropriate registry of deeds or town hall, wherever the property filings are recorded. You can ask other unit owners in the complex for a reading. Or if you're really concerned, you can hire an appraiser to analyze the market for you. General economic conditions have everything to do with the rate of appreciation of real-estate values, but if condo values are soaring everywhere except in the development you're considering, you need to wonder why. It's possible that you've stumbled onto a big bargain, but it's also possible that you've stumbled onto big problems.

The Bottom Line: What It Will Cost You to Buy

If you've completed your detailed examination of the house (or the condo) and it still looks good to you, you should have two major questions in mind: What will it cost you — *total* — to buy it? And what will it cost you — *total* — to live in it?

BUYING IT

The cost starts with the amount you agree to pay the seller for the house or condo. But the real cost must also include any repairs or improvements, major or minor, that you decide are necessary, along with all the additions, subtractions, and alterations you feel you can't live without.

Go back to the detailed notes you made as you walked through the house. If the roof has to be replaced, that's at least a $3,000 expenditure, more or less, that must be factored in depending upon the cost of labor and materials in the area in which you live. Is there a new furnace in the immediate picture? Add another $1,000 or so. Are the front stairs rotting away? Does the foundation need some work?

Keep adding things up. Include absolutely everything you consider to be essential, no matter how inexpensive you think it's likely to be. Those small items add up quickly, and all will contribute to the real bottom-line price you must pay. For the smaller jobs, such as replacing loose bricks, repairing railings, and the like, estimate the cost as well as you can, making sure to be on the high side.

How can you even guess at these costs when your only experience with household repairs has involved calling a landlord to report a leaky faucet? Well, help is available from several sources. The easiest and perhaps best solution is to find a friend who either is in the construction business or knows enough about home repair from personal experience to look at the house you're considering with a somewhat educated eye. Just try to be sure that the consultant you pick to work with really knows more about these things than you do.

Another possiblity is to take your list of what you think needs doing (along with such details as the room dimensions) to a home-improvement center that caters to do-it-yourselfers. Many of the salesmen in these companies know a lot about home renovation projects and may be able to shed some light on the expenses you're facing.

Another good source is a reputable home inspector. You don't customarily call in an inspector until you've decided to buy and have signed a Purchase and Sale agreement (see chapter 11), but if you think you're getting serious about a place that looks, even to your uneducated eye, as if it's going to require some major work, then you might bring in an inspector to go through the house with you before you make an offer. That way you'll get a clearer idea of what you might be taking on. If you do ultimately choose to buy this house, the inspection will already be done, and you'll save some time. If you decide the repair costs are too great, the approximately $200 to $500 you've spent on a preagreement inspection will have saved you from much greater expenses down the road.

Obviously you don't want to get a preagreement inspection for every house you feel interesed in. This is a step that should be reserved for homes that look good but have potentially troublesome problem areas.

A less expensive alternative to calling in an inspector is asking a contractor to give you an estimate on the costs of the needed work. You should definitely do this if you're contemplating such major work as new siding, a new roof, or a new family room. Most contractors will provide such estimates free, and few will charge you more than $100 or so for their time. It is so costly and frustrating to get involved with unanticipated repair problems that *not* taking this step would have to be reckoned an utterly false economy. Spend the money. Find out what you need to know. Hundreds of thousands of dollars and long years of commitment are involved. Do it right.

On the other hand, I'm not saying you've got to bring in an army of hired experts for every house you consider. The point, rather, is this: don't agree to buy a house that will need extensive work without getting a sound general idea of what it will cost you to fix it up.

When you've finished calculating the essentials, turn to your list of the less essential work you'll want to do. These are the changes that aren't necessary for structural or health reasons but *are* necessary — at least in your mind (and it's your castle) — to make the home work for you. Will all the kitchen appliances have to be replaced, for instance? Does the bathroom need new fixtures? Do you have to remake the attic into a bedroom? All such changes add to your bottom line.

Of course, you don't have to do all these things right away. A broken furnace you must correct *now*. A radon problem you must correct *now*. But adding a sunroom, changing the wallpaper, upgrading the fixtures, and the like are improvements that can be made one by one as your time, finances, and personal priorities permit. This is the joy (and the frustration) of owning a home — there's always *something* to do to it.

For now, however, you should focus on what absolutely has to be done to make the house livable for you. And you really have to be realistic about this. Don't grit your teeth and say you can live with something that you know will make you miserable within a month. If you know something has to be done, be sure you'll be able to afford to do it. And if you can live without a certain alteration for a while, do that. Give the house a chance to show what it can do. It often turns out that a year of living in a house changes a new owner's mind completely about what needs to be done to it.

So take another look at your to-do list and pare it down to those items that you cannot omit or postpone. Estimate what those necessary fixes and changes will cost you. Add the sum to the seller's asking price. You may find, lo and behold, that the great $100,000 bargain you've stumbled upon will actually cost you twice that by the time you've made it livable on your terms.

Avoid despair. The key question is this: after you've spent a grand total of $200,000 to buy and upgrade this $100,000 house, how will it compare to other houses that are selling for $200,000 to begin with? Could you buy a house that meets your needs for $200,000, and would you like it as well as this one? Would you like it better?

If you can get essentially the house you want for the same total money without doing any extensive work, that's probably what you should do. On the other hand, if a comparable ready-made house in the same neighborhood would cost $250,000, then it makes good economic sense to buy the fixer-upper and get going.

Your assessment of the additional repairs and improvements needed and what they will cost should influence your calculation of how much you're willing to pay for the house. The seller may be asking $125,000, but if you see $20,000 in essential repairs, maybe you'll only want to offer $105,000. That's the sort of give and take you should expect in the negotiations leading up to the signing of the offer and the Purchase and Sale agreement (covered in detail in chapter 11). The point of this exercise is simply to encourage you to be realistic about how much you're likely to end up paying for a certain house and about what to expect for your money.

LIVING THERE

Your decision to buy a house should also be based in part on how much it's likely to cost you to live there.

Take a careful look at the owner's heating and utility bills for the past year or two (brokers generally have this sort of information at hand). Add those costs to the amount you'll be paying in principal and interest payments.* Plug in an accurate estimate of the property-tax and insurance bills. Explore the tax bill in some detail. Ask the owner whether the property is assessed at full value or at some portion of full value. If full valuation is used, find out when the property was last assessed and when the next assessment is due. Will the transfer of ownership trigger a reassessment? If so, when is it likely to be reflected on your tax bill? What about local tax rates? How long has it been since the last increase? What is the likelihood of another increase in the near future? New homeowners are almost invariably strapped for cash during the first year or so; the last thing you need to discover is that your property tax is about to be raised to twice what you can afford.

To your estimate of total living costs you should also add something for maintenance. I would assume that something will go wrong and that it will probably be the one most expensive thing to fix. A reasonable figure would be from $50 to $100 a month, depending on the age of the house and the condition of its vital systems.

Your moment of truth is when you add these numbers up and come up with your estimate — and it is only an estimate at this point — of what it's going to cost you, bottom line, to buy and live in this particular house on a month-by-month basis. Can you write a check (or checks) for that amount every month? Before you decide bravely that you can, remember that you'll still have most of the same expenses you had as a renter. You'll still have to eat food, wear clothes, and pay the dentist.

So be careful here. The closer the house brings you to your financial limits, the warier you should be of getting in over your head. Most people wind up buying the most expensive house they can afford. I agree that there is a certain solid logic in that approach, since the long-term tendency is for property to in-

---

* Since you know the purchase price and the amount you have available for a down payment, you can estimate your payments fairly easily, as shown in chapter 2.

crease in value over time. But it's not sound management of one's affairs to buy so close to one's debt limit that the slightest setback can threaten financial disaster. Make sure you can live more or less comfortably, and at least adequately, with the numbers you see.

Then make your offer.

ELEVEN

Putting It in Writing

MAKING THE OFFER

You've finally found a home you like, the price is in the neighborhood of what you expected to pay, and you've thought about it, fought about it, and lost sleep over it, but at last you're sure this is the house for you. Now what?

Your next step is to let the buyer know that you're interested in the property. You do this by making an offer to purchase it. That doesn't necessarily mean offering to pay precisely what the seller is asking; you might decide, for example, that while the asking price is $225,000, you don't want to pay more than $210,000. Your reasons might be that the house has to be painted, that it has structural or design flaws that you believe reduce its value, that you think the asking price is greater than fair market value, or simply that the market is slow and you think you can get away with a lower bid. In a more active market, with several buyers vying for every house, you might be less comfortable with this last strategy.

I can't teach advanced negotiation techniques in this book. All I can suggest is that you should do your homework, then let common sense be your guide. Be realistic about what the house is worth to you, what you can afford to pay for it, and how appealing you think it's likely to be to other buyers. If this is the only two-family home in the area in good condition to come on the market in the past year, you're likely to have stiff competition, but don't let yourself be stampeded. Not getting the house would be a bummer, but it'd be a worse bummer to wake up with a huge mortgage on a house you never really liked that much to begin with.

Suppose you decide to make an offer close to the asking price but a little below it. One of three things will now happen: (1) the seller may accept your proposal, in which case you have an agreement; (2) the seller may reject your offer outright, leaving it to you to decide whether to make another offer or walk away; or (3) the seller may reject your offer but make a counteroffer, which *you* then must decide whether to accept or reject or counter with yet another offer.

This process of negotiating the price begins with the buyer's submission of a written "offer to purchase" the property for a specified price, subject to any specified conditions or contingencies the buyer thinks are important. (More about these below.) In many jurisdictions, the offer to purchase is a binding legal document. It commits the buyer to sign a more complete document, known as a Purchase and Sale agreement, sometimes called a contract for sale. In some areas it's common to skip the offer to purchase and go directly to the P&S (as the trade calls it).

Whenever you're asked to sign a document, however, remember that there are generally legal implications. The time to consult your attorney is *before* you make a written commitment, no matter how straightforward and "informal" it may seem. Trying to save money by waiting to see your attorney later is a false economy. In some areas it's not at all common for buyers (or sellers) to be represented by an attorney in the home-purchase process, but I'm convinced that buyers are better off with an attorney on their side from the beginning of the negotiations. It's easier and far less expensive for an attorney to help you avoid problems at the offer-to-purchase stage than to have to try to extract you from unwanted commitments later on.

Don't regard the offer as "just an offer," reassuring yourself, or relying on the assurances of others, that any problems can be "worked out in the P&S." That may or may not be true. Your signature on the offer may bind you to sign a Purchase and Sale agreement, which in turn could obligate you to buy the property under terms you don't like and without basic protections or "contingencies" (see below) that you'll want to have.

Also, don't be misled by the fact that many real-estate contracts are entitled "standard form," as if they were drafted originally by Moses and haven't been altered since first appearing in tablet form. Not so. These "standard forms," which tend to be weighted in favor of the seller and broker, can be, regularly are, and usually *should* be altered to fit the individual situation and to represent the buyer's interests more fairly.

BINDERS, DEPOSITS, AND INTEREST

When you submit your offer, you're required to provide "binder" or "earnest money" as evidence of your serious intent to purchase the property. The size of the binder varies but is generally not less than $500 or more than $1,000. Be reluctant to plunk down much more than that at the offer stage.

If your offer is accepted, you'll proceed to the drafting of the more detailed Purchase and Sale contract — the P&S. When that agreement is signed, you'll be required to place a deposit on the house in an escrow account; the deposit is usually between 5 and 10 percent of the purchase price. (Even if you plan to put 20 percent down, you shouldn't tie up that amount in a deposit on a P&S.) Be sure that the P&S clearly states who will hold the deposit (it's usually either the broker or the seller's attorney), what conditions it will be held under, and what will happen to the money if either the buyer or the seller defaults on his or her legal obligations under the agreement.

The P&S should also specify whether or not interest will be earned on the deposit. If it will be, the P&S must say who will get the interest that will accrue on the deposit while it's being held.

Industry practices vary on all of these matters, but as a rule, the individual holding the deposit is not required to place it in an interest-bearing account (or to account for any interest earned) unless he or she is specifically instructed to do so. The buyer and seller must therefore decide whether they want an interest-earning arrangement. If they do, it should be specified in the agreement.

The next question is how to allocate the deposit's earned interest. There is no absolute legal requirement in most cases, and industry practice varies according to locale. Sometimes it goes to the buyer and sometimes to the seller; sometimes the buyer and seller divide it. The interest can also "follow the deposit," meaning that it goes to whoever ends up with the money.

Pay careful attention to any language referring to the seller's right to keep the deposit as liquidated damages *"unless he otherwise notifies you."* It's that "unless" clause that can mean trouble. It does not mean, as you might assume, that if you renege on your offer to purchase, the seller will just keep your deposit and there make an end of it. Rather, it means that the seller will keep your deposit and *still* be in a position to sue you for additional damages, or even to require "specific performance" — that is, require you to go through with the transaction under the terms you had previously accepted. Therefore, many buyers' attorneys will insert language in the P&S that specifically limits the seller's default damages to the amount of the deposit.

THE KEY CONTINGENCIES

Any condition that must be met before you purchase the property, or before the seller sells it, is a *contingency* of the sale. All such contingencies must be specified in writing, preferably in both the offer to purchase (if there is one) and the Purchase and Sale agreement. Think of contingencies as the equivalent of fire escapes. They represent avenues of exit from the agreement if one of the conditions you've identified as essential (your ability to obtain a mortgage, for example) is not fulfilled. Any number of contingencies may be inserted, but there are two basic protections that you as the buyer will always want to have: a financing contingency, which addresses your ability to obtain a mortgage; and an inspection contingency, which covers a structural home inspection and in some cases a pest inspection as well.

THE FINANCING CONTINGENCY

The financing or mortgage contingency clause makes your obligation to buy the property contingent on your ability to obtain financing under specified terms and conditions. Often the "standard" contingency language talks only about the buyer's ability to obtain a mortgage. But it's in your interest as the buyer to specify the maximum interest rate and the type of mortgage that you're willing to accept.

The boilerplate language in many agreements refers to "current market rates and terms." Avoid that. What it means is that you'll have to accept any mortgage offered you (assuming you qualify) even if current rates are 25 percent and the only mortgages available are adjustable-rate loans that are adjusted every other week with no limit on how high the payments can go. You wouldn't like that.

Prudent buyers tell their lawyers to make sure the documents contain a much more specific contingency clause, something that reads, for example, like this:

> This purchase is contingent on the buyer's ability to obtain a thirty-year fixed-rate mortgage at no more than 13 percent plus two points or a one-year adjustable-rate mortgage at no more than 10 percent with two points and with interest-rate caps of no more than 2 percent per adjustment and 6 percent over the life of the loan.

You may choose different figures, and your lawyer can guide you through that. The general idea is to establish some reasonable financial limits on your obligation to go through with the transaction.

The financing contingency clause should also specify how much time you have in which to obtain an *unconditional* written commitment for a mortgage. Some loan approvals are contingent on everything in the world; make sure your mortgage contingency clause makes it clear that a conditional commitment is not enough to bind you. If you don't get an uncluttered mortgage approval on terms acceptable to you within the specified period, you will then have the options of either canceling the transaction, requesting an extension from the seller, or proceeding with the deal without being assured of the financing.

It's important that the financing contingency clause leave a reasonable amount of time for the buyer to obtain a lender's commitment. Allowing too little time will place you in the position of having to seek an extension from the seller, who isn't usually required to give you one. If the seller has another buyer waiting in the wings, or if another buyer has come along and made a better offer since your P&S was signed, your need for more time could give the seller the excuse he or she wants to get out of his or her commitment to sell the property to you.

How much time you should allow depends on market conditions and industry standards, which can vary from one area to another. There have been periods when it was taking lenders as long as 120 days to process loan applications. In down markets, some lenders say they can turn around a loan request in a matter of days. As a rule, thirty days should be sufficient in most areas under most normal conditions; forty-five to sixty days is even more comfortable, and you lose nothing by asking the seller to agree to that.

The "good-faith" requirement.   The financing contingency clause is designed primarily to ensure that the buyer has adequate time to obtain a mortgage and the ability to cancel the transaction without penalty if he or she is unable to do so. But the agreement shouldn't be one-sided. The seller's interests should be protected too, and most sellers, reasonably, will insist that the buyer make a "good-faith effort" to obtain financing. That usually means more than spending a month trying to persuade your father to lend you the money. The seller wants to avoid a situation in which the buyer, for whatever reason, simply changes his mind after signing the P&S and either fails to apply for a loan or makes no serious attempt to obtain one.

The question, then, is what constitutes a "good-faith effort." And the answer is that there is no firm legal rule in place. So this is an issue that buyers and sellers can and should negotiate. Some sellers want buyers to apply to two or three lenders at least; the attorneys I know think that one application is usually enough. They insert language specifying that the buyer is not required to apply to more than one lender or to pay more than one application fee. The important thing here is to be sure that any "good-faith" requirement is spelled out clearly in the P&S. This is your only way to know with certainty what is required of you. What a court might later infer from ambiguous wording could hurt you more than you would think it could.

THE INSPECTION CONTINGENCY

This is another must in any Purchase and Sale agreement. It provides for a structural inspection of the property and in many cases a pest inspection as well, at the buyer's expense, and makes the sale contingent on the results. If the inspection reveals that termites have more equity in the house than its owner, or that a central support beam has rotted beyond repair or the foundation is crumbling, you want to be able either to walk away from the deal or to reopen the discussion about what the purchase price will be.

So watch out for wording that allows you to cancel a transaction only if "serious" structural flaws are discovered. "Serious" is in the mind (and pocketbook) of the beholder. Chipped paint in the living room might seem "serious" to some buyers, while a collapsing roof might seem only a minor, cosmetic flaw to some sellers. Avoid provisions, too, that give the seller the option of paying for any repairs required. You may well want to negotiate such an agreement later, but for now you also want the option of backing out of the transaction rather than allowing the seller to pay for the repairs and hoping the work will turn out to be acceptable.

The best and cleanest inspection contingency clause states simply that if the buyer is not satisfied with the inspection results, he or she can cancel the transaction within a specified time period. That period (usually around ten days) should be long enough to allow the parties to renegotiate the terms if flaws are discovered and the buyer still wants to make a deal, but short enough that the seller is not forced to keep the house off the market for weeks waiting for an indecisive buyer to decide what he or she wants to do.

Pest inspections. The purpose of a pest inspection, obviously, is to determine whether there are rodents, termites, or other nonhuman neighbors that you would consider undesirable. While a structural inspection is absolutely essential before you purchase any residence, the pest inspection generally isn't necessary in new construction. But it's a good idea in resale homes, even if they're relatively new, and lenders sometimes require it as a matter of course.

Arranging for the inspection. The best way to find a home inspector is not by asking the broker or seller to recommend one. The broker has an obvious (and legitimate) interest in seeing the deal go through, and there exists at least the possibility that an inspector who is referred by the broker might be subject to subtle or not-so-subtle pressure to ignore or downplay any problems that might derail the transaction. It's much better to get a recommendation from your attorney, or from friends or acquaintances who have used an inspector in the past.

In most states home inspectors, unlike brokers, do not have to be licensed (one exception is Texas, which recently enacted a licensing law); in fact, almost anyone can hang out a sign offering "professional inspection services." Distinguishing between a real professional and a self-proclaimed expert who may know less about the workings of a house than you do may not be easy. But there are some indicators to watch for. Although inspectors usually aren't licensed, they may belong to a professional trade association. That's usually a good sign. As with brokers, it's no guarantee of professionalism, but it is an indicator of some level of commitment to the profession.

One especially important question to ask any home inspector is how long he's been in the home-inspection business. A former real-estate agent who became an inspector six months ago because he wasn't selling enough homes probably isn't your best bet. A structural engineer or a former home builder who's been in the home-inspection business for ten years is much closer to the kind of person you're looking for.

In addition to wanting your inspector to be knowledgeable and experienced, you also want him to be bonded. That way you'll have some assurance of being compensated if the inspection fails to note a flaw that becomes a costly problem for you after you purchase the home.

Ask your inspector what the inspection will cover, how long it will take, and what it will cost. Some structural inspections will cover pests, but others specifically exclude that area. Expect your inspection bill to run anywhere from $200 to $500, but also be prepared for deviations from the range. Inspection costs vary widely depending on the market area and the property involved.

What should you expect for your money? The inspector should give you a top-to-bottom analysis of the home, spotting existing and some potential problems, recommending solutions and estimating the cost of any needed repairs. If the roof needs to be replaced, if there is or has been a leak in the basement, if the foundation has been weakened, or if the heating system is on its last legs, the home inspector should alert you to the problem. And he should do so in a written report.

But there are some things even the best home inspector can't do. He can't see through walls. He can't guarantee that a heating system that seems to be in good working order when it's tested will never need to be repaired or replaced.

There are also some things the inspector should *not* do. He should not refuse to give you a written report or tell you that you cannot provide a copy of it to the seller. The home inspection is valuable to you only if you can use it to exercise the inspection contingency clause. In order to do that, you usually have to produce some evidence to show the seller that flaws were found. If the inspector is not confident enough of his findings to put them in writing — for the seller as well as for you — then you should find yourself another inspector.

Another real benefit of the home inspection — one that's often overlooked by buyers — is the opportunity it affords to be taken on a tour of the house by an expert. An hour or two spent with a good inspector can give you a tremendous amount of useful information about a house, in terms not just of what's wrong with it, but of how it works. This is a chance to find out, before the lights go out, where the fusebox is located; a chance to learn, before you move the wrong wall, where the support beams are.

It will be an invaluable, one-time-only learning experience, and you owe it to yourself not to miss it.

If you're buying a hundred-year-old home, you'll obviously want an inspector to review it. But what about a newly constructed dwelling? Again, typically you'll find that a pest inspection isn't necessary (unless the lender requires it), but a structural inspection is just as essential here as it is with a much older home. The walls may be freshly painted and the ceilings unstained, but did the builder actually use the materials specified in the plans, or did he take some shortcuts that could cost you money down the road?

Condominium inspection.   Condominium buyers must face a few additional considerations. Your inspector should go over not only your unit but the common areas as well. After all, you're buying a percentage interest in the building as a whole, and you need to know what condition it's in. Are there potential problems around the corner? An aging roof? A decrepit heating system? Make sure your inspector has access to the roof and the boiler room, because that's the only way you'll be able to answer those questions.

OTHER CONTINGENCIES

Financing and inspection contingency clauses have become almost standard insertions in most Purchase and Sale agreements, but they are by no means the only ones that a buyer or seller might want to specify.

It's becoming increasingly common, for example, for buyers to insist on a radon contingency clause, making the purchase contingent on the satisfactory outcome of a test to determine radon levels in the dwelling. In areas where lead paint is a problem, a lead paint inspection contingency clause is also common. If lead paint or radon is discovered, the buyer and seller can negotiate terms for dealing with the problem.

Your purchase of a property can be made contingent on virtually anything you consider essential to the sale. The seller, of course, has the right to reject any contingency clause you propose, and you in turn have the right not to purchase the property unless conditions that are important to you are included in the contract. If you've found problems you want corrected, you can specify that the seller must complete the repairs he or she has agreed to by a certain date. If the work isn't finished on time or to your satisfaction, you have a legal out, if you want it.

In the purchase of multifamily property, it's common to specify that the dwelling will be delivered "free of all tenants," which gives you the option of either finding new tenants or negotiating new leases with the existing residents. If you decide on the former course, the "free of all tenants" clause places the onus of evicting the current occupants on the seller. (More about this below, under "Drafting the Documents.")

Sometimes, special conditions of the sale are specified in "riders" or "addenda" to the agreement, rather than in contingency clauses. There really isn't much difference, except that riders are often tacked on at the end, rather than being inserted in the body of the agreement.

One common rider provides that the seller will deliver any special documents required for the purchase by a specified date. If the seller has agreed to provide the buyer with a second mortgage, that agreement, typically, would be spelled out in a rider. A rider might also contain any specific representations made by the seller — for example, that the septic system was in good working order, or that the roof had been replaced within the past year.

DRAFTING THE DOCUMENTS

THE OFFER TO PURCHASE

As I noted earlier, the offer to purchase and the Purchase and Sale agreement are legal documents. They should be written carefully, scrutinized closely, and drafted or at least reviewed by an attorney before you sign. The offer is usually shorter than the P&S, but it contains some of the same information. For example, make sure that the two key contingencies (inspection and financing) are specified in the offer as well as in the P&S. If they are not mentioned in the initial agreement, you may not be able to insist that they be included in the final purchase contract.

At a minimum, the offer should contain the following:

1. *A complete property description.* This means not just the address, but a precise description that includes the amount of land, the boundaries, the place where the owner's deed is recorded, and so on.

2. *The amount of any deposit or binder accompanying the offer.* This should be no more than $500 or $1,000, or whatever is common in your area.

3. *What's included or not included in the sale.* For instance, the refrigerator is part of the deal, but the dining-room chandelier isn't.

4. *Any additional contingencies.*

The offer should also indicate what happens in the event of a default by either party. (For example, if the seller changes his mind and refuses to go through with the transaction, or if the buyer reneges for reasons other than those covered in the contingency clauses).

Additionally, the offer should specify the date and time by which the offer must be accepted or rejected by the seller. As a general rule, the less time allowed for a response, the better. Three days is usually about right. That's long enough for you to have to spend agonizing over whether you're going to get the house or not. Moreover, you want to minimize the seller's ability to use your offer as a bargaining tool to encourage another interested buyer to increase his or her offer.

Your offer should also establish a date by which the Purchase and Sale agreement must be executed. This time should be relatively short, but it should take into account the fact that the agreement will have to be negotiated between the buyer and the seller and their respective attorneys (if the parties are represented by counsel), and sometimes the broker as well. Allow enough time for some unpressured give-and-take, and enough time for the attorney — or attorneys — to do the final drafting after an agreement has been reached.

Again, there's no rule of thumb for the timing here, but the attorneys I know say they like to see two weeks between the signing of the offer and the deadline for executing the P&S. This is usually more than enough time to produce the final agreement.

Many offers contain language requiring the buyer to sign a "standard form" Purchase and Sale agreement. Don't even consider accepting that language unless you read that standard form contract first and find its terms acceptable as they stand. Since that usually won't be the case, you'll be better off with language requiring you to sign a P&S that's "mutually agreed to" by both parties. That makes it clear that if you don't like the terms of the P&S, you're not obligated to sign it.

The date for delivery of the deed — that is, for the final closing — should also be specified in the offer. This should allow enough time after the signing of the Purchase and Sale agreement for you to obtain financing and for the lender's attorney (or the escrow or title company) to perform the title search and complete preparations for closing. You should check with your attorney to see what kind of time period is reasonable, given market conditions and industry practice in your area.

Standard-form agreements often specify where the loan closing is to occur. In some jurisdictions, that's usually the office of the lender's attorney. In others, the closing occurs at the office of the escrow company or at the registry of deeds. To avoid problems, the attorneys I know insert language permitting reasonable changes in the time and location of the closing. Avoid a situation in which the closing location specified by the standard P&S is neither convenient nor practical.

THE PURCHASE AND SALE AGREEMENT

If you take my advice and retain an attorney, the particulars of the transaction will be almost completely worked out before you get to the P&S. In fact, as I noted before, a draft P&S agreement is often used instead of the preliminary offer. If the seller accepts the draft, the contract is completed. Alternatively, as with the offer proper, the seller can make a counteroffer by changing some of the provisions of the draft P&S agreement and sending it back to the buyer for approval.

Bypassing the offer stage can have many advantages. It can save time, because the buyer and seller move more quickly to the signing of the detailed P&S agreement. Working out those details in the initial stages will also make it clear early on if there are disagreements between the seller and the buyer serious enough to break the deal.

Brokers and sellers sometimes object to going directly to the P&S, however, primarily because they're concerned about something known as "buyer's remorse." This is a common and almost inevitable reaction on the part of buyers who look up, realize that they've just taken on the largest financial obligation of their lives, and say, "What have we done? How are we ever going to pay for this? Is this house really worth the fortune we've agreed to pay for it?" Such thoughts generally come in the middle of the night, and most buyers recognize them for what they are — namely, signs of panic. From the perspective of the seller and the broker, though, the little bit of extra time that's required to draft the P&S (rather than just signing the simpler preliminary-offer form first) may give the buyer too much time to get nervous.

While buyer's remorse is more common, "seller's remorse" can also be a factor, particularly in a hot real-estate market. Sometimes sellers have second thoughts about whether they really want to sell a home in which they have been happy for a long time. Sometimes their concerns are more practical — they discover that the house they're buying won't be ready on time, for instance, or they get a better offer from another buyer.

You want the P&S to be detailed and complete, but you don't want the negotiations to drag on for so long that the deal goes flat. If you've thought seriously about buying a home and re-searched your purchase carefully, then any feelings of remorse on your part will be fleeting. And it's in your best interest to be sure the seller doesn't have a chance to think twice about the transaction. The remorse you really want to avoid is the remorse that comes from discovering that the seller has just sold the house you wanted to someone else for $15,000 more than he or she had agreed to accept from you.

MAKING IT RIGHT

A good Purchase and Sale agreement reflects the circumstances and concerns of the buyer and seller involved, as well as the peculiarities of the market in which they are located. For that reason, what's considered important or "standard" may vary from agreement to agreement or from location to location.

The P&S will contain many of the components of the offer but will be much more detailed. First, it will clearly identify the parties to the transaction in the same form in which they hold or will hold title to the property. For example, if the property is owned by a husband and wife as tenants by the entirety (a form of joint ownership), then the husband's name alone on that P&S won't do you much good, since the property cannot be sold without the wife's consent. If the property is owned by a corporation, trust, or estate, then the individual or individuals authorized to sign on behalf of that entity should sign the P&S, and you or your attorney should be reasonably satisfied that the authorization is valid.

Next, as in the offer, the property itself should be identified as completely as possible. The size should be specified, along with a "title reference" showing where the current owner's title is recorded. A description of the property by "metes and bounds" is usually helpful, too. You're going to want to be sure that what you've agreed to buy is consistent with what the seller is authorized to sell you. For example, the P&S may refer to a three-acre lot, but the title search may show that the seller owns only two and a half of those acres, and the neighbors may not be willing to donate the extra land to you.

One of the most important things the P&S should do is lay out, in detail, what is and what is *not* to be included in the sale. If the seller intends to remove a tree, a fence, or the living-room chandelier, that should be spelled out and agreed upon. If the sale includes the draperies, the dishwasher, and all the air-conditioning units, this too should be stated. Specificity and completeness are the keys here. Many a transaction has been scuttled literally on the verge of the final handshake because the disposition of a seemingly minor item — a rug or a refrigerator — was not agreed on in advance.

Another key provision in the P&S is language giving the buyer the right to inspect the property within a specified period (usually twenty-four hours) before the closing. This enables the buyer to be sure, for example, that the chandelier that is supposed to be included in the purchase is still hanging in the hallway. The inspection also allows the buyer to determine that the property has not been damaged since the purchase agreement was signed.

Sometimes special documents are required in order to record the deed, to obtain permits or licenses from the city, county, or state, or to obtain the loan and title insurance. When this is the case, the P&S agreement should ensure the cooperation of the seller in obtaining those documents. One example would be a release authorizing the sale of a house that is part of the estate of someone who has died. Another example: federal law now requires that the proceeds from the sale of real estate be reported to the Internal Revenue Service on a 1099 form. The purpose of this law is to make it harder for people to avoid reporting the capital gains they realize from the sale of real estate. Reporting is generally the responsibility of the closing attorney, but the seller is required to furnish the proper information and often must sign affidavits or other documentation of the sale or the selling price.

In addition, title-insurance companies and lenders also often require that the seller execute affidavits affirming the purchase price, any secondary financing that is being provided, the existence of any liens, and various other facts. The documentation needed from the seller can be extensive, so it's a good idea to insert language in the P&S specifically requiring the seller to provide the requested information and assistance.

Practices vary as to who is to take care of title searches, title insurance, plot plans, and the like, but these obligations should be specified in the P&S, even if local statutes dictate precisely who is responsible for what. Too many closings have been delayed because a document necessary to complete the transaction wasn't provided by the party responsible for bringing it.

Another important detail that must be included in the P&S, obviously, is the purchase price. Equally important is the amount of any funds paid, or intended to be paid, by the buyer as deposits or binders (see above). The form in which any payments must be made (check, cashier's check, or whatever) should also be specified. Generally, the amounts due at the closing must be paid in cash or by certified, cashier's, or treasurer's check. If a certified check is required from the closing attorney, it could delay the release of the funds to the seller by one to three days.

(Cash can also be a problem, however. A seller who wants to be paid entirely or even partly in cash may be trying to prevent documentation of the sale — to avoid tax liability or for other possibly illegal reasons. To avoid paying transfer or capital gains taxes, for example, some sellers will ask that part of the purchase price be paid in cash and that there be no documentation reflecting that fact. The result is that the records show the selling price as being lower than it really was. Have no part of such transactions. It is a violation of federal law — and usually state law as well — to lie about the selling price of a property. Participating in such a scheme could make you party to tax evasion or worse. If you're approached with a request or suggestion of this kind, consult your attorney right away.)

The P&S should further specify the quality of the title the owner is going to convey. What this tells you is the extent to which the seller is guaranteeing that the property is without title flaws. There are several different kinds of deeds you might receive; the most common are the quitclaim deed, the general-warranty deed, and the special-warranty deed. They reflect different degrees of assurance as to the title's quality. The problem is that the definition of each type of deed can vary considerably from one area to another. Your attorney will know the difference and be able to tell you what to expect in your area.

EASEMENTS, RESTRICTIONS, AND ENCUMBRANCES

Any easements, deed restrictions, or encumbrances you have agreed to accept with the property should all be specified in the Purchase and Sale agreement. An "easement" is a right granted to another party to use the property, usually for limited purposes.

A utility easement, for example, which would give a utility company access to your property in order to reach wires, cables, or pipes, may be quite acceptable, since it usually won't interfere with your use of the property for residential purposes. But if that easement entails a sewer pipe that runs diagonally across your backyard four feet down — where you had intended to put the swimming pool — then you may want to reconsider your purchase.

A "deed restriction" is anything that limits your use of the property. There might be a prohibition, for instance, on the construction of any additional structures on your lot.

An "encumbrance" is anything that clouds your title to or ownership of the property — such as a lien filed because the owner failed to pay a water bill, an outstanding mortgage, or the like.

You may not find out about these title problems until after a title search is performed, but any that are known at this point should be stated in the P&S.

Whatever you do, until you know exactly what they are, don't accept language saying that you'll accept the title subject to any easements, restrictions, or encumbrances of record. Don't agree in advance to pay full price for a property that you may not be able to use as you had planned.

THE FREE-OF-ALL-TENANTS CLAUSE

Most buyers assume that when they purchase a home, it will be vacant when they're ready to move in. To make sure that will be the case, Purchase and Sale agreements typically specify that the property will be delivered "free of all tenants."

That may seem unnecessary in a single-family home; the sellers, after all, must be aware that they'll have to leave. But these transactions don't always go precisely as planned. The sellers, for example, may be intending to move into a new house, and perhaps it won't be finished by the promised date. In those circumstances some sellers will ask to be allowed to continue living in the house as tenants of the new owner, for a specified period after the closing.

Such arrangements are generally workable, but they're fraught with potential problems. What happens, for instance, if the time for their departure comes and the sellers still aren't ready to leave? Take that a step further and imagine that you in turn are still in an apartment you're expected to vacate to make way for the new tenants your landlord has found to replace you.

It's far cleaner and less complicated simply to insist that the premises be vacant and ready for you to take possession immediately after the closing. If you're going to accept another arrangement, your attorney should spell out the terms in the Purchase and Sale agreement. If the sellers are to remain in the house after the closing date, the provision should specify (a) the date by which they must leave, (b) the rent they are to pay during their occupancy period (the higher the better — you don't want this arrangement to be too comfortable for them), and (c) the penalty they must pay for every day they remain beyond the specified termination date. Again, the penalty should be high enough to discourage them from overstaying their welcome.

THE MULTIFAMILY DWELLING

The free-of-all-tenants language is even more critical when you're purchasing a multifamily residence, one or more units of which are occupied by tenants. You may want to keep the current tenants, but you'll probably want to renegotiate the terms of their existing leases or rental agreements. The rents charged by the previous owner may have been sufficient to cover his or her $25,000 mortgage, but they may fall far short of what you need to offset your mortgage of $150,000.

The free-of-all-tenants provision is important for other reasons as well. The existing tenants may have been living in these units for years, with only minimal increases in their rent, making them resistant to your efforts to require them to pay more after you take possession. The tenants may be friends of the old owner, who, to protect them, may try to sign them to long-term leases shortly before he or she sells the property. And, yes, the new owner is usually obliged to honor these leases if they are in effect when he or she takes possession — unless, again, the onus of eviction is placed on the seller by means of a free-of-all-tenants clause.

There are some alternatives to insisting that the owner evict all existing tenants. One is to negotiate new leases or written rental agreements with the tenants *before* you buy. That's an option you may want to consider, since there are definite advantages to inheriting desirable tenants rather than having to go through the often difficult process of finding them yourself. But don't count on being able to negotiate new lease terms *after* you've bought — unless you don't mind the prospect of a (possibly prolonged) period during which you're collecting less rent than you need, or possibly no rent at all.

Another alternative to a free-of-all-tenants requirement is to reduce the purchase price significantly, or hold a significant portion of it in escrow, to defray the costs and the loss in rental income you will incur if you have to go through the process of evicting the tenants yourself. How much of an offset is reasonable depends on the costs and market conditions in your area. Where the rental market is tight (limiting the options available to the tenants if they are forced to relocate) and the eviction process difficult (which means your legal costs will be high), a purchase-price reduction or escrow requirement of up to $10,000 is not out of line.

ADJUSTMENTS

In the interests of avoiding disagreement later on, the P&S agreement can include a clause on how to handle adjustments for charges and credits that are still outstanding when the transfer of ownership occurs. These include such things as property taxes that may not yet be due, water and sewer charges incurred by the seller for which he or she has not yet been billed, fuel oil left in the tank, and so on. Practices vary, but the general rule is that the seller should pay his or her fair share of, or should receive a fair credit for, those charges or credits accrued up to and in some cases including the date of the sale, with the buyer taking over after that.

For example, suppose the community sends out its tax bills

twice a year, for the periods from January 1 to June 30 and from July 1 to December 31. If the tax bill for the first six months has not been paid by the date of the closing, and the new owners take possession on April 1, then the new owners should be responsible for half the tax bill (from April through June), and the sellers should pay for the first three months, during which time they still occupied the residence. This might be handled by a clause in the Purchase and Sale agreement calling for the sellers to place in escrow an amount equal to their anticipated share of the tax bill.

Similarly, if the heating-oil tank is half full when the sale is completed, the P&S agreement typically requires that an adjustment be made at the closing to compensate the seller for the unused fuel.

Industry practices and methods of computing these charges may vary from one area to another. But the more specific you can be in the Purchase and Sale agreement about what the charges are and how they are to be handled, the better your chances of avoiding last-minute (and potentially costly) surprises.

CONDOS — SPECIAL CONSIDERATIONS

A condo purchase entails a few special considerations that should be addressed both in the offer and in the P&S agreement.

The documents should specify the name of the condominium, the owner's unit number, and the owner's percentage interest in the condo as a whole. Both documents should also include all the contingencies noted earlier, plus an additional one: your obligation to purchase the unit should be made contingent on an attorney's review and approval of the condo documents. The primary documents, as you will recall from chapter 9, include the master deed, a sample unit deed, and the rules and regulations, bylaws, and budget for the current year and for the previous three to five years (if the condo has existed that long).

The buyer should insist on a review contingency of this kind, but it's also common and reasonable for the seller to require that any such review be completed within a fairly short period of time — say, two weeks.

Another provision unique to condo purchase documents is a requirement that the seller (and/or the condominium association) provide all the additional documents required for the mortgage application and for the closing of the loan. These additional documents include (a) affidavits or statements showing the number (and percentage) of units that are owner-occupied and the number of units that have been sold or are under agreement for sale; (b) descriptions of the insurance policy or policies covering the unit, the condominium as a whole, the condo association, and the condo management; and (c) documentary proof that all condo fees and assessments have been paid and that any local rent-control, security-deposit, and condo-conversion laws have been complied with.

BROKER REPRESENTATIONS

The Purchase and Sale agreement, obviously, must be signed by both the buyer and the seller. In many areas, however, it is common for the broker also to be a party to the contract. Generally this is of minimal interest to the purchaser, since the broker typically represents only the seller. In some instances, though, you should be concerned about the broker's rights and obligations as a party to the contract.

For instance, many P&S agreements state that the broker is making (or explicitly is *not* making) certain warranties about the property. If any representations have been made to you, they should be stated in the P&S with as much specificity as possible. Examples of the representations a broker might make include assurances that the roof is "brand-new," that the heating system "will last a hundred years," or that the zoning laws will permit you to put the "in-law apartment" up for rent. Any representations that you're relying on in purchasing the property should be included in the P&S.

It's usually a good idea to have the broker certify that he or she is licensed in the jurisdiciton and that he or she has complied with the Code of Ethics of the National Association of Realtors.

If your broker is a Realtor (a member of the National Association of Realtors), he or she is already ethically bound by that association's code, but putting a clause in the P&S adds a clear legal obligation to an ethical obligation that already applies. Such language is particularly important if there's no statute in your state specifically requiring brokers to disclose any adverse information that might affect the purchaser's decision.

Finally, any representations made by the seller should also be stated in detail in the Purchase and Sale agreement. Be wary of any language asserting that no representations have been made. First of all, it's hard to imagine how a house could be sold without either the seller or the broker or both saying something about it beyond "Here's the house." If either the seller or the broker seems reluctant to see his or her oral representations put into writing, your warning light should go on. He or she has either told you something that isn't true or neglected to tell you something that you need to know. Be hard-nosed about this. If the owner and the agent aren't willing to stand behind what they've told you about the house, then you shouldn't be willing to buy it.

But let's suppose there's nothing wrong with your purchase and that your agreements are negotiated and signed smoothly. The next step along the home-purchase path is to find and apply for a mortgage.

TWELVE

Shopping for a Mortgage

You've established your priorities and researched the markets. After weeks of searching, you've finally found the house for you. You've resolved the potentially sticky points and signed the Purchase and Sale agreement.

"Now," you say with a sigh of relief, "all I have to do is get the mortgage."

Would that it were that simple. Shopping for a home, finding it, and bargaining for a good price, alas, are just the beginning, because the next thing you have to do is to find a mortgage.

Obtaining a mortgage *used to be* fairly simple. For one thing, there used to be only one kind of loan available — namely, a thirty-year fixed-rate mortgage. Today the mortgage menu looks like a bowl of alphabet soup, full of ARM's, GPM's, GEM's, and the like in what can seem an endless and hopelessly confusing mess. How do you make a valid choice?

The application process itself is much more complex, too. When your parents bought their home, maybe twenty-five or thirty years ago, they faced very little paperwork. They may have filled out a simple one-page application or been given their loan on a handshake from a local bank president who attended the same church and had known them all their lives. Today's mortgage folders, in contrast, can look like unabridged copies of *War and Peace*. And you can forget doing business on a handshake. Borrowers who go through the mortgage-application process today sometimes feel as though they're being scrutinized for top-secret security clearance.

The major reason for all the changes is the evolution of the secondary market (see chapter 2). This term, you'll recall, refers to the individual and institutional investors that purchase the loans originated by local lenders. For mortgage seekers, the existence of this secondary market means three things: (1) more paperwork; (2) a longer wait for loan approval; and (3) stricter rules for qualifying.

In this chapter I hope to convey a good general sense of what's likely to be required of you, and to provide a framework of basic terms and concepts. It won't make you an expert on home-mortgage finance, but it will show you that there's order to the apparent chaos after all, and help you get your bearings. And I hope it will steel you to the rigors of the process.

THE NEW ABC'S OF MORTGAGES

The best place to start the tour is with a review of the major kinds of mortgages you may encounter.

My list of the major options runs to ten items. Even so, the list doesn't begin to be inclusive. An inclusive treatment of the universe of mortgages would consume a book by itself, and even if such a book were to be compiled, it would be out of date and incomplete by the time it got published.

The following paragraphs, nonetheless, will give you a working concept of the mortgage options that you're most likely to run into.

FIXED-RATE MORTGAGE (FRM)

This is the standard mortgage model, the vanilla ice cream on the mortgage menu. It is the oldest, most easily understood type of mortgage. Its primary attraction is that the interest rate and the amount of the payment remain fixed for the life of the loan, typically either fifteen or thirty years. If the rate is 11 percent when you get your mortgage, it'll still be 11 percent when you make the last payment or sell the house to a new owner, unless you yourself initiate some kind of change.

ADJUSTABLE-RATE MORTGAGE (ARM)

As its name very well tells you, this kind of mortgage has a rate that can change from time to time over the course of the loan. How much and how often it changes depends on the lender's specific policy and on the "index" being used. (Lenders use a variety of formulas to calculate their rates, but all are pegged to some well-established, well-known statistical measurement of the economy. This measurement is taken as an "index" for the lender's interest rate. If the index moves, your interest rate will move, too.)

Thus, two basic questions to ask about any ARM are how often the rate is adjusted and what index governs the adjustments.

Most lenders offer ARM's that are adjusted either every year (a one-year ARM) or every three (a three-year ARM). Some ARM's are adjusted every six months, but I'm not a big fan of an arrangement that could change the amount of my mortgage payment more than once a year.

Lenders typically peg their one-year ARM's to the one-year Treasury Bill (or "T-Bill") index and their three-year ARM's to the three-year Treasury Bill index. Those indexes reflect the rates paid to investors who purchase those federal government securities. The rates are determined by the results of open market auctions, which are held every week. The Treasury Bill rates are published regularly by many newspapers, including the *Wall Street Journal*, so ARM borrowers who want to obsess about their loans can monitor fluctuations every week. Less obsessive borrowers will probably be content to check the rates every month or so, particularly as the review period for their loan approaches, so they'll have a general idea of what kind of adjustment to expect.

When the time comes to adjust your loan, the lender will look at the movement of the appropriate index during the adjustment period. If the index has moved up, you *will* pay more; if it has moved down, you *may* pay less. The actual adjustment will be calculated by means of a formula that is often lender-specific.

Have the lender's agent explain this formula to you in detail when you apply for the loan.

The disclosure requirements for ARM's are extensive. Under a federal law passed in 1988, lenders must supply loan applicants will exhaustive information about the index and how it has performed in the past. They must also provide you with examples showing what will happen to your mortgage payments under assumed "worst-case" rate changes during your adjustment period. Don't just stuff these papers into a drawer along with all the other unread material you collect during your trip through the mortgage-application process. Read this stuff carefully and make sure you understand it — the mortgage you save may be your own.

An essential question to ask about an ARM is whether there are any limits on how much your rate can be raised, both at each review and over the whole term of the loan. Without limits of some kind — known as "caps" — you'll have no way to predict how much your rate (and thus your monthly payments) might change. Neither will you know for sure whether you'll be able to afford the increases that may hit you.

The "capping" system has become more standardized over the past several years and is now fairly uniform, chiefly because capping is required by the secondary market. Most lenders limit periodic adjustments to 2 percent at each review, and lifetime adjustments to 5 or 6 percent. So if your ARM rate starts out at 8 percent, you know it will never increase more than 2 percent per adjustment, and that it will never exceed 14 percent over the life of the loan.

Another important ARM concept is the lender's "margin." This is the profit the lender adds to the index rate to determine what your adjusted mortgage rate will be at each periodic review. Say you get a one-year ARM with a beginning index rate of 8 percent. Suppose the lender's margin is 3 percent, which is typical in some markets. Let's assume that at the end of the first year, the index has not moved at all. It's still at 8 percent. But your adjusted rate is going to be 11 percent — that is, the index rate of 8 percent plus the lender's margin of 3 percent.

This shows why it's important to have a cap or limit on periodic increases and why it's advisable to avoid the "deeply discounted" ARM's that some lenders use to attract borrowers in a competitive lending market. A deeply discounted ARM is one in which the starting rate is below (and sometimes *far* below) the governing index.

Let's say the ARM index is at 9 percent, but the lender offers a starting rate of 8 percent for the first year. Come the first adjustment, the index is still at 9 percent, but that deeply discounted ARM is going to jump, and I do mean *jump* — first from the starting rate of 8 percent to the governing 9 percent index, then up again by the lender's 3 percent margin.

So unless your bank deal includes a cap on periodic adjustments, you could find yourself "adjusted" from an 8 percent mortgage one year to a 12 percent mortgage the next. (If you had a standard 2 percent–per–adjustment cap, your adjusted rate wouldn't be able to exceed 10 percent.) Consider what that uncapped adjustment would mean in dollar terms on a $100,000 mortgage. Your starting principal and interest payments of $733.77 would increase to $1,028.62. Most household budgets would be hard pressed to absorb a jolt like that. The technical term for an adjustment of that magnitude, by the way, is "payment shock"; it can be a definite pain.

One solution some lenders have come up with for the payment-shock problem is to limit the *dollar* amount by which monthly payments can increase, but at the same time to put no restrictions at all on the size of adjustments allowed.

Sound weird? Take a one-year ARM that starts at 10 percent. At the end of a year, let's say, the index movement puts the adjusted rate at 12 percent. This means that your payments on a $100,000 loan ought to increase from $877.58 to $1,028.62. But the lender limits increases in your monthly payments to $50 per adjustment; therefore your new payment will be only $927.58. But this is $101.04 less than what you actually owe under the new interest rate, and don't imagine that the lender just forgets about it. Rather, the lender adds it to the *principal* balance of your loan. This is known in the trade as "negative amortization." What it means is that your loan balance, instead of building down month by month, can actually increase! Imagine your surprise when you decide to sell your home, only to discover that you owe the bank more than you borrowed to begin with.

Clearly, ARM's can be complicated, with fine print within fine print and footnotes to footnotes. It's important for you to understand how they operate. This is the only way to be certain that any loan you accept will be structured comfortably for you and will meet your financial needs.

Indeed, at this point you might well be wondering who would want an ARM if it's so complicated and strewn with perils. The answer is simple. Most borrowers would probably prefer the certainty of a fixed-rate mortgage, but when interest rates are high, many of us can't qualify for a fixed-rate loan. The advantage of the ARM is that it's typically offered at rates below (sometimes considerably below) the fixed-rate alternative. As a result, borrowers who can't afford the fixed-rate loan may find the ARM their only option.

It's really not a terribly risky option if you're pretty sure of seeing your income increase over the next several years. Even a deeply discounted ARM should cause you no fear if you know you can handle whatever the interest-rate climate can dish out.

Moreover, the many buyers who know they'll be transferred in two years would be well advised to take an 8 percent ARM with a 2 percent adjustment cap rather than an 11 percent fixed-rate mortgage. For the first year they'll have an 8 percent mortgage. At the end of the year, even in the worst case — if the maximum adjustment is indicated — they'll still be better off than they would have been with the 11 percent fixed-rate mortgage. And at the end of the second year, when another worst-case adjustment could take the ARM rate up to 12 percent, they're about to sell, move on, and buy again.

It's also possible, of course, that the ARM index may go down. If that happens, your rate will go down automatically, and *maybe* your monthly payments will also go down. That depends on the margin (reductions usually being capped in the same way as increases). If you have a fixed-rate mortgage, the only way to take advantage of declining rates is to refinance, and that's a costly process.

If you find yourself considering an ARM, you should also be aware that many lenders apply more conservative underwriting standards to ARM's than they do to fixed-rate mortgages. For example, some lenders will insist that the monthly housing payments for ARM borrowers not exceed 25 percent of their income, while they'll qualify fixed-rate borrowers whose payments represent up to 28 percent of income. The rationale behind this is that it is better for ARM borrowers not to start out on the edge of their affordability limits, since there's a certain risk that their mortgage payments will increase.

CONVERTIBLE OPTION

Fixed-rate and adjustable-rate mortgages represent the primary options available to home buyers today, and the convertible mortgage represents something of a compromise between the two. It's designed for those who want the advantages of the ARM but also want to limit the risk of rising rates.

Under this arrangement, the buyer starts out with an ARM but has the option of converting to a fixed-rate mortgage at specified points during the loan term. That's the first thing to understand about convertibles. You usually cannot just switch whenever you get nervous about the economy and want to lock in a fixed rate; you typically have to convert at the times the lender has designated for you to exercise that option. Lender programs vary widely, so make sure you understand exactly how flexible your program is going to be. When can you convert? How often do you get to consider the option?

Also ask whether there are any up-front fees involved. Will you have to pay more for an ARM with the conversion feature than for an ARM without it? Are there additonal fees due if and when you do decide to convert?

And most important, find out what the lender's actual conversion rate is. Most lenders will not simply let you convert to whatever the prevailing fixed rate happens to be when you're ready to make the switch. Conversion formulas vary from lender to lender, and they're generally complicated. The best way to get an idea of how they work is to ask lenders offering convertible mortgage loans what the conversion rate would be today for an ARM borrower who decided to convert. In most cases the conversion rate will be somewhat higher than the same lender's fixed rate. In other words, the conversion rate is higher than the rate you'd pay if you were to go through the process of refinancing — that is, rewriting the loan at the lower rate.

That doesn't mean, however, that the convertible option isn't worthwhile sometimes. The conversion should involve less paperwork and be less costly than a straight refinancing. But you need to know whether you'll have to pay any points or other fees at the time you convert. If you will, you must consider how those costs would compare with the cost of refinancing.

Whether the conversion option makes sense for you will depend in part on how much of a premium you'll have to pay for it in up-front fees and higher rates. It will also depend on how long you plan to be in the home. If you're going to occupy the house for only a year or two, it's unlikely that you'll be able to recover the costs of refinancing before you move. But obtaining an ARM with the conversion option, on the other hand, might enable you to get a low rate at the outset, with the knowledge that you could protect yourself, by locking in a rate, should the interest-rate trend turn against you. That might be security worth having in an uncertain economy, especially if you don't have to pay hefty refinancing fees in order to get it.

If you plan to stay in the home long-term, however, you'll have to sharpen your pencil and do some figuring. It's not an easy calculation. First you need to work out the up-front cost of a straight refinancing. Then you have to look at the difference between the monthly payments: how much would you have to pay per month at the refinanced rate? How much would you have to pay at the higher conversion rate? Then take the difference between these two figures and multiply it by the number of months you expect to stay in the house.

To illustrate, suppose it would cost you $2,500 to refinance (a realistic figure). The 0.5 percent higher conversion rate, on the other hand, would result in monthly payments $65 higher than you'd pay with simple outright refinancing. If you figure on being in the house at least five years, then you're talking about a difference, at $65 per month, of $780 a year and $3,900 over a five-year period. Which means that you're paying a premium of $1,400 for your conversion option, not counting any extra initial fees that may have been involved. On the other hand, you'll be spreading that cost over five years, as opposed to coming up with $2,500 in a lump sum to cover the refinancing cost, and not a few buyers will find that convenient.

It's a complicated exercise. There's no easy way to determine whether or not the conversion option makes sense for you. But if no up-front fees are required for the option and the interest rates are the same for convertible ARM's as for conventional ones — in other words, if it won't cost you anything — I'd say go ahead and take it. Otherwise, break out the calculator to see what the cost of the conversion option is really going to give you. Before you accept a conversion feature, be sure that you understand its terms, costs, and limitations and have a clear picture of its real value to you. Be sure you not only get what you want, but want what you get.

BUY-DOWN

The ARM with a conversion option is a fairly recent addition to the mortgage menu. The buy-down, on the other hand, has been around for some time, coming in and going out of fashion as interest rates go up and down.

The goal of a buy-down is to make a home mortgage affordable for a borrower who's having trouble meeting the lender's standard qualification ratios. That goal is accomplished by, in effect, "buying down" the borrower's rate for a certain period of time. To explain: suppose that the borrower needs an $80,000 mortgage but can only qualify for the loan at a 10 percent interest rate, which would make for monthly payments of about $700. Suppose the prevailing rate is 11½ percent, which would mean payments of almost $800. The borrower cannot qualify.

At that point the buy-down becomes an option. What happens in a buy-down is that either the seller, the builder (if it's a new house), or the buyer pays a lump sum into a fund that is then used to pay the lending institution for the lower rate for a certain period, usually no more than three years. During this buy-down period, the borrower makes payments at the 10 percent level, but each month the lender withdraws enough money from the buy-down fund to make up the difference between what the borrower is paying ($700) and what he or she would be paying at prevailing rates ($800).

You may wonder why a builder or a seller would want to participate in a buy-down. Why not simply lower the selling price if the buyer is having trouble qualifying? Similarly, if a buyer has enough cash to put into the buy-down fund, why not add that amount to the down payment instead and thus reduce the mortgage?

The answer to both questions lies in the fact that a relatively small amount of money is needed in a buy-down. Typically, the same amount of money applied to the down payment would have much less of an impact. To illustrate: using the above example, let's say the seller is willing to kick in $3,000, either by lowering the asking price or by funding a buy-down. A reduction in the purchase price would mean the buyer has to borrow only $77,000 instead of $80,000. The monthly payment at the prevailing rate (11½ percent) would be almost $763, which is still beyond our buyer's reach. That same $3,000 invested in a buy-down, however, would provide an extra $100 per month toward the borrower's mortgage payment for 30 months — enough to bring the buyer within the lender's affordability guidelines.

On its face, this solution seems ideal. The seller is able to sell the home at the asking price, whereas without the buy-down, he or she would have had to reduce the price by almost $10,000 in order to qualify the same buyer. The buyer, meanwhile, is able to overcome the interest-rate obstacle and get a foot in the ownership door.

But what happens when the buy-down period ends? The basic assumption of the buy-down arrangement is that your income will increase sufficiently during the buy-down period so that, by the time it ends, you'll be able to afford the payments at the higher rate. Or, failing that, you'll be able to either sell the property or refinance it within the buy-down period. But what if these assumptions collapse? What if you're no more able to afford the higher payments at the end of the buy-down period than you were at the beginning? What if the market is slow? What if all you'll be able to do, short of foreclosure, is accept refinancing at unfavorable terms?

Before you decide that a buy-down is the right mortgage product for you, you need a solid, clear answer to that question. If you can't make the higher payments that will start hitting you after three years, and you can't find another source of financing, you might have to sell the house or default on the loan and lose the house in foreclosure. There's nothing good there.

GRADUATED-PAYMENT MORTGAGE (GPM)

The GPM is another mortgage designed for people who are having trouble qualifying for a mortgage at current rates but have reason to expect that their income will increase over time. The idea here is that the starting rate is below that of a fixed-rate and possibly that of an adjustable-rate mortgage, but it increases at specified increments during the first five to seven years, then levels off.

One disadvantage of the GPM is that its final interest rate is often higher than the rate on either the fixed-rate or the adjustable-rate alternative. Another drawback is that some GPM's have limits on payment increases, which can result in negative amortization (the unappealing prospect I discussed earlier in this chapter). And like the buy-down, the GPM carries the inherent risk that the borrower's income won't keep pace with the required interest-rate and payment increases. So think twice about this one, too.

GROWING-EQUITY MORTGAGE (GEM)

This is a variation on the graduated-payment mortgage theme. It's designed not for borrowers who are having trouble qualifying but for those who are anxious, for whatever reason, to pay off their mortgage as soon as possible. To that end, the interest rate remains fixed, but the amount of the monthly payment increases according to a prearranged schedule, with the higher payments going to reduce the principal balance. The result is that the mortgage is repaid in fifteen to eighteen years instead of the more typical thirty years. This can be an appealing arrangement to someone who is expecting regular income growth and wants to build equity quickly.

There are some potential disadvantages to this type of mortgage, however. First, the down-payment requirements and effective interest rates for GEM's are often higher than for other mortgage options. And aside from the risk that the borrower may not be able to keep up with the required payment increases, there's also the question of whether this is the best use of those funds. In other words, is it better to use that additional money to pay down the mortgage or to invest it in other ways?

An even more serious concern for some borrowers is the tax impact. Mortgage-interest payments are deductible, but with a GEM, with an ever-increasing portion of the monthly payment going to reduce the principal, the tax deductions for interest payments will be reduced over time. And the reduction will be more rapid than with the standard repayment schedule. For borrowers in a high tax bracket, that could be a serious drawback, especially after the tax-reform legislation of 1986, which eliminated virtually all interest deductions available to consumers except that for mortgage interest.

FIFTEEN-YEAR MORTGAGE

An alternative to a growing-equity mortgage is a conventional fixed-rate mortgage with a term of fifteen rather than twenty-five or thirty years. Like the growing-equity mortgage, the fifteen-year mortgage enables borrowers to repay their loan more quickly, which means they build equity faster and pay less interest over the life of the mortgage. The advantage of the fifteen-year plan is that the payments are fixed. You don't have to worry about coming up with progressively more money for monthly payments over the term of the loan. Like the GEM, the fifteen-year mortgage will require higher monthly payments than will the thirty-year alternative. On a $100,000 loan at 10 percent, the borrower with the thirty-year mortgage will pay $878, compared to payments of $1,074 on the fifteen-year alternative. On the other hand, the borrower with the fifteen-year note pays only $93,320 in interest over the life of his loan, while the borrower with the thirty-year note has interest payments totaling $120,760. (The actual savings may be even greater, since the rate on the fifteen-year mortgage is often a bit lower than the rate on the thirty-year alternative.)

Yes, the interest savings are dramatic, but you should take those numbers with a grain of salt. First of all, most people don't remain in their home for the full thirty-year term of their mortgage; in fact, the average actual life of a mortgage is closer to seven to ten years. The shorter your time frame, the less significant the benefits of the fifteen-year loan. On the other hand, if you're planning to stay put for a while and you're looking at the equity in your home as a source of financing for the college tuition bill that you'll be facing in ten years or so, then the fifteen-year option may be a sensible alternative.

The affordability factor is also a concern, though, as it is with a GEM. Can you comfortably handle the higher payments required by the fifteen-year mortgage? And even if you can, does that represent the best use of your funds?

One final point to consider in connection with both fifteen-year and growing-equity mortgages: most lenders today will allow you to make extra payments toward principal without penalty, if you want to do so, on a standard fixed-rate or adjustable-rate loan. That represents another way of repaying your loan more quickly without being locked into a repayment schedule that you might not be able to meet every month. But it only makes a noticeable difference if you're disciplined enough to pay more than you're required to each month. The fifteen-year note and the GEM impose a payment discipline that most of us would be hard-pressed to impose on ourselves unaided.

BIWEEKLY MORTGAGE

Another option for people who want to repay their loans sooner is the biweekly mortgage. Instead of making a single mortgage payment each month, borrowers who choose this option make two equal payments monthly. Under that repayment schedule, which can work well for someone who is paid twice monthly, the borrower actually winds up making an extra payment every year. As a result, as with the GEM and fifteen-year mortgages, the loan is repaid and equity is built more quickly, and interest costs are consequently lower. There's nothing wrong with this, but remember that you could accomplish the same goal by making additional payments on your own, without being locked in to a twice-monthly repayment schedule that you might not always find convenient.

FHA LOANS

In their assessment of the available loan options, many borrowers overlook two mortgage programs that can be worth considering: those mortgages insured by the Federal Housing Administration, and those guaranteed by the Veterans Administration (see the following section).

FHA loans in particular are often ignored today because the below-market interest rate that used to be one of the program's primary attractions has been eliminated. But these loans can still have some definite advantages, primary among them being a relatively low down-payment requirement. The lowest down payment required on non–federally insured loans is 5 percent, but in practice most borrowers today must come up with a minimum of 10 percent down. An FHA loan requires only 3 percent down on the first $25,000 of the purchase price, and 5 percent down on any amount above that. On a $100,000 loan, for example, a conventional borrower would have to come up with at least $10,000 as a down payment, while the FHA borrower would need less than half that amount.

Another advantage of both FHA and VA loans is that they are fully "assumable" by other borrowers. To "assume" a loan is essentially to step into the shoes of the seller and take over the responsibility for paying off his or her loan. This can be an attractive arrangement if the rate on the seller's loan is significantly below the prevailing mortgage rates that would otherwise be available to the borrower.

Take a seller who has an $80,000 FHA loan written at 6 percent, with an outstanding balance of $60,000. The selling price of the house is $100,000. The buyer assumes the $80,000 mortgage, which relieves the seller of the need to pay off the $60,000 balance. To complete the purchase, the buyer will either have to make a $40,000 down payment or finance a loan for some portion of that amount. Let's say the buyer has only $20,000 available for a down payment. That would leave $20,000 to finance at the prevailing rate of 11 percent. The monthly payment on the assumed mortgage would then be the sum of $480 (the payment on the original FHA loan) plus $190.60 (the payment on the new $20,000 loan at 11 percent), or a total monthly payment of $670.60. If the buyer didn't assume the seller's mortgage, however, and instead put $20,000 down and obtained an $80,000 mortgage at 11 percent, the monthly payment would be $762.40. So in this case the assumable mortgage could make a significant difference — $91.80 a month — to a buyer on the margin of affordability.

The numbers don't always work out this way, though. The higher the rate on the mortgage being assumed, the less advantageous it's going to be. So if you run into the possibility of assuming a mortgage, be sure to study the numbers carefully to make sure it'll be worth your while.

If you're the seller, having a mortgage that can be assumed by another borrower can be a definite advantage if interest rates are much higher than the rate on your mortgage, since that may increase your chances of finding a buyer. (ARM's, by the way, are almost invariably assumable, but fixed-rate mortgages usually aren't.) There is one caveat here, however. With a VA loan, you want to be sure that the buyer assuming the loan is eligible in his or her own right for VA financing. Otherwise, you'll continue to be liable for the loan, even though the new borrower has assumed responsibility for making the payments.

You don't have to meet any membership or income requirements to qualify for an FHA loan, but there's a limit on the size of the mortgage you can obtain under this program. In markets where home prices are high, these ceilings can make the FHA program unworkable. Currently the maximum loans allowed in "high-priced" areas are $101,250 for a single-family home or condominium, $114,000 for a two-family, $138,000 for a three-family, and $160,000 for a four-family dwelling.

These are the maximums, however. The ceiling in some markets is as low as $67,500 for a single-family home. For someone putting down the minimum amount, the maximum purchase price, in a high-priced area, would be only about $105,000. That won't get you very far in areas such as New York and Los Angeles and Boston, where the average price for a single-family is more than $180,000.

VA LOANS

Loans guaranteed by the Veterans Administration have most of the advantages of FHA loans, and then some, but they also have eligibility restrictions. They are available only to veterans of the armed services, those currently in the service, and their spouses. VA loans typically are half a percent or more below prevailing market rates, and they can be obtained with no money down. The VA does not actually limit the size of the mortgage a lender can approve, but it does limit the portion of the loan on which repayment is guaranteed to the lender.

This has the effect of limiting the amount lenders are willing to lend under the program. The size of the guaranteed portion has recently been increased, so that on loans of about $45,000 or more, the VA will now guarantee 40 percent of the principal amount, or $36,000, whichever is less. For loans with a principal balance below $45,000, the VA guarantee will cover 50 percent.

What that means as a practical matter is that a VA borrower who doesn't put any money down will be able to pay up to about $144,000 for a home. (Lenders typically want the VA guarantee plus the down payment to equal at least 25 percent of the mortgage amount.) Under the old VA guarantee of $27,500, the maximum purchase price with no down payment was only about $110,000.

The major drawback to a VA loan is the number of discount percentage points (known simply as "points") lenders charge to bridge the gap between the market rate and the VA rate. The borrower is allowed to pay only one of those points, plus a 1 percent financing fee. Any additional points required must be paid by the seller, and not all sellers are delighted to do that. On the other hand, sellers in a slow market who are anxious to make a deal will often pay the discount points and (though they are not technically supposed to do so) make up the difference by increasing their asking price. There's no limit on the price of homes that can be purchased with VA financing, except that it cannot exceed the VA's appraised value for the property.

One serious disadvantage of both FHA and VA loans is the amount of paperwork involved. It can take considerably longer in some markets to get an FHA or VA loan approved than it does to obtain a non–federally insured mortgage. Government efforts to streamline the procedures have made this less of a problem than it used to be, but you may find some sellers and brokers hesitant to work with buyers who are planning to seek either FHA or VA financing. That doesn't mean you should ignore these options, but you should be prepared to overcome some resistance to them. If the housing market is slow, on the other hand, you may find some brokers and lenders aggressively pushing these programs in order to increase the pool of eligible home buyers.

SELLER FINANCING

One other option to consider is a form of "seller financing," where the owner provides some of the money needed to complete the sale. Seller financing is most common when high interest rates make it difficult for buyers to qualify for mortgages, and this arrangement can in fact facilitate transactions that might not otherwise occur.

For example, the seller might offer to pay closing costs for a buyer who can't clear that financial hurdle; or, if the buyer needs a $150,000 mortgage but can only qualify for $125,000, the seller might "take back" a second mortgage to fill that gap. The buyer is able to complete the purchase, and the seller doesn't have to lower the price.

That looks like a win-win situation, and, indeed, it may be in some cases. But there are potential problems here, for buyers and sellers alike. Most seller financing involves a relatively short-term note (usually with a term of three to five years). The buyer may pay interest only during the loan period, but will face a "balloon payment" at the end, which means that the entire principal amount borrowed from the seller will have to be repaid all at once. Unless the buyer anticipates a windfall that will make such a lump-sum payment possible, he or she will have to find some other means of repaying the loan. The assumption is that the buyer will be able to refinance the bank mortgage and thus obtain the funds needed to repay the seller. And that may work out. But if the property hasn't appreciated much, or if the buyer still can't qualify for a larger loan, then both buyer and seller are going to have a problem. The buyer could be forced to sell the house (or lose it in foreclosure) to pay off the seller, and the seller, who may have been counting on the nice lump-sum payment, may have to decide whether to extend the loan or take back the house instead.

SPECIAL PROGRAMS

In addition to the mortgages I've described so far, buyers may find that special programs designed primarily for first-time home buyers are available in many states. The details of these programs vary from state to state, but most provide below-market-rate mortgage money to eligible borrowers — that is, borrowers who meet specified income and purchase-price limitations.

Although these programs have been quite helpful for many first-time buyers in many states, there are two reasons for not emphasizing them too much. First, the funding available for these programs is usually limited; only a small number of the borrowers who can qualify for these programs are actually able to obtain financing through them. Second, there's a strong effort now under way in Congress to eliminate or severely restrict the use of the tax-exempt bonds that provide the financing for these programs. So there's a good chance that the funds available to help first-time home buyers will be even more restricted in the future, and perhaps may not be available at all.

WHERE TO LOOK

Now that you have a general idea of what kinds of mortgages are available, you're ready to start shopping for the loan program that will best suit your financial needs. Where do you start your search?

Depending on where you live, you'll find home mortgages available at commercial banks, savings institutions (savings banks, savings and loan associations, cooperative banks, and credit unions), and mortgage companies.

Commercial banks and savings institutions are also known as depository institutions. In addition to making home mortgages available, they provide other kinds of consumer and business loans and accept deposits, offer checking and savings accounts, and provide a variety of other services.

Mortgage companies, on the other hand, are in business for only one purpose — namely, to write home mortgages and sell them on the secondary market. All mortgage companies operate in that way. Some depository institutions handle their residential mortgage business through mortgage-company subsidiaries. Other depository institutions have mortgage departments that function much like mortgage companies in that they sell all (or nearly all) the loans they originate on the secondary market.

A lending institution that retains rather than sells its loans is known as a "portfolio lender." Because portfolio lenders don't have to worry about selling their loans to investors, you may find their loan requirements somewhat more flexible than the requirements of secondary-market lenders, who have to toe the secondary market's underwriting line. But you will also often find that portfolio lenders charge a somewhat higher rate for their loans.

HOW TO LOOK

Because so many lenders today are selling or planning to sell the loans they originate, you'll find a good deal of similarity in the kinds of mortgages they offer and even in the rates they charge.

There are some differences, however, and sometimes they can be important to the buyer. For example, while mortgage rates usually seem to be fairly uniform, at times they can vary dramatically. Market conditions can change rapidly, and not all lenders make the same assumptions about interest-rate trends. So there may be periods when one lender's rates are significantly higher or lower than the rates charged by other lenders.

It's a mistake to assume that all loan programs and all lenders are alike. It definitely pays to shop around. It also pays to make sure your information is current. Most lenders establish their rates every week, and the lender with the lowest rate one week may no longer be lowest the following week. Shopping for a mortgage is a bit of a grind, but it's an important grind. You won't enjoy it at the time, but in the end you'll be glad you did a good job of it.

POINTS

One of the first terms you'll hear when you start asking lenders about their rates is "points." A point represents one percent of the mortgage amount. On a $100,000 mortgage, one point would be $1,000.

Most lenders charge one point or more to cover the cost of originating and processing the loan. This is different from the application fee that borrowers pay, which covers the cost of the lender's determining whether the borrower can qualify for the requested loan. Typically the points have to be paid in a lump sum at the closing (see chapter 15), though sometimes lenders want some of the points paid up front, with the application and/or upon the borrower's acceptance of the lender's commitment. (Sometimes you can "lock in" an interest rate by paying a point up front. More about this below.)

No matter when you have to pay them, points raise the cost of obtaining the loan. The only good thing about points is that they're usually tax-deductible, so long as they represent the prepayment of interest and are "necessary and common" in the community in which you obtain the loan. If you pay more points than most other lenders charge, however, you may have to amortize their cost over the life of the loan rather than deducting all of them from your taxes in the year in which you incurred them.

KEY QUESTIONS

The first question to ask when you survey your potential lenders is what kinds of loans they offer. Be sure when you compare loan programs that you're not comparing apples and oranges — that is, don't compare one lender's fixed-rate mortgage with another's one-year ARM.

Once you've determined which kinds of loans are available, the next step is to ask lenders about their prevailing rates. This harmless-sounding exercise will teach you right off the bat that comparing the offerings of different lenders isn't easy. One lender will tell you it's charging 10½ percent plus three points for its fixed-rate mortgage, while another will quote a rate of 11 percent plus two and a half points. Yet a third lender may rattle off several different fixed rates, depending on how many points the borrower pays.

How can you tell which represents the best deal for you? By looking at the *annual percentage rate,* or "APR," which all lenders are required to quote when borrowers inquire about the mortgage rates. The APR represents the *real* cost of the money you're borrowing, with the interest rate plus all points and other fees combined. The lender is required to tell you what its fixed rate is (say, 10½ percent plus two points), but it's also required to disclose its APR (say, 11.095 percent). And that last figure, the APR, is what shows you how the absolute cost of one loan stacks up against that of another.

In addition to asking lenders about their current rates, you must also ask about their *down-payment requirements.* Some lenders will still offer loans to borrowers who put only 5 percent down; others won't look at anything less than a 10 or 15 percent down payment. Often the rate that borrowers must pay and the income-to-debt ratios they must meet will vary, depending on how much they can put down and the kind of loan they want. Some lenders, for example, apply more conservative ratios to ARM borrowers than they do to borrowers obtaining fixed-rate loans, as we noted earlier. Some lenders may also require a higher down payment on an ARM than on a comparable fixed-rate mortgage. And some lenders are more or less conservative in their underwriting requirements than others.

One good question to ask lenders is what ratios they use to qualify borrowers. Some allow housing debt to equal 28 percent of income; others set their limit for all borrowers at 25 percent. Further, the type of loan and the amount of the down payment involved may determine how the ratios are applied. Some lenders will go to the high end of the ratios (28 percent or more) for a borrower who is putting 20 percent or more down or has extensive assets. A borrower with a problematic job who puts down the minimum amount will either be qualified closer to the 25 percent ceiling or else not be qualified at all.

It's important that you learn as much as you can about how particular lenders qualify borrowers. Find out how much flexibility they permit. Then decide where you want to apply.

The lender's *loan-commitment policy* is another area of interest for you. At what point will the lender guarantee the rate quoted, and for how long? Some lenders may lock in the rate when you submit your application; others may not commit to a rate until a day or two before the closing. Some will give borrowers the option of locking in the rate at the time of their application by paying an extra point or two, or letting the rate float until shortly before the closing. Be sure you understand what the lender's rate-lock policy is.

Should you lock in the rate? The advantage to locking in is that you'll know the rate won't soar to uncomfortable heights before you close on your loan. If the interest-rate environment is volatile and you're worried about your ability to qualify if the rate moves up even a hair, this might be a viable option, depending on how costly it is and on the nature of the guarantee. Be aware, however, that a rate-lock that lasts only thirty days from the time of your application may not be worth much, since chances are good that it'll take the lender six weeks or so to process your application. Unless the time frame is realistic — at least sixty days — there's probably no point in bothering with a rate lock.

Remember too that a rate lock can work against you if rates

fall before closing, leaving you locked into a higher-than-market rate.

What other fees will be charged? The lender's rate is your primary concern, but not your only one. There may not be much variation in the mortgage rates quoted by different lenders, but their other fees may vary considerably.

Ask first about the *application fee*. How much is it? Will all or part of it be applied toward your closing costs? Is the fee refundable in whole or in part? If it is, under what circumstances? How much does the lender charge for the property appraisal and for legal costs (which are typically passed on to the borrower)? How long will it take the lender to process the loan?

Take the answer to that last question with a grain of salt. Few lenders like to admit that their processing time is longer than the market average. And in fairness to the lenders, it must be said that delays often can't be anticipated. If it takes you or your employer a long time to provide some required documentation, it could throw the whole schedule off. Still, it's worth asking lenders how long they expect a routine approval process to take.

Some lenders in some markets promise loan commitments within one or two days. Before you get involved with such a lender, however, make sure you understand precisely what kind of commitment is actually being offered. It may be that the lender can complete the review process in an extraordinarily short period of time, but it's also possible that the lender's idea of a "commitment" is to look at your income and debt ratios and tell you that you fall within its lending guidelines. The "commitment" it offers says it will give you a loan of a specified amount *contingent upon*, among other things, a satisfactory credit check, an acceptable property appraisal, and the receipt of all required documentation. In other words, this lender is going to have to do precisely what every other lender does to process your loan. The next-day "commitment" is not a commitment at all, but rather a prequalification test that you could easily have run on your own. Some of these instant-commitment plans are really good, honest deals, but many provide you with far less in terms of speedy response than they pretend to.

LENDER LOCATION

In a competitive market, many lenders will send representatives to your home or to the broker's office or virtually anywhere you say to do the paperwork. But once you've made the transition from buyer to owner and are sending in your mortgage payment every month, the location of the lender's office becomes important. If there's a problem — if the payment isn't credited properly or the lender doesn't make your property-tax payment on time — it's a lot easier to deal with an office in your area than one in another state. (Yes, a bank in one state can write a mortgage in another.)

Many of the lenders you encounter may be branches of institutions located in other regions. That's not a concern if there's a local office through which your account can be handled. Nor should you be concerned as to whether or not your loan is to be sold on the secondary market; that's also common. What you do need to know is whether the *servicing* of your loan is going to be sold, as well as the loan itself. The fun starts when you need to contact the computer center in Idaho that handles loan collections for the mortgage company in California that bought the loan package from the local bank that gave you your mortgage in Grover's Corner. You don't always have a choice, but if and when you do, remember that it's generally better to deal with a local entity. The more distant corporation will almost certainly be less responsive, and that's something you most definitely do care about, because lenders and loan servicers sometimes screw up. Sometimes they fail to credit a payment; sometimes they credit it improperly. Sometimes they collect tax-escrow payments but neglect to pay the borrower's bill on time. Such problems are hard enough to unravel when the processor is sitting across the desk from you and thinks you might grab him by the throat. It can be almost impossible to convey a sense of urgency to someone who's sitting in front of a computer in an office a thousand miles away.

QUALITY OF SERVICE

The considerations noted above tie into the somewhat elusive questions of quality of service and reputation. Elusive, I say, because judging the kind of service that potential lenders will give is an inexact science. How much can you tell from the way clerks answer the phones and quote their companies' rates?

You may be able to tell more than you might think, though, if you pay attention to certain details. Are the lender's representatives reasonably pleasant and well informed? Do they seem to care whether you apply or not? How responsive are they to your questions? Are they willing to sit down with you and guide you through the mortgage-financing maze?

You can tell still more from talking with people who have dealt with the institution in the past. The best recommendation is from someone who has obtained a mortgage with that lender (or has decided not to!), or perhaps from the attorney representing you.

The broker who is helping you find a home is not generally the best source of advice on where to go for a loan. True, brokers know the market and have current information on what loans are being offered. But remember, the broker usually represents the seller, and his or her commission is contingent upon the consummation of the sale. Consequently, he or she may be more inclined to send you to the lender that processes loans the quickest. What you're looking for, however, is not just the lender with the fastest processing time (though that may be important), but the one that offers you the best mortgage deal.

Talk to friends and acquaintances. Check with the local Better Business Bureau and the federal or state regulator responsible for supervising any lender you're considering. At the very least, be sure that there's no long history of consumer complaints outstanding against the lender or lenders you have selected to apply to.

HOW MANY APPLICATIONS?

Not to put all your eggs in one basket is generally good advice, regardless of the endeavor; but with mortgage-application fees running at between $250 and $500 a shot, there's probably a limit to how many baskets you're willing to spring for.

Further, if your loan is rejected by one lender, chances are pretty good it will also be rejected by other lenders for the same reasons. This is because the secondary-market guidelines are so pervasive. That isn't invariably the case — a more flexible portfolio lender might make a loan that a secondary-market lender couldn't — but the point is that you don't necessarily quadruple your chances of promptly obtaining a mortgage by applying to four lenders at the same time. You do, however, quadruple your application costs.

Some attorneys say one application is enough; others say two are safer in terms of maximizing the prospects of getting a loan, since it's possible that one lender will read your application differently from another or be more willing to work with you to help you qualify. Making two applications also protects you in terms of the "good-faith" requirement I mentioned in chapter 11.

Once you've decided what kind of loan you want and where to apply for it, you're ready to begin the application process.

Buckle up and take a deep breath. This part can be bumpy.

THIRTEEN

The Loan-Application Process

We've talked about what you should ask lenders when you're deciding where to apply for a loan. Now it's time to discuss what lenders are going to ask *you* in the process of deciding whether they're going to approve the loan you're requesting.

The lender's exhaustive analysis of your application is designed to answer two fundamental questions: (1) are you able to repay the loan? and (2) are you likely to?

The answer to the first question is largely a function of the income-to-debt ratios we described in chapter 2. To refresh your memory, the rule of thumb used by most lenders holds that your monthly housing expenses (principal, interest, taxes, insurance, and, if applicable, condo fees) should not exceed more than 25 to 28 percent of your before-tax income. Your housing expenses plus all your other installment debts combined should not total more than 33 to 36 percent of your gross income.

These calculations tell lenders something about your capacity to repay. Equally important is their assessment of your willingness to do so. The only real method they have of evaluating your future performance as a borrower is to look at your financial record.

ARE YOU A GOOD CREDIT RISK?

The infrastructure of the mortgage-loan industry includes a gigantic network for collecting and distributing credit data of all kinds on the consumer public. Here we'll take a brief look at how the credit-reporting system works, and then we'll walk through the application process itself in the lender's shoes.

THE CREDIT-REPORTING SYSTEM

From the time you obtain your first credit card or open your first charge account, you begin developing a credit history. And while you probably aren't aware of it, there are agencies that keep track of your repayment record. These credit-reporting agencies don't exactly open your mail, but they do receive reports from creditors (credit-card issuers, retailers, and others) indicating whether or not you're paying your bills on time. If you ever missed any payments, paid late, or defaulted on a loan, then that information was probably reported to one or more of the credit-reporting agencies. If it was, it will appear on the credit record the lender is going to see.

It's a good idea, therefore, to take a look at your credit report before lenders start looking at it. Since more than one credit-reporting agency may have a file on you (because different companies provide credit data to different agencies), it's a good idea to survey all the agencies in your area. There are usually only three or four, and they're listed in the Yellow Pages under Credit or Credit Rating and Reporting. Federal law requires the agencies (for a ten- to twenty-dollar fee) to give you the substance of the information contained in your credit report when you ask for it. In fact, if you are denied credit and act within thirty days, the credit-reporting agency must show you your file without charge.

(The credit-reporting agencies don't have to give you the actual written credit report, by the way — although many will do so voluntarily — but they must provide the substance of that report. Some agencies will give you the information over the phone; some require that you actually visit their office. My advice: you're better off with a written report.)

The reason for this exercise is that you want to see what lenders are going to see when they request a copy of your credit report, and you want to make sure the information contained in each of the reports is accurate. Sometimes mistakes are made.

The billing dispute you thought had been resolved may still be carried as an unpaid bill, or there may be an unpaid balance due on a charge account that you don't even have. It's easier to correct mistakes like that ahead of time than in the middle of the application process, when you're struggling to meet an agreed-upon closing date. If there's anything in the reports that you disagree with, the agency is required to double-check the information and correct any inaccuracies. If you still disagree with the agency's conclusions, then you have a right to insert your version of the dispute in your credit record.

The basic rule of the mortgage-application process is to be honest and forthcoming. Don't withhold information. Don't try to disguise the facts. If there's adverse information about you in your record, the lender will uncover it sooner or later. From your perspective, the sooner such problems are faced and dealt with, the better.

Credit blemishes in your past will not necessarily kill your chances for a loan now if you have clearly put your affairs in good order in the meantime. But any lapse must be explained, no matter how insignificant you may think it is, and any explanation must be documented.

Some problems are easier to explain away than others, such as an occasional late payment on a credit card or bills paid late because you were out of the country. But a pattern of late payments, even on relatively small debts, will raise red flags for loan officers. They are trying, after all, to evaluate the seriousness with which you view your credit obligations.

Defaults or regular late payments on major credit obligations — auto or student loans, for instance, or rent — will be all but impossible for a loan officer to overlook. If you couldn't make your rent payments on time, how can the bank expect you to treat your mortgage payments any differently?

Even these serious past credit problems may not stand in your way now, however, provided you can explain why they shouldn't. The missed rent payments, for example, won't appear so ominous if they were caused by an illness or temporary loss of work and you made them up promptly and haven't committed any further credit sins since.

It's difficult to get credit approval if there are defaults or very late payments in your record, and it's extremely difficult (though not impossible) to overcome a bankruptcy. From a lender's perspective, declaring bankruptcy is a way for someone to walk away from past obligations. If you've ever done that, the lender may find it hard to believe that you would never do it again, even though a home loan typically is a secured transaction that is not discharged in a bankruptcy.

There are some signs, though, that attitudes toward a past bankruptcy are becoming a little less rigid. The more or less formal rule used to be that the once-bankrupt applicant had to demonstrate a flawless credit record for at least seven years after the bankruptcy. The applicant had to show that the reasons for the previous failure were unique and unlikely to recur. Under recent changes in secondary-market guidelines, however, many lenders will now give the former bankrupt another shot after three years, again provided that the failure is not deemed likely to recur and provided that the applicant's credit record during those three years has been excellent.

HIS AND HERS

What happens with a couple borrowing together, combining their incomes, if only one of them has a good credit record? One bad credit history between the two of them will not necessarily spoil the deal, provided that the income of the good-credit partner is sufficient by itself to qualify for the mortgage. If both partners' incomes are needed, then both credit records must be acceptable to the lender.

DOCUMENTATION

In addition to being able to explain any problems in your credit history, you must be prepared to document virtually all of the information you supply.

I put it that strongly despite the recent appearance of lenders who promise virtually instant qualification with pratically no documentation requirements. Such programs are variously described as "no-documentation," "limited-documentation," or "mini-documentation," options, and they can seem attractive at first glance, since this would seem to speed up the application process and make things easier for you.

You should look into this type of service in great detail before you decide to try it out, however.

First, such programs are for the most part available only to buyers who put down a minimum of 30 percent. That criterion will exclude the great majority of first-time buyers right off the bat, though it may appeal to trade-up buyers who have the ability to make a larger down payment. These programs may also work well for self-employed borrowers, individuals who have strong financial positions but might not look that way on paper by the lights of the secondary market.

Second, not all of the lenders that promise speedy approval are as clear and precise in their descriptions of their programs as they might be. Some are in fact willing to approve a loan to high-down-payment borrowers without verifying their income and assets. If you tell them you're earning $300,000 a year, they'll try to believe you. Far more of them, though, *will* verify that information. They'll issue a quick *conditional* commitment based on the information you provide, but then they'll check it, and when they find out that you're actually earning $30,000 a year instead of $300,000, they'll take their commitment back and have the law on their side. As with every other aspect of getting a mortgage, be sure to read and understand all the fine print.

Following are the major areas in which documentation will be required.

EMPLOYMENT AND SALARY

Lenders will not take your word for what kind of job you have. They want written verification from your employer of several bits of data: your current position, how long you've held it, your current salary, and your prospects for continued employment. The information usually won't be accepted if it's hand-delivered by the loan applicant.

In a large company especially, it's not unusual for the lender's request for this information to wind up on the bottom of someone's in-basket. It's not a bad idea, therefore, to find out who in your company is likely to receive the verification request and then politely but firmly bug that individual to respond as quickly as possible. This is the kind of small detail that can hang up an otherwise smooth mortgage application for weeks.

Your employer can verify your base salary, but if you need overtime income to qualify for the loan, you'll have to provide the lender with your W-2 forms for the previous two years, in order to prove that you've consistently earned the overtime you're claiming.

The lender's primary concern is to make sure you're working where you say you are and earning the salary you claim. But the length of time you've held your current position is also important. Lenders are just as concerned about your income's stability as they are about its size, so a recent job change will draw the attention of the mortgage underwriter. This won't be any problem if you've moved from one company to another in your field to accept a better job, but if you've held ten jobs in the past two years, all of them in different fields, the lender will be nervous regardless of your current earnings. Similarly, if you're employed in an industry in which layoffs are a regular occurrence, you may have a hard time getting a mortgage even if you meet all the other loan guidelines.

SELF-EMPLOYMENT

The need to see strong evidence of employment stability and security makes many lenders wary of self-employed borrowers, and they therefore generally ask them tougher questions, demand more complete documentation from them, and sometimes impose stricter underwriting requirements on them.

To verify your income if you're self-employed, you'll have to submit copies of your personal federal tax returns for at least the past two years, as well as (if applicable) your partnership or corporate tax returns for the same period. These returns have to be signed by all the parties that filed them. (If you're a sole proprietor, you won't have a separate corporate or partnership return; all the necessary information should be included on your personal tax return.)

Be aware that the lender will use your adjusted gross income, as reported on your tax returns, for purposes of calculating your income-to-debt ratios. This means that paper losses you may have legitimately taken to reduce your tax liability, such as depreciation, will also reduce the income level that the lender uses to determine what size loan you can qualify for.

Typically, lenders want to see that you've been in the same business for at least two years. A shorter period of time might be accepted if you were employed in the same or a related field for several years before striking out on your own, and if you can demonstrate, through market-feasibility studies, audited financial statements, and other supporting materials, that your new venture has a reasonable probability of succeeding.

If you're self-employed, you will at a minimum have to provide the lender with a current profit-and-loss statement, a current balance sheet, and profit-and-loss statements and balance sheets for the previous two years.

GIFTS

Lenders typically will not allow you to borrow the amount needed for your down payment, but an outright gift of all or part of the amount is usually acceptable. This practice has become almost commonplace, in fact, given the difficulty that many first-time buyers face in saving 10 percent or more of the purchase price of most homes.

The source of the gift is important to the lender. It doesn't have to be your parents, but it should generally be a family member. The closer the relationship, the better, from the lender's point of view. The lender wants to be sure that the gift really *is* a gift, that it's not a secret loan that will have to be repaid. That's why a "gift" from a friend or even an employer is likely to be viewed with suspicion. As an official at Freddie Mac told me, "If it's coming from your seventh cousin twice removed, we'd look at it a little differently" than if it were coming from a parent, a sibling, or even an aunt or uncle.

If you're using a gift to help cover all or part of your down payment, the lender will want a letter from the donor specifying the relationship and confirming that the amount is an outright gift and won't have to be repaid. The lender will verify the source of the gift in order to ascertain, among other things, that the benefactor has the resources to make the contribution and is not in fact borrowing the money.

Secondary-market rules don't limit the size of the gift you can receive, but if you're putting less than 20 percent down, you may run into a problem with the mortgage-insurance companies. (Mortgage insurance, you'll remember, is required if you put down less than 20 percent.) Some of the major insurers require that borrowers come up with at least half of their down payment from their own funds.

So if you're making a 10 percent down payment and are required to obtain mortgage insurance, you could cover 5 percent with a gift, but the remaining 5 percent might have to come from your own funds. And the gift would have to come from an "immediate family member" (a parent, grandparent, sibling, or child) under the mortgage-insurance rules, which in some respects are more restrictive than the general secondary-market standards. (Not all mortgage-insurance companies have the same policies. Some companies may be less restrictive, but be prepared for the worst.)

OTHER ASSETS

One of the blanks on the mortgage application invites you to list "other income" that the lender might consider in determining your eligibility for the loan you want. It may be, for example, that a borrower has a limited salary but receives a substantial sum every month from a trust fund, from other investments, or from alimony payments. If these are stable sources, the lender will include them in the calculation of the borrower's income-to-debt ratios.

You'll want to detail as assets here such things as stocks and bonds, money-market funds, real-estate holdings, trust funds, and any other investments you may have, noting any income these assets provide on a regular basis. Your checking and savings accounts will usually be listed in another section of the application.

Again, every asset you cite will be verified by the lender. For instance, the lender will contact the bank at which you have your checking and savings accounts to verify the balances. Many borrowers are unpleasantly surprised to receive bills from their banks charging them for providing that verification. That's a common practice in many areas; you might ask your bank if and how much it charges for the service.

One of the things the lender will be looking for in the analysis of your assets is some assurance that you will have sufficient funds on hand to pay the closing costs, which are described in detail in chapter 15. These costs include any points the lender is charging, the mortgage-insurance premium (required if you're putting down less than 20 percent), and a host of other expenses. In addition, most lenders want you to have cash reserves on hand after the closing equal to at least two months' housing payments. That's something to keep in mind when you're deciding how much of a down payment to make.

In the evaluation of your financial resources, lenders will consider nontaxable income such as social-security, child-support, or disability payments. In fact, due to the nontaxable nature of this income, many lenders will consider it at 120 percent of its face value, but you must document it. If you're including child-support payments in your assets, you must provide a copy of your divorce decree, any separation agreement, and possibly also a twenty-three-month payment history to prove the regular receipt of the payments you're claiming.

RENTAL INCOME

If you're buying a multifamily property, lenders will consider the rental payments in their calculation of your income. The secondary-market rules governing precisely how rental income is calculated and what percentage of the rents will be counted in qualifying you for a mortgage are in the process of being revised as I write. But in general you should expect lenders to accept less than 100 percent of your rental income. And they will look at net income, minus expected maintenance costs and anticipated vacancy periods.

In most cases you'll have to supply the lender with copies of the leases currently in effect or with letters from existing tenants verifying their acceptance of the rent you intend to collect. If you plan to increase the rent, you may need a letter from a real-estate expert indicating that the rent you plan to charge is realistic in that market.

GETTING THROUGH THE PROCESS

The mortgage-application process has been described as slightly less comfortable than Chinese water torture, but I think that probably understates the pain. All I can do to ease it for you is to give you a good idea of what's coming. If forewarned is at all forearmed, then it will help you to have a sense of what lies ahead.

Here is what you should expect to happen, pretty much in the order in which it will most likely occur.

THE GOOD-FAITH ESTIMATE

When you submit your mortgage application (or within three business days afterward), the lender is required to provide you with what is known as a "good-faith estimate" of the closing costs that you are likely to have to pay. These cannot be specified finally at this time because the lender cannot predict in advance precisely what all of the closing expenses will be. For example, the fee for the title search will most often depend on how complicated it turns out to be. There shouldn't be a tremendous difference between the estimate and the actual costs, but on the other hand, you shouldn't expect the esimate to be to the penny, either. A federal law called the Real Estate Settlement Procedures Act requires a lending institution to give the borrower its best information in advance on all the costs with which he or she will be confronted at the closing.

GETTING CHECKED OUT

The lender should prequalify you on your first visit. That is, the lending agent will use the information you provide on your credit-application papers (your income, employment, assets, and so on, as described above) to see whether you will qualify for the requested loan if all your information does check out.

This will be done in the lender's office, and it won't take very long at all. The arithmetic is simple, and you'll either fall within the income-to-debt ratios specified by the secondary market or you won't. If you don't (and if it's clear that nothing you can do will make it possible for you to qualify), you can't have the loan you want. If you do, the lender's credit-research staff will begin the much slower and more detailed process of nailing down your numbers and your credit background.

THE APPRAISAL

In negotiating the Purchase and Sale agreement, you and the seller settled on a purchase price; but even so, the lender will commission an independent professional appraisal of the property in order to determine its current market value.

The lender is not concerned that you may be paying more than the property is worth. That's your business. But the lender does want to know that the value of the property will support the mortgage.

If you're paying $200,000 for a house and putting 20 percent down, the lender will assume that the $160,000 you want to borrow represents 80 percent of the property's value. If it turns out that the property is only worth $180,000, then instead of giving you an 80 percent loan, the lender would actually have financed almost 90 percent of the purchase price without intending to do so.

Most of the time the lender's appraised value and the agreed-on purchase price will not differ much. If they do, however, the lender will base the loan on the lower of the two figures. So in our example, the lender might say, "I'll still give you the $160,000 loan, but that's a 90 percent loan, not an 80 percent loan, which means that you'll have to obtain private mortgage insurance." Or instead, "Sorry, the maximum I'll finance on this property is 80 percent, or $144,000." If that occurred, the buyer would have three options: to come up with a larger down payment to close the gap; to try to persuade the seller to reduce the price; or to walk away from the deal, hoping that the wording of the Purchase and Sale agreement's mortgage contingency clause provided a comfortable escape.

In determining the value of the property, the appraiser will look at sales of comparable properties in the neighborhood and at the condition of the house itself. If there are any health-code or safety-code violations, a lender generally will approve the loan only if the violations are corrected before the closing or if the buyer can show sufficient assets to be able to correct the problems on his or her own. If the seller agrees to make repairs that are required by the lender, make sure that the work is completed before the closing.

THE TITLE SEARCH

Another milestone you must pass on the path to your mortgage is the title search. Required by the lender, this is a search of the ownership documents to verify that the individual who is selling the property has the legal right to do so. One of the most important questions that the title search will answer, therefore, is whether or not the person selling the property actually owns it.

Don't laugh. Most real-estate attorneys have stories about people who have tried to sell property fraudulently. One of my favorites involves the wife who, after a spat with her husband, tried to sell their home while he was away on an extended business trip. The title search showed that they owned the property jointly, which meant that the husband's signature was required, so the sale didn't go through.

Not all title flaws are known by the sellers. You can't even rely on the fact that the sellers themselves may have bought the property not long ago and were able to finance the sale. This doesn't necessarily mean they have a good title; after all, title abstractors and attorneys make mistakes. In addition to verifying the ownership of the property, the lender is also looking for any "encumbrances" on the title. These are such things as liens or attachments filed by creditors trying to collect unpaid bills, or liens filed by local, state, or federal government entities for non-payment of taxes. Any such claims against the property must be resolved before the lender will approve the mortgage.

In addition to the title search, the lender will also order a plot plan or survey, which will confirm that the property's boundaries are as described in the Purchase and Sale agreement. The plot plan might show, for example, that the roadways in the condominium development don't conform to secondary-market requirements. And it's not uncommon to discover that a fence constructed by the seller extends a few inches onto a neighbor's property (or vice versa), or that structural additions such as a tool shed or swimming pool violate local zoning codes. If the seller built the shed himself, he may not have bothered to get the building permit that was required. Or perhaps he located the shed closer to the property line than zoning rules allowed. There are any number of possible violations of that kind, some of them easily corrected (an errant tool shed can be moved) and some more difficult to handle. What do you do about the swimming pool that's partly on the neighbor's property? You might be able to persuade the neighbor to sell you that portion of his land, or you might have to fill in the pool.

Your Purchase and Sale agreement should require the seller to give you a "good, clear record and marketable title" (as standard legal boilerplate has it) and should further require him or her to expend reasonable effort and money to do so. If he or she is still unable to provide a good title, you should have the right to walk away from the deal. If the title problems are serious, you may have to do just that.

Some lenders won't order the title search until after all the other verifications have been completed and a loan commitment has been issued and accepted by the borrower. The advantage to this is that the buyer doesn't have to pay for the title search until and unless it's clear that the loan application is going to be approved. The disadvantage is that it takes longer to complete the process, which may make it difficult to meet the closing date you've agreed to.

Given that concern, some lenders will order the title search at the beginning of the application process and require the loan applicant to pay for it regardless of whether or not the loan is utimately approved. (In some markets it is the listing broker, rather than the seller, who actually orders the title search.) A few lenders will order the title search in advance and absorb the cost themselves if the application is rejected. Policies vary widely, so this is another good thing to ask about when you're deciding where to apply for a loan.

In some areas the title search is handled by the attorney representing the lender, who in turn will often hire a title abstractor· to gather the documentation required. In other areas, closings are dealt with by "escrow companies" rather than lenders, and they handle the title search as well. The cost of the title search and the responsibility for paying for it vary according to who does the work and the market area. But you should expect to pay at least $200 for a basic title search, and if it turns out to be particularly complicated, it can cost much more than that, rising in bad cases to more than $1,000.

TITLE INSURANCE

All lenders that sell their loans on the secondary market, as well as most of those that don't, require buyers to hold "title insurance." Like mortgage insurance, a lender's title-insurance policy protects the lender's stake in the property — in this case, against any title flaw that might be discovered at some future date.

Take a worst-case situation. A month after you buy a house from the estate of someone who has recently died, the former owner's long-lost son reappears to claim his inheritance, which is now your house. If his claim to the property is valid, the lender's title-insurance policy would pay off the mortgage, but you'd be out of luck. Your down payment and any other costs you incurred in purchasing the property would be in jeopardy, and any legal costs you accrued in trying to defend your title or seek damages would be your responsibility.

However remote such a risk may seem, you still might want to protect yourself from that kind of loss by purchasing a *buyer's title policy.* You have to pay for the lender's policy anyway, and the cost of an owner's policy, purchased at the same time, is not that great. In some states the lender's attorney is required to certify title to the borrower up to the purchase price; if there's a title flaw, the lender's malpractice insurance should cover it.

But even if you get the lawyer's certification, an owner's policy is still a good idea. For one thing, if you're covered, not only will the insurance company pay off if you do lose a claim, it will also defend you against any claims that threaten your title. If the title is certified, the lender's malpractice insurer will also pay off eventually, but you'll first have to lose your title case and then sue the attorney to recover whatever damages you've suffered.

Title-insurance premiums vary from state to state, but on the average, a lender's policy costs $2 per $1,000 of the mortgage, while the lender's and owner's policy combined would cost around $3 per $1,000. (The most expensive title-insurance costs in the country are in Texas, where premiums average $7 to $8 per $1,000.) On an $80,000 mortgage, you'd be looking at a one-time charge of roughly $160 (payable at closing) for a lender's policy versus about $240 for a combined buyer's and lender's policy.

To reiterate, the owner's title-insurance policy will cover the legal costs involved in defending a title claim. Even if you win, these costs can be high. And if you lose, the insurance will "make you whole" by reimbursing you at least for the equity you already have in the property.

Some title-insurance companies offer an inflation-protection clause. This isn't available in all states or from all companies, but it's worth asking about. The closing agent, who is usually the agent for several title-insurance companies, is a good person to start with. It's easiest to obtain your title-insurance policy this way, but you're also free to find another title agent to write the policy (and certify the title) for you.

Your standard coverage will be based on the purchase price of the property. If you pay $100,000 for a house and take out an $80,000 mortgage, and then somehow lose the title, the insurance company will pay off the $80,000 mortgage and pay you the difference — in this case, $20,000. But what if the loss comes not a month after you move in but after you've owned and occupied the property for five years? By that time appreciation may have boosted the property's value from $100,000 to $150,000. The outstanding mortgage is about $75,000 at this point, and that amount is paid out to the lender. You've got $75,000 in equity based on the current value of the property, but the base policy won't pay more than the original purchase price. This means that the most you can collect, after the mortgage is repaid, is $25,000. An inflation-protection policy would leave you in a better position to go out and buy another property in that inflated market.

If you do decide to buy an owner's policy, whether it has the inflation protector or not, make sure to read the fine print so you'll know exactly what the policy covers and what's excluded from coverage.

THE COMMITMENT

You're sure your income is large enough. You know your application is complete. Your credit record is the envy of all. Nothing could possibly go wrong.

So why haven't you heard anything? After four weeks of sweating it out, and despite repeated assurances from the loan officer (whom you've called daily) that all is well, even the most confident borrower is bound to get a little nervous. But finally you open the mailbox and find an envelope from your bank, nervously tear it open, and read the first sentence: "We are pleased to inform you. . . . " You're so relieved that you don't bother to read the rest.

But you should.

The typical lender's commitment letter will say that the loan you requested has been approved at the interest rate you expected and under terms that have already been explained to you in detail by the lender's agent. The letter will also tell you what your monthly payments will be. It will state how many points you must pay and when you must pay them (for instance, you may be required to pay one or more of those points on acceptance of the commitment, with the balance due at the closing). It will list all the other costs that you'll be expected to cover and outline what documents you'll be required to submit at the closing. In addition, the letter will tell you if there are any conditions you must meet before the closing. If there are outstanding building-code or zoning violations, the letter will specify that those problems must be corrected before the closing. If you don't meet those explicit conditions, the lender won't sign off on the loan.

The purpose of the commitment letter is to tell you that your application has been approved. Some commitment letters are more equivocal than they appear to be, however, which is why you must read yours carefully. Take the following example, invented but based on a real experience with a lender that was promising commitments within two weeks at a time when most other lenders were taking at least eight weeks to process applications:

> Congratulations. Sockittome Bank is pleased to inform you that your application for a mortgage loan of $250,000 at an interest rate of 400 percent has been approved, contingent on the following: (1) verification of your employment and income; (2) verification of the appraised value; (3) a satisfactory title search; and (4) anything else we think of between now and the closing.

Actually, such a letter makes no commitment at all. It's only a note saying that your stated income qualifies you for the loan, which is something the real-estate broker could have told you early on and probably did. All this lender is agreeing to do is to make the loan *if* all the ordinary verifications really do check out.

This is know in the trade as a "noncommitment commitment," and it can be very dangerous to a home buyer's financial health. The danger is that a buyer will get a letter such as this, read the first words, assume that the mortgage is all set, and let the date for exercising the mortgage contingency clause lapse without notifying the seller that the mortgage has not yet been approved. That buyer is going to be in big trouble if the lender finds something he doesn't like and rejects the application. A great many buyers have wound up forfeiting hefty deposits because the lender's "commitment" turned out not to be a commitment after all.

So make sure the commitment letter you get really *is* a commitment. And pay particular attention to language that will appear somewhere around the last paragraph. That's the part that tells you how long the rate lock-in (if there is one) will remain in effect. As I mentioned earlier, not all lenders will commit to a rate much in advance of the closing date, and those that do will usually charge you a point or more for that rate security. Be sure that the lender's commitment lasts long enough to give you a reasonable chance of completing the purchase before it expires. In that respect, anything less than thirty days is essentially meaningless in most markets.

When it comes to commitments, the borrower has few options other than to shop around. What's available will depend entirely on the interest-rate climate and competition. In 1987 most lenders were offering liberal rate locks because rates were relatively stable. As I write today, in the fall of 1988, it's hard to find many rate locks at all, since lots of lenders got stuck in 1987 when rates veered suddenly upward.

If you aren't able to close before the commitment expires, it doesn't necessarily mean that the lender will withdraw approval of your loan, though that is a possibility. It does mean, however, that you may no longer be able to obtain the loan you wanted at the rate the lender had agreed to. So if your commitment for a 10 percent fixed-rate loan expires before you're able to close and you aren't able to exercise the right of escape in your mortgage contingency clause, you might have to accept an 11 percent loan (or an adjustable-rate mortgage that you'd rather not have) in order to meet your obligation to the seller to complete the purchase within the time stated in the Purchase and Sale agreement. This is why it's necessary to ask lenders about their commitment policies before you decide where to apply.

HOW LONG?

For the buyer whose home purchase depends on the outcome, the wait for a mortgage approval can seem endless. But how long does the process normally take?

That depends on a number of variables, not the least of them being how quickly the borrower provides the information and documentation that the lender requires.

You have little control over most aspects of the approval process (the title search and appraisal, for example, are out of your hands), but there are some steps you can take to help speed the process along. Make sure, for example, that all the information you provide is accurate and complete, and that any credit problems in your record have been resolved. Find diplomatic ways of pestering your employer and the bank or banks at which you have savings and checking accounts to insure that they process the verification requests from your mortgage lender as soon as they receive them. If those requests wind up at the bottom of a stack of papers, as they often do, the loan approval can be delayed.

One of the most important things to do is to stay in close touch with the lending officer who is handling your loan. Don't wait for the lender to call to tell you that there are problems; you may not hear anything at all until you get a letter saying your application has been denied. You certainly don't want to find out two days before your mortgage contingency clause is set to expire that your application is still incomplete. It's far better to find out about potential problems while you still have a chance to correct them without having to beg the seller for an extension of the deadline set down in the Purchase and Sale agreement. So don't be shy about calling the lending officer to see how things are going.

DEALING WITH REJECTION

Certainly you can go to another lender if your application is rejected. And you don't have to worry that the second lender will be biased against your application because you were rejected elsewhere.

But before you go running off to apply at another institution, find out why you were rejected at the first one. If it's because you failed to meet one of the secondary-market standards, then you'll almost certainly be rejected by the next lender for the same reason.

If your application is rejected for any reason at all, the first thing you should do is contact your loan officer to learn why. The federal Equal Credit Opportunity Act (ECOA) requires the lender, on request, to send you a written explanation of the reasons for the denial within thirty days of the decision. You should also be aware that federal law (and state law, too, in most places) prohibits lenders from rejecting your application because of your sex, marital status, age, race, religion, or national origin.

You may discover that the reason for the rejection is a relatively minor, easily corrected problem. Maybe a missing document can be supplied, or a mistake in your credit report can be clarified. If that's the case, then your application can probably be reactivated and the approval process completed without too much delay. But even a short delay can be costly when interest rates are rising, causing you to lose an attractive rate or perhaps even resulting in your losing the house to another buyer. That's why it's essential that your application be as complete as you can make it. There are more than enough things that can go wrong with a mortgage application; you don't want to add to the list.

If the problem with your application turns out to be more serious, first make sure that you understand the reason for the denial. And don't give up too easily. Perhaps there's something you can do to turn the decision around. For example, if the lender finds that you don't meet the income-to-debt ratios (it would be far better, of course, for you to have discovered this earlier by prequalifying yourself — see chapter 2), you might be able to get around it by coming up with a larger down payment or by paying off some of your other outstanding debts. If you can't qualify for a fixed-rate mortgage at current rates, perhaps you could handle an adjustable-rate mortgage that starts off lower. Heed all the warnings noted earlier about not winding up with a loan you really can't afford, but be sure to explore all your options before deciding that your loan application is a lost cause.

If it turns out that you can't make this particular deal work, consider changing your frame of reference a bit. If you've been looking only at single-family detached dwellings, this may be the time to consider a condominium, which may be less expensive, or a two- or three-family home, where the rental income may be enough to help you qualify you for the loan.

If the problem is sheer affordability, go back to the market and look at less expensive homes, perhaps in areas that you rejected initially because you thought they were too far from your workplace or because you didn't like the homes themselves as much. If you've been unwilling to compromise up to now, this may be the point at which you realize that some kind of compromise is going to be necessary. Sometimes it takes a jolt such as rejection of their mortgage application to make buyers realize that in order to achieve the dream of home ownership, they may have to give up, at least for a while, the hope of purchasing the home of their dreams.

For buyers who are finding it difficult to obtain a mortgage on their own, another option is to purchase a property jointly with an unrelated individual or another couple. You may not be able to afford a single-family home, but what about sharing the ownership of a two-family with a like-minded couple? Or even sharing a single-family with an individual with whom you think you can live comfortably? Lenders *will* consider applications filed jointly by unrelated parties; in fact, such arrangements have become rather common as home prices have increased. Bear in mind, however, that your coborrower(s) will also have to be deemed credit-worthy by the lender. So before you get too deeply involved in a joint-purchase plan, make sure any co-borrowers have large enough incomes and good enough credit histories to enable them to qualify for their share of the mortgage loan.

Joint-ownership arrangements have some drawbacks, of course. You should be certain, for example, that your partners will take their ownership obligations seriously. They must make their portion of the mortgage payments on time and share your views on the upkeep of the property. More than one fine friendship has been destroyed by a partnership in property ownership. What happens when one owner wants to replace the heating system or repair the roof, but the other one thinks the expenditures are unnecessary? What do you do if one person wants to sell but the other isn't ready to move?

Those are just some of the major issues that need to be anticipated and addressed in writing in this kind of arrangement. The best way to handle it is to treat it like the business transaction that it is. The agreement should be on paper and should be as detailed as you can make it. All parties to it should be represented by their own attorneys to ensure that everyone's interests are provided for.

COMPLAINING

If you believe the lender rejected your application without justification (that is, if you think you were the victim of illegal discrimination), you can file a complaint with the agency that regulates the lender you're involved with. Depending on the type of institution, that could be a state banking department, the Federal Reserve Board, the Comptroller of the Currency, the Federal Home Loan Bank Board, the National Credit Union Administration, the Federal Trade Commission, or some combination of these. The regulatory structure for financial institutions is complex. If you're unhappy with the lender's decision and are not sure how to proceed, someone in your state's bank-regulatory agency should be able to either hear your complaint or tell you where it should be filed.

But we're going to assume here that you won't have to worry about that. Since you had the good sense to read this book, we'll assume that you applied its lessons, prequalified yourself, straightened out your credit records, and decided on a house that you know you can afford. Your loan application has therefore been processed routinely and accepted by the lender.

Which means that the worst of this process is over. But don't pop the cork yet. You still have to get through the closing.

FOURTEEN

Closing

You're almost a homeowner now, but you have one more step to negotiate: the closing. How this is handled will differ in different jurisdictions, but most commonly the closing is a formal meeting at which the ownership of the property is transferred from the seller's hand to yours. This is also sometimes called the settlement because the purchase itself and other smaller outstanding debits and credits are all settled at this time.

The participants in this session may or may not include the seller, whose presence is sometimes not required, the seller's attorney, and the broker, who usually does choose to be present. (If there was a selling broker as well as a listing broker, he or she may attend, too.) The buyer has to be present, however, and so does the closing agent, who is often (though not always) the lender's attorney and who acts as a sort of master of ceremonies, making sure that all the necessary papers are signed and all the required documents recorded. If you follow my advice, you'll also have your own attorney present at this meeting. This is in all likelihood the largest financial transaction you have ever been involved in. When tens and hundreds of thousands of dollars are about to change hands, you'd be penny-wise and pound-foolish in the extreme not to have your lawyer there, just to insure that everything is right from your point of view.

Those who have been through a closing typically remember the experience as a blur. A friend told me after buying her first house, "I just remember a blizzard of paper and signing documents and checks one after another. At some point, I don't think I even read the words anymore. Whenever anyone put a paper in front of me, I just signed it."

Her experience was typical. The closing can be confusing and even intimidating. But perhaps knowing a little about what to expect, and specifically knowing what kinds of documents you'll be asked to read and sign, will make your closing, when you get to it, a little less overwhelming than it was for my friend.

The closing process actually begins several weeks before the closing meeting. The lender's letter of commitment, which tells you that your loan request has been approved, also specifies many of the conditions required for closing (see chapter 14). Once you've accepted the lender's offer of a mortgage, the lender will contact its "closing agent" (an attorney in some areas, an escrow agent or a title company in others) and instruct the agent to set the closing wheels in motion.

In most locales, the steps that must be taken before the closing will include the following: (a) ordering a title abstract, which is a report on the ownership of the property you're buying, and a plot plan or survey, which shows the boundaries of the lot and the location of the house and any other buildings on that lot; (b) ordering a certificate showing any liens outstanding for the nonpayment of local taxes or other local charges, or the absence of any such liens; and (c) checking local documents that will itemize any outstanding assessments against the property for municipal improvements (sometimes a community will add a road or sidewalk that benefits only a few residents and will assess them for a portion of the cost).

Who is responsible for ordering and paying for these various documents and services varies according to standard practice in different places. I'll get into more detail about the costs below.

Once the closing agent receives all the documents ordered and has determined that everything is in order, a date and time for the closing will be set, after consultation with the lender and the attorneys (if any) for the buyer and the seller. Often schedules will conflict, making it impossible to accommodate the preferences of everyone involved. In those instances it's usually either the closing agent or the terms of the Purchase and Sale agreement that dictate where and when the closing is to be held.

BEFORE THE CLOSING

Long before the date for the closing arrives, you and your attorney should go over the lender's commitment letter to check on what the lender is going to require of you.

The letter should tell you whether you or the seller will be required to provide any additional documents at the closing, and it should specify what forms of payment may be used for the various charges you will have to pay. Usually personal checks are acceptable only for relatively small amounts, if at all. You should expect to provide certified checks, cashier's checks or treasurer's checks to cover the down payment (or the balance of it) and the bulk of the closing costs. Bear in mind that it can take time to transfer funds from the stock market, a money-market fund, or an out-of-state bank. Make sure the funds you'll need for the closing are liquid and readily available to you. Also determine in advance how your checks should be made out (that is, to a certain bank, to yourself, to an escrow company, to an attorney for the bank, or to an attorney for a client's account).

In addition to checking your commitment letter for any special closing requirements, you or your attorney should also contact the closing agent at several points well before the closing date to find out whether everything is on track and to confirm that you're aware of all that will be asked of you at the closing. A little extra work in advance will avoid unnecessary confusion later, which could prolong or possibly even delay the closing.

Another vital preclosing step you should never skip is the last-minute inspection. Your Purchase and Sale agreement should contain language giving you the right to inspect the property within twenty-four hours of the closing so you can ascertain that the property is in the same condition as when you agreed to buy it. You don't want to wait until *after* the closing to open the door of the house you've bought and discover, for example, that a storm has just left three feet of water in the basement, or that all of the fixtures you thought were part of the deal have been removed.

CLOSING COSTS

The costs buyers have to pay can vary tremendously from one area to another, depending in large part on who's responsible for what. What is standard practice in most areas will obviously not include every variation that can be encountered in all the thousands of communities in which closings regularly occur.

You'll recall that the lender is required to provide you with a "good-faith estimate" of your closing costs within three business days after you apply for a loan. Remember that it's just an estimate. You won't find out until shortly before the closing occurs precisely what those costs will actually add up to. If you are trying to calculate how much to set aside, as well you should, the Mortgage Bankers Association suggests a rule-of-thumb estimate of anywhere from 3 to 6 percent of the mortgage amount. On an $80,000 mortgage, therefore, you should estimate closing costs of between $2,400 and $4,800.

The precise breakdown of the costs you must pay will be contained in the RESPA statement (also called a "Hud-one" in honor of the HUD-1 form). You'll find a copy of this form reproduced on pages 198–199. RESPA stands for Real Estate Settlement Procedures Act, and it's only one of the many documents you will receive at the closing.

Page 2 of this form will contain two columns, one listing payments for which the buyer is responsible, the other detailing the seller's costs. The items in the buyer's column typically will include the following.

FEES YOU PAY THE LENDER

Lines 800 through 814 itemize these fees, which include loan-origination or loan-discount fees (legalese for the "points" you pay), appraisal fees, charges for credit reports obtained by the lender, fees for any inspections required by the lender, mortgage-insurance-application fees, and, if an outstanding loan is being assumed or taken over by the borrower, assumption fees.

HUD-1 Rev. 5/76   FORM RSD-101A

Form Approved
OMB No. 63-R1?01

A. U.S. DEPARTMENT OF HOUSING AND URBAN DEVELOPMENT	B.	TYPE OF LOAN	
	1.___ FHA 2. ___ FMHA 3. ___ CONV. UNINS. 4. ___ VA 5. ___ CONV. INS.		
	6. File Number	7. Loan Number	
	8. Mortgage Ins. Case No.		

SETTLEMENT STATEMENT

C. NOTE: This form is furnished to give you a statement of actual settlement costs. Amounts paid to and by the settlement agent are shown.
Items marked "(P.O.C.)" were paid outside the closing; they are shown here for informational purposes and are not included in the totals.

D. NAME OF BORROWER:

E. NAME OF SELLER:

F. NAME OF LENDER:

G. PROPERTY LOCATION:

H. SETTLEMENT AGENT:
   PLACE OF SETTLEMENT:

I. SETTLEMENT DATE:

J. SUMMARY OF BORROWER'S TRANSACTION		K. SUMMARY OF SELLER'S TRANSACTION	
100. GROSS AMOUNT DUE FROM BORROWER:		400. GROSS AMOUNT DUE TO SELLER:	
101. Contract sales price		401. Contract sales price	
102. Personal property		402. Personal property	
103. Settlement charges to borrower (line 1400)		403.	
104.		404.	
105.		405.	
Adjustments for items paid by seller in advance		*Adjustments for items paid by seller in advance*	
106. City/town taxes to		406. City/town taxes to	
107. County taxes to		407. County taxes to	
108. Assessments to		408. Assessments to	
109.		409.	
110.		410.	
111.		411.	
112.		412.	
113.		413.	
114.		414.	
115.		415.	
120. GROSS AMOUNT DUE FROM BORROWER		420. GROSS AMOUNT DUE TO SELLER	
200. AMOUNTS PAID BY OR IN BEHALF OF BORROWER:		500. REDUCTIONS IN AMOUNT DUE TO SELLER:	
201. Deposit or earnest money		501. Excess deposit (see instructions)	
202. Principal amount of new loan(s)		502. Settlement charges to seller (line 1400)	
203. Existing loan(s) taken subject to		503. Existing loan(s) taken subject to	
204.		504. Payoff of first mortgage loan	
205.		505. Payoff of second mortgage loan	
206.		506.	
207.		507.	
208.		508.	
209.		509.	
Adjustments for items unpaid by seller		*Adjustments for items unpaid by seller*	
210. City/town taxes to		510. City/town taxes to	
211. County taxes to		511. County taxes to	
212. Assessments to		512. Assessments to	
213.		513.	
214.		514.	
215.		515.	
216.		516.	
217.		517.	
218.		518.	
219.		519.	
220. TOTAL PAID BY/FOR BORROWER		520. TOTAL REDUCTION AMOUNT DUE SELLER	
300. CASH AT SETTLEMENT FROM/TO BORROWER		600. CASH AT SETTLEMENT TO/FROM SELLER	
301. Gross amount due from borrower (line 120)		601. Gross amount due to seller (line 420)	
302. Less amounts paid by/for borrower (line 220)		602. Less reductions in amount due seller (line 520)	
303. CASH (___ FROM) (___ TO) BORROWER		603. CASH (___ TO) (___ FROM) SELLER	

CAT. NO. FF00112
ES 355 (1-84)

L.	SETTLEMENT CHARGES	PAID FROM BORROWER'S FUNDS AT SETTLEMENT	PAID FROM SELLER'S FUNDS AT SETTLEMENT
700. TOTAL SALES/BROKER'S COMMISSION:			
BASED ON PRICE $ @ %=			
Division of Commission (line 700) as follows:			
701. $ to			
702. $ to			
703. Commission paid at Settlement			
704.			
800. ITEMS PAYABLE IN CONNECTION WITH LOAN			
801. Loan Origination Fee %			
802. Loan Discount %			
803. Appraisal Fee to			
804. Credit Report to			
805. Lender's Inspection Fee to			
806. Mortgage Insurance Application Fee to			
807. Assumption Fee to			
808.			
809.			
810.			
811.			
812.			
813.			
814.			
900. ITEMS REQUIRED BY LENDER TO BE PAID IN ADVANCE			
901. Interest from to @$ /day days)			
902. Mortgage Insurance Premium for months to			
903. Hazard Insurance Premium for years to			
904.			
905.			
100. RESERVES DEPOSITED WITH LENDER			
1001. Hazard Insurance months @ $ per month			
1002. Mortgage Insurance months @ $ per month			
1003. City property taxes months @ $ per month			
1004. County property taxes months @ $ per month			
1005. Annual assessments months @ $ per month			
1006. months @ $ per month			
1007. months @ $ per month			
1008. months @ $ per month			
1100. TITLE CHARGES			
1101. Settlement or closing fee to			
1102. Abstract or title search to			
1103. Title examination to			
1104. Title insurance binder to			
1105. Document preparation to			
1106. Notary fee to			
1107. Attorney's fee to			
(includes above items numbers:			
1108. Title insurance to			
(includes above items numbers:			
1109. Lender's coverage $			
1110. Owner's coverage $			
1111.			
1112.			
1113.			
1200. GOVERNMENT RECORDING AND TRANSFER CHARGES			
1201. Recording fees: Deed $:Mortgage $: Release $			
1202. City/county tax/stamps: Deed $:Mortgage $			
1203. State tax/stamps: Deed $:Mortgage $			
1204.			
1205.			
1300. ADDITIONAL SETTLEMENT CHARGES			
1301.			
1302.			
1303.			
1304.			
1305.			
1306.			
1307.			
1308.			
1400. TOTAL SETTLEMENT CHARGES *(enter on lines 103, Section J and 502, Section K)*			

HUD

The undersigned acknowledge receipt of this settlement statement and agree to the correctness thereof. Furthermore we acknowledge receipt of the proceeds detailed above and approve the disbursement itemized therein.

SELLER _____   BORROWER _____

SELLER _____   BORROWER _____

ADVANCE PAYMENT FEES

Among the items for which the lender requires payment up front is what is called "odd days' interest," which you will find at line 901. This is the interest on the mortgage calculated from the closing date (or, in some areas, the date when the deed is recorded), when you take possession of the house, until the first day of the following month. For example, if your closing is on June 20, there will be ten days' worth of interest due to cover the period of time between the closing and the end of the month. If the closing were held on June 2, however, almost an entire month's worth of interest would be required. That's why many buyers try to close as near to the end of the month as possible, to reduce the amount of cash they'll need for the closing.

There may seem to be a long gap between the closing and the receipt of the bill for your first mortgage payment. Don't get nervous, and definitely don't assume that the lender has forgotten your payments. Most mortgages call for the payment of interest "in arrears." That means that the payment due on June 1 is for interest accrued during the previous month. In other words, the check you send the bank in June is for the May mortgage payment. If you close on June 20, your payment for July won't be due until August 1.

INSURANCE PREMIUMS

Lines 902 and 903 on the RESPA statement itemize the insurance premiums due, if any. Line 902 refers to mortgage insurance (see chapter 2). Line 903 is applicable only if the lender is paying for your hazard insurance directly. Lender practices in this area vary. Some lenders insist on making the insurance payments themselves, collecting and escrowing insurance payments each month just as they do the property-tax payments. Others let buyers handle the insurance payments on their own; most will simply require you to provide them with a binder showing that you have obtained hazard insurance and (often) also a receipt verifying that the first year's premium (and sometimes the first year's plus the first two months' worth of the following year's) has been paid.

One important detail to check on is how the lender wants to be named on your insurance policy. Many will insist on being named as the "loss payee, as its interest may appear." The idea of this requirement is to prevent a borrower from burning down his heavily mortgaged house and then cheerfully accepting the insurance payment for the casualty loss. As the loss payee, the lender will be assured of being reimbursed for the amount of the outstanding mortgage. This is one of those details that if not attended to properly can throw a wrench into the closing wheels.

RESERVES

Lines 1001 through 1008 on the RESPA statement deal with the reserves that you must deposit with the lender. The lender receives these now (and sometimes continues to receive them on a monthly basis, right along with your mortgage payments) to pay for insurance (if any), taxes, and local assessments. Local practice will vary, but most lenders will require the escrowing of mortgage-insurance but not hazard-insurance premiums. Whether tax payments must be escrowed will depend, again, on local laws, the amount of the down payment (escrowing is more likely to be required of borrowers who put less than 20 percent down), and the lender's policy.

MORE CHARGES

Other closing-related charges are itemized on lines 1101 through 1113 and lines 1301 through 1308. Often these involve payments to entities other than the lender or the lender's attorney or closing agent. For example, the title abstract (line 1102) is often prepared by someone hired by the lender's attorney to perform that task, and the fee is passed on to the borrower. Other fees you will find in this section include general settlement or closing fees, the fee for the title-insurance binder (if any), document-preparation costs, notary fees, and the lender's attorney's fees. Sometimes several of these items (typically closing, title-examination, document-preparation, and notary fees) will be included in the fee for the lender's attorney (which you pay) and will not be broken out separately.

TITLE INSURANCE

Charges related to title insurance are itemized on lines 1108 through 1110. The lender and the rules of the secondary market (see chapter 12) generally require that you maintain title insurance up to the amount of the mortgage. Getting an owner's title policy, so that you'll be covered up to the purchase price of the property, is usually a good idea, but it's optional. Any title-insurance premiums you pay will be one-time charges, providing coverage for as long as you own the property. As a general rule, the title search and the title insurance are paid for by the buyer, but in some states the seller foots those bills.

RECORDING AND TRANSFER FEES

Most states impose a tax on the transfer of property and require the payment of a fee for recording the purchase documents. Those fees, which vary widely across the country, are itemized on lines 1201 through 1205 of the RESPA statement. Common (though not universal) practice calls for the seller to pay the transfer taxes and the fees for recording any documents needed to deliver good title to the buyer. The buyer usually must pay for the recording of the mortgage and all items related to it.

STILL MORE FEES

Continuing down the RESPA form, you'll find a section marked "Additional Settlement Charges" (lines 1301 through 1308). This is where the lender will note such miscellaneous expenses as the cost of a survey or plot plan (paid for by the buyer, in most jurisdictions) and the costs of messengers, express mail, and other services used to expedite the delivery of documents and checks. Again, local practices differ, but generally the buyer pays unless the expedited service is specifically for the benefit of the seller (for example, to speed the payoff of the seller's outstanding mortgage, saving an additional day or two of interest payments).

SETTLEMENT CHARGES

The list of closing fees will seem endless, but eventually you'll come to line 1400 on the RESPA statement, which will give you the grand total of all the settlement charges you must pay. This number should be the same as the number entered on line 103 on page 1.

Also on page 1 (lines 101 through 105), you'll find the total of all the costs related to the purchase of the home, representing the contract sales price plus the total of all the settlement costs itemized on page 2. There's also a place here to enter the payments due the seller for any personal property (appliances, furnishings, or the like) that you have agreed to purchase with the house, but attorneys I know who handle real-estate transactions suggest that those payments be made separately, outside of the closing. That simplifies the closing and also minimizes the risk that a relatively minor dispute over a lamp or a rug will foul up the entire procedure.

ADJUSTMENTS

An important part of the closing involves making "adjustments" to reimburse the seller for items he or she has paid for in advance that should be the obligation of the new owner. One example, explained in some detail in chapter 12, is the payment of property taxes. If the seller has paid his or her taxes through December and the closing occurs July 1, he should be reimbursed for six months' worth of taxes. These adjustments in the seller's favor will be entered in lines 106 through 115. On the other hand, if the seller owes money on the tax bill, say for the three months preceding the closing, that amount should be credited to the buyer, thereby reducing the total due the seller. Adjustments in the buyer's favor will show up on lines 210 through 219.

Another example of a common closing adjustment involves the monthly condominium fee. If the seller has already paid the June fee and the closing takes place on June 15, you will owe him or her for one half of the fee. Sometimes additional adjustments, such as payment for any fuel oil remaining in the tank at the time of closing, are required, and they will be listed on lines 204 through 209 of the RESPA form. Such adjustments are often made outside of the closing, again, in order to limit as much as possible the details that have to be handled during an already complicated session. For the purpose of calculating these adjustments, the seller should bring to the closing his or her final utility bills, the last tax bill received, and any bills for filling the fuel tank.

STILL MORE ADJUSTMENTS

On lines 201 through 219, you'll find an accounting of amounts paid by or on behalf of the buyer. For example, the deposit you made when you signed the Purchase and Sale agreement should be credited here, reducing the amount due the seller. The principal amount of the mortgage you've received will also be listed as a credit, since you don't have to come up with those funds yourself; the lender will write that check for the seller.

If you're assuming any loans the seller has outstanding (a rare occurrence these days), those amounts too will be deducted from the total you have to pay the seller. Some banks will also give you a credit in this section for the application fee you paid. It's not a universal practice, but in a competitive market, it becomes more common.

The total amount credited to the borrower will appear on line 220 and again on line 302. That sum is subtracted from the gross amount owed by the borrower (given on line 120 and restated on line 301) to yield the bottom line (303) — that is, the total amount the borrower must pay at the closing. If there have been substantial adjustments for amounts unpaid by the seller, it's possible that line 303 will show an amount due to the buyer. It's much more likely, however, that you'll have to write out a substantial check, the amount of which should equal (or be very close to) the amount you were told in advance to bring to the closing. Discrepancies sometimes occur because of mathematical errors or mistakes in filling out the RESPA form. Small differences shouldn't bother you; they can usually be handled with a personal check. Differences of several thousand dollars are another matter, though. If they do occur, you'll be glad you were clever enough to have your attorney sitting at the table with you.

TRUTH IN LENDING

At some point during the closing, you'll begin to feel as if you're drowning in a sea of paper. At just about that time, the closing agent will introduce the "truth-in-lending disclosure statement."

This document, like the RESPA form, is required by federal law. It was designed to give borrowers more detailed information about the mortgage they receive. As a practical matter, however, it may do more to confuse borrowers than to inform them. But if you're among the few consumers who actually read this document, you'll see first a spot for the annual percentage rate (APR). That figure, as you'll recall from chapter 13, represents the total annual cost of your loan, with the points and other fees you pay factored in and restated as part of the rate. Your note and other documents related to the mortgage will refer simply to the mortgage rate alone, not the APR.

The truth-in-lending statement also contains some valuable and, for some buyers, frightening information, including:

1. The total amount you're financing. Since the federal government does not consider points paid and prepaid finance charges to be amounts financed, this figure will be your loan amount less any of these charges that may apply.

2. The total amount of interest you will pay over the term of the loan if you don't sell the property, prepay the mortgage, or make any additional prepayments toward the principal.

3. The combined total of the principal and interest payments you will make over the life of the loan. This will be an enormous sum. It is known to have induced feelings of vertigo in even the most courageous borrowers.

Once you make it past that section, the truth-in-lending statement gets a bit more reasonable. Here you'll find information on how much your monthly payments will be, when they'll begin, and how long they'll last. If the mortgage has an adjustable rate, the truth-in-lending statement will specify how and under what circumstances the rate can change, what index is being used, what the lender's margin is, and what caps (if any) there are on the periodic adjustments and over the life of the loan.

The disclosure statement will also detail the filing fees you have to pay, specify when late charges become due (if you make your mortgage payment after the date required), and indicate whether there will be any prepayment penalty if you repay your loan before the end of its specified term. (Prepayment penalties are far less common today than they were a decade ago.) This section will tell you, too, if you will be entitled to a refund of any portion of the finance charges (odd days' interest or points) if you pay off early. This is unlikely in today's market.

The statement will also disclose the fact that the lender can require you to maintain hazard insurance but cannot compel you to purchase credit life insurance. This last is a policy sold by lenders to assure the repayment of your mortgage in the event of your death. There are many different ways of obtaining coverage of this kind; which option is best depends on your individual financial circumstances and a range of other factors, including what other kinds of insurance you have. This is a question you might want to discuss with an insurance agent you trust.

Finally, the truth-in-lending statement will indicate whether someone buying your house can assume your mortgage under the terms given to you. Adjustable-rate mortgages sold on the secondary market can usually be assumed; fixed-rate mortgages typically can't be, except for VA and FHA loans, which are by law assumable.

After you've waded through the truth-in-lending disclosure statement, you'll be required to sign it. That step must be completed before you sign the next two critical closing documents: the note and the mortgage.

THE NOTE

The note represents your promise to pay the lender or its assignee according to the agreed terms. It sets forth the principal amount, the name of the lender, the address of the property, the interest rate, the date on which your payments must be made, and the location to which they must be sent. If your loan has an adjustable rate, the note will specify the index used, the margin, the caps (if any), the adjustment dates, and the method by which the adjustments will be calculated. (Much of this same information is included in both the truth-in-lending statement and the mortgage.)

The note also explains your rights to prepay the loan and specifies any prepayment penalties that will apply if you do. In addition, the note details the penalties that will be assessed against you if you default and describes the conditions under which you can be required to repay the full outstanding amount before the end of the loan term. The loan can usually be "called" by the lender if you fail to make the required payments, if you transfer all or part of your interest in the house to someone else without the prior written consent of the lender, or if you violate the terms of your note or mortgage in any other way.

One additional point about the note: it's a negotiable instrument, like a check, so you should never sign more than one copy of it.

THE MORTGAGE

The mortgage is the legal document that secures the note and gives the lender a claim against your house if you default on the note's terms. It represents an "encumbrance" on the property until the loan has been repaid.

The mortgage restates much of the information contained in the note: the borrower's name, the lender's name and address, and the amount being borrowed. In addition, the mortgage specifies the date by which the last payment must be made under the note. Its basic terms provide that the principal and interest and any tax and insurance payments required will be paid in a timely manner; that the buyer-borrower will not permit the attachment of any liens (for nonpayment of local property taxes, for example) that might take priority over the mortgage; that the borrower will maintain hazard insurance as agreed; that the property will be adequately maintained and not allowed to deteriorate; that mortgage insurance, if required, will be maintained by the borrower; and that the lender will have the right to inspect the property after giving reasonable notice (the document should also state how much notice is to be given).

The mortgage provides, too, that if the borrower fails to comply with these requirements and continues not to comply after receiving notice, the lender can demand full payment of the loan balance. This last provision is subject, in some cases, to the buyer's rights to reinstate the mortgage, guaranteed by law in many states.

In addition, the mortgage provides that if the borrower defaults, the lender can foreclose on the property, sell it, and use the proceeds to pay off the outstanding loan and the foreclosure costs, returning anything that might be left to the borrower — that is, unless there are second mortgagees standing in line who would have to be repaid first.

The bottom line is that as long as you pay what you have agreed to pay when you have agreed to pay it, and take good care of the property, you won't have any problems. But if you don't, you could lose your house, along with some or all of the equity you have in it at the time.

While I'm on this unpleasant subject, there's one additional point to make. If you default on your mortgage, the lender is not limited to foreclosing on the property in order to satisfy the note. If the lender sells the property in good faith, and the price it brings is not sufficient to pay off the loan balance, then the lender can sue you personally on the note. In fact, the lender doesn't have to deal with the property at all; it can simply sue you on the note alone. That's not common, but it is possible. For example, in a situation in which the real-estate market was depressed and the borrower had significant assets other than the house, the lender might decide that pursuing the note alone would offer better and faster prospects of recovery than selling the house.

RIDERS

In addition to the mortgage itself, there will often be a number of riders that are incorporated into the mortgage and become part of it. If you're obtaining an adjustable-rate loan, for instance, there will be an adjustable-rate rider, which will simply restate the terms of the note you signed.

If you're buying a condo, there will be a condo rider to set forth some of the additional requirements that apply to condos. Chief among these is the requirement that the buyer comply with the condo documents and maintain appropriate hazard and liability insurance. This rider will also specify what will happen in the event that the entire condo building is condemned — that is, declared unsafe for occupancy or taken by the state or local government under its power of eminent domain. Finally, the rider will outline the lender's rights if the buyer does not pay the condo dues or assessments. Generally the lender has the right to make those payments itself and add the cost to the borrower's loan balance.

If you're buying a two- to four-family house, then a two- to four-family rider will normally be required. This will provide that the property will be used in accordance with its current zoning classification (unless the lender agrees to a change) and that the borrower will comply with all laws and regulations applicable to the property. This rider will also typically state that, except in certain limited instances, the buyer will not permit the attachment of any liens without the lender's prior written permission. In addition, the rider will require the borrower to maintain rent-loss insurance and will limit the borrower's rights to reinstate the mortgage in the event of a default. (The reinstatement rights are usually more liberal for a single-family homeowner.) Finally, the rider will provide for the transfer of existing leases and rent payments to the lender in the event that the buyer defaults on the mortgage.

STILL MORE PAPERS

After you've read and signed the note and the mortgage, you'll probably be asked to sign a typed copy of the application you filled out at the time you first applied for the loan. Some of the details may no longer be accurate, but the information on the application should reflect the conditions that existed at the time you submitted it.

The next flood of papers that you (and often the seller, too) will be required to sign will be a set of affidavits, some mandated by state law and others by the secondary market or the lender. These affidavits cover a wide range of matters and vary from one region of the country to another. Typical sets of documents might include affidavits attesting to the following:

1. The presence or absence of urea formaldehyde foam insulation (UFFI), lead paint, and radon.

2. Your intention to occupy or not occupy the property.

3. Your compliance with local and state laws, ordinances, and regulations covering such things as lead-paint removal and smoke-detector installation.

Many of these affidavits will contain language specifically indemnifying the lender should your statements — or the seller's — turn out to be false.

On the secondary-market side, Fannie Mae and Freddie Mac require an affidavit from both the seller and the buyer stating the purpose of the loan, the purchase price, the amount of the borrower's down payment, the amount of the first mortgage, the initial monthly payment under the note, and the terms of any subordinate financing (for example, if the seller is providing a second mortgage). You may also be asked to attest that there is no subordinate financing in place other than what has been disclosed, and to affirm that you will or will not occupy the property as your principal residence.

Take these affidavits seriously. If you provide false information (by fudging the purchase price, for instance, as sellers sometimes want buyers to do, or by failing to disclose secondary financing), you could end up facing criminal penalties and running the risk that the lender will exercise his right to call your loan — that is, to demand that you repay the outstanding balance immediately, and in full.

Most of the required affidavits have to be signed by the buyer, but the seller may also have to sign statements certifying that there are no "mechanics' liens" in place. These are liens filed by contractors who do work on a house for which they are not paid. This is an important affidavit to have from the seller because it's always possible that a mechanics' lien might not be discovered until after the closing. Requiring sellers to attest, under threat of penalties, that there are no such encumbrances discourages them from accidentally "forgetting" to disclose them.

The seller also has to sign an affidavit testifying to his or her US citizenship. This is because special tax laws apply to foreigners selling real estate. In addition, the seller must provide the information that the closing agent needs to complete the 1099 form now required by the IRS, which reports the purchase price that the buyer pays the seller.

It's a good idea to include language in the P&S requiring the seller to cooperate by signing the necessary affidavits and providing all the specified information. Several real-estate attorneys have told me that they've seen many deals either made needlessly complex or killed outright because the seller refused to cooperate at the closing and was not explicitly required to do so by the terms of the P&S.

THE DEED

The deed is one of the most important documents in the closing stack. It's the document that transfers ownership from the seller to you. The seller should bring (or send) the deed, properly signed and notarized, to the closing. The deed will specify how you will own the property, so there are some essential decisions to be made before you get to the closing.

One such decision is what name or names to put on the deed. Do you want to own the property in your name alone, or do you want to own it jointly with your spouse or with another individual, related or not? Your choices here will depend in part on the lender's requirements. For example, if the mortgage is approved for you and your spouse, the lender will want both of your names on the deed. If the mortgage is your obligation only, then the lender will want the property owned in your name alone. The reason for this is that should you happen to default, it will save the lender the trouble of foreclosing on a party who has no obligation at all under the mortgage.

There are some differences in how ownership interests are defined in different states. But the chief options are fourfold:

1. *Sole ownership.* Self-explanatory.

2. *Joint tenancy.* A form of joint ownership in which the surviving owner automatically gets the deceased owner's share in the property.

3. *Tenancy by the entirety.* A joint-ownership form for married couples only, which typically can be severed only by the mutual consent of the parties. If one owner dies, the share passes automatically to the other owner.

4. *Tenancy in common.* With this method the property is owned jointly, but if one owner dies, his or her shares go to his or her heirs instead of to the other owner.

RECORDING THE DOCUMENTS

After all of the papers have been read and signed, all the fees paid, and all the necessary adjustments made, the next step is to record the mortgage, the note, the deed, and all the other requisite documents, usually at the registry of deeds or the town clerk's office.

The closing agent will generally not release the checks to the seller or the broker until the transaction has been recorded and the buyer has become the official owner of record. That's an important consideration for sellers because it sometimes results in an unanticipated delay before they receive the proceeds from the sale. If the closing occurs late in the day on Friday, for example, the recording may not occur until Monday, and the checks may not be released before late that day or even the next. For someone planning to sell one property and simultaneously purchase another with the proceeds, even a short delay can create serious problems.

CHECKLIST

Just to be safe, let's run down a list of the items that have to be provided at the closing.

The lender must provide:

1. The RESPA statement
2. The truth-in-lending disclosure statement
3. The mortgage
4. The note
5. Applications for any escrow accounts required for the buyer
6. The check for the seller

The seller must provide:

1. The deed
2. Final utility bills
3. Final tax bills
4. Any documents required to clear the title
5. Any special certificates (for smoke-detector installation, lead-paint removal, and so on)
6. Any special documents that are needed (as with a condo purchase)
7. The key to the house, the single item most often forgotten

The buyer must bring:

1. The purchase money required for closing costs and any adjustments to be made at the closing. The total due here will include the amount of the down payment you're making, less the deposit you've already put down.
2. The insurance policy or binder
3. Any additional documents the lender has requested
4. Your checkbook, for small adjustments (but ask ahead of time whether your personal check will be acceptable)

I would add (have I said this before?) that you should also bring your lawyer. No, it's not a legal necessity, but the closing process can sometimes stumble over significant questions, and if that happens in your case, you'll be very glad to have your lawyer there.

Buying the house is not the end of the house-buying story. Stick with me for two more chapters, and we'll survey some of the basics that new homeowners have to know.

FIFTEEN

Living Happily Ever After

This is the bravo moment. You've done it. You've bought a house in America. You own part of the Dream. Have some champagne.

In the process you've also acquired myriad responsibilities and concerns that had no place in your life as a renter. There are mortgage payments to make. There are records to keep. There is maintenance work to do and to oversee.

Most of us learn what we have to know about taking care of a mortgage and a house as we struggle to do it. There really is no substitute for that, no shortcut around it, but the following brief compilation of hints for the new owner is based on the collective wisdom of a good number of real-estate professionals with many years of experience. As your first year as an owner will very likely teach you, you'll have no need of someone else's list to find something to do to the house, for the house, or because of the house, but this will give you an advance sense of what ownership entails.

MORTGAGE PAYMENTS

Every month you'll receive a statement from your lender reminding you that your mortgage payment is due — or, if you have a coupon book, you'll have to remember to send it on your own. In many areas the wording of the mortgage will specify that a penalty is due if the payment is made more than a stated period, usually fifteen days, after the due date. Many borrowers therefore assume that as long as the payment arrives before the penalty is assessed, it's still on time. Not so. The payment is in fact due on the due date. If it comes in after that, even if it's early enough to avoid the late-payment penalty, it's still technically late, and many lenders will record it that way.

Even though the lender usually can't foreclose on you if your payments consistently come in within this imaginary "grace period," you may still have to pay a price for your tardy ways. Those late payments may show up as such on your credit record, for instance, which would adversely affect your ability to get credit in the future from another lender. Or later on, if rates change to the borrower's advantage and you should want to refinance your mortgage (see below), your record of late payments could weigh against the approval of your application. Take the due date seriously; make a habit of paying the mortgage bill on time.

If you should have a problem making a payment, let the lender know right away. Don't make the lender come to you. Most of them will be more willing to work out a solution with you (perhaps by refinancing the loan or otherwise altering the loan terms) if you approach them as soon as you see a snag ahead. Don't just fall behind.

REFINANCING

Since you just obtained a mortgage and began making the payments, it may seem a bit soon to be talking about refinancing it. But let me mention a few considerations.

If you've gotten a fixed-rate mortgage and rates begin to fall, your thoughts may turn to the idea of refinancing at a lower rate. Don't be too hasty. Whether refinancing is a good idea for you or not depends on a number of factors, including the cost of the transaction and the length of time you plan to remain in the home. The industry rule of thumb holds that refinancing usually doesn't make sense unless rates fall at least two percent and you can recover the cost of refinancing within two years.

INSURANCE

When you obtain your mortgage, the lender will probably require you to buy insurance coverage equaling the home's replacement cost — what it would take to replace the structure in the current marketplace. (That figure generally should not include the cost of the land, which, presumably, would *not* have to be replaced.)

Beyond that, however, it's up to you to see that your insurance coverage remains adequate. Among other things, you should make sure that your policy has an inflation rider that increases your coverage automatically as the value of your house rises through inflation. Typically, insurance companies require that you have coverage equaling at least 80 percent of the replacement cost of your property. If your coverage falls below that level, most insurers will pay only a portion of any claim for damages. Let's assume, for example, that you have only $100,000 in coverage and the replacement cost of your home is $200,000. If you incur storm damages of $30,000, the insurer may cover only half that amount, because your insurance covers only half the replacement cost. If you had coverage equaling at least 80 percent of the value ($160,000), however, the insurer would probably reimburse you for the entire amount of your loss.

Review your coverage periodically to be sure it's adequate for your needs in view of your property's changing value.

FURNISHING AND RENOVATING

You've just moved in. Most of your belongings are still in boxes. But you've decided that the first thing you want to do, starting right now, is redo the first-floor bathroom, buy new furniture for the living room, and strip the wallpaper from every wall in the house.

Stop. Put your hands in your pockets, seal your wallet, tie yourself to a chair. Don't do anything major right away.

Acquiring a home entails some adjusting. Your mortgage payment is probably a good deal higher than the rent you've been paying, so first off you need some time to get used to the new cash regimen you'll be living under. Too many new buyers realize in pain that they had no idea how much it cost to run a house.

Taking your time will not only give you a more realistic view of what you can handle financially, it will also give you a chance to reconsider your first impulses before you start making costly and irreversible changes.

That holds for furnishings as well as renovations. Your ideas of what you want and need may change as you see how the house works for you. It may turn out that the room you planned on decorating first isn't used nearly as much as the room you thought you'd save for last. As you assess your financial situation after the purchase, you may decide that the living-room furniture you were sure you'd hate in the new house will do nicely, thank you, for another year or two. On the other hand, you may find that you really can't wait six months or a year to add that second bathroom after all, unless you're willing to farm out your teenager.

The message here is simple common sense. Go for a slow, smooth transition. You'll probably be living in this house for a good while; don't try to do everything at once, even if you can afford it.

WORKING WITH CONTRACTORS

If you do decide that work, major or minor, is in order, there are several ways you can move to protect yourself with contractors. The most important are the following.

1. Have a written contract, preferably negotiated by an attorney, that specifies in detail the work to be done, the materials to be used, the costs involved, and the date by which the work is to be completed.

2. Try to include a penalty clause in the contract that will require the contractor to compensate you, at a specified rate, for every day the project remains uncompleted beyond the specified completion date. I say "try" because it's a provision that's very difficult to negotiate, and contractors fight hard to avoid it.

3. Agree on a price for the work, but don't pay it all at once. Lenders typically advance funds in stages as the work progresses. Even if you're using your own rather than borrowed money, you should follow the same approach. Make sure to hold back the last part of the money due the contractor so that you'll have some leverage in ensuring that the "finish work" — often the most frustrating part of any project — is completed to your satisfaction. Once a job is substantially complete, builders often move on to their next big project, leaving the new homeowner to fume helplessly over unfinished work that the builder plans to complete when and if he can get around to it. Avoid builder-inserted clauses that require payment of virtually the entire amount due when the work is "substantially complete."

4. Be as specific as possible about the work you want done, and try not to make any changes in the plans once construction is under way. Every time you change your mind about something, the cost of the job goes up, often disproportionately in relation to the size of the changes you want to make.

5. Choose a reputable contractor, preferably someone recommended by a friend or acquaintance familiar with his or her work. Ask the contractor what kind of warranty he or she provides (if any), and make sure he or she is bonded. Otherwise you may have little hope of recovering anything if the contractor takes your money and leaves you with an unfinished or perhaps shoddily finished addition.

BUDGET

One thing you *should* do right away, however, is establish a household budget with two categories — one for regular maintenance and repair, the other for more extensive renovations and decorating.

For maintenance, depending on the age and condition of the house, you should allocate about 1 percent of the purchase price annually. You may find this high; it may be conservative. I've found, though, that you rarely make a mistake by assuming that something that's capable of failing *will* fail, and planning accordingly.

Your budget for decorating and rehab work will depend entirely on what you decide you want to do and how much you can afford to spend. The important thing is to have a plan and a timetable for implementing it: you're more likely to get major projects done if you plan for them in advance and tackle them one or two at a time.

MAINTENANCE

Home maintenance is a book in itself. *Many* books. But the following checklist of the fundamentals, based on information compiled by the American Society of Home Inspectors, will get you correctly oriented.

Tasks can be broken down into those you need to do regularly (more than once a year) and those you need to do annually. On the needs-regular-attention list:

1. Check the basement for dampness after every heavy rainfall.

2. Check faucets for leaks. Don't forget outside faucets.

3. Remove sediment from the hot-water heater. Try it first on a monthly basis.

4. Change or clean the filters on your furnace and air-conditioner as specified by the manufacturer, or every six to eight weeks during the heating and cooling seasons.

5. Drain the low-water cutoff of steam heating systems in accordance with the manufacturer's instructions, or every two to four weeks.

6. Clean humidifiers every two months or so during the heating season and have them checked when you have the heating system serviced, preferably once a year.

7. Trip the circuit-breakers every six months or so. This will brush the contacts and keep them from sticking due to oxidation. Check the ground-fault circuit interrupters every month.

Every spring or fall, or both, you should:

1. Check chimneys for damaged chimney caps and loose or missing mortar.

2. If you have a fireplace, be sure its damper works. Clean the flue (or have it cleaned professionally) if needed. You'll probably need the services of a professional chimneysweep every four or five years, depending on how much you use your fireplace and the type and moisture content of the wood you burn.

3. If you have a septic system, have it pumped every two to four years, depending on usage and the number of people in your household.

4. If you have an oil heating system, clean and service the equipment in the fall.

5. Check the roof for damaged, loose, or missing shingles. Make sure your gutters and downspouts are clean and correctly directing water away from the foundation.

6. Check flashings around vents, skylights, chimneys, and the like for leaks.

7. Check the condition of the exterior paint every spring. Do touch-up work as needed. Trim adjacent shrubs and trees.

8. Drain exterior water lines, sprinklers, and pool equipment in the fall if you have freezing winters where you live.

9. Check your weather stripping and caulking in the fall to make the house weather-tight for the winter.

10. Close crawl vents at the beginning of winter and open them at the beginning of summer, except in areas of extreme humidity.

11. Check for signs of dampness or condensation throughout the house, particularly in the attic and around the chimneys.

SIXTEEN

Debt and Taxes

Tax laws have always been complex, but they're even more so now that Congress has undertaken to simplify them. This chapter can't begin to cover all the intricacies of the tax code, and it shouldn't be taken as a substitute for the professional tax-planning advice you may need. But it will give you a general idea of the deductions available to you as a property owner, and it will anticipate some of the questions that may come up when you next sit down with your IRS forms.

MORTGAGE INTEREST

You've no doubt heard that tax advantages rank as one of the primary benefits of owning your own home. That has always been true, but it's even more important today because the massive overhaul of the federal tax laws in 1986 eliminated virtually all of the deductions available to consumers, except those related to home ownership.

Homeowners are allowed to deduct the interest paid on money borrowed to purchase or improve a first or second home, up to a maximum mortgage total of $1 million. If you borrow $150,000 to buy your house, then borrow another $75,000 for a summer home, the interest you pay on both mortgages will be fully deductible. If the combined total of the mortgages on your first and second homes exceeds $1 million, however, the interest on the loan amount above that is not deductible. And if you own more than two homes, you can claim a residential-mortgage-interest deduction only on two of them, though the interest on the other properties may be included in the deductions allowed for the ownership of rental property, if indeed you rent them out (see "Vacation and Rental Property," below).

The mortgage-interest deduction is important to you not only because it's sizable, but also because, once again, it's just about the only significant deduction left to consumers now that the deductions for interest on consumer loans are being phased out. In the early years of your mortgage, when the bulk of your monthly mortgage payment is being applied to the interest charges, the size of your deduction is greatest. As your loan ages and you reduce the principal, the amount being applied to interest declines, and the size of the deduction is reduced.

POINTS

Points represent charges that borrowers are required to pay lenders in advance during the process of obtaining a mortgage. Under certain conditions, the IRS allows you to treat these charges as prepaid mortgage interest, which is deductible.

The conditions are: (1) you may deduct points paid only on the purchase of a primary residence, not on the purchase of a second home; (2) the payment of points must be an established practice in the area; and (3) the number of points you pay must not exceed the standard for the community. To illustrate: if most lenders in your area charge two points and you paid five, not only should you have your software checked, but you'll also be able to deduct only two of those five points in the year in which you obtained the loan. The remaining three points can be deducted, but the deduction must be spread over the lifetime of the loan. That is, if you have a thirty-year mortgage, you can deduct one-thirtieth of the total deduction each year for thirty years, or until the loan is repaid. There's still a benefit, but it's not quite so interesting, especially considering that most people sell their homes within six or seven years.

Another big detail about points is that they can't be deducted in the year in which they are paid if what you're doing is refinancing an existing mortgage. As with points paid in excess of the market standard, points paid in connection with the refinancing of an existing mortgage must be deducted proportionately, over the life of the loan. There have been some efforts in Congress to amend that requirement, but so far they haven't been successful.

PROPERTY TAXES

Any state or local real-estate taxes you pay are also deductible from your federal tax bill.

CONDOS AND COOPERATIVES

If you live in a condo, the interest you pay on your mortgage is deductible, and so are your property-tax payments, just as if you owned a detached single-family home. No deduction is allowed, however, for your monthly maintenance fee on a condominium.

The situation with cooperatives is a little different. The interest on the cooperative-share loan you obtain to finance the purchase of your unit is deductible, just as the interest on a home mortgage loan would be, but only if the cooperative meets one very important condition: at least 80 percent of the income earned by the cooperative corporation must come from the fees paid by residents of the cooperative development. This means that if there's commercial space in the building, or if the cooperative has funds invested, those sources can't produce more than 20 percent of the corporation's total income without jeopardizing the interest deductions available to the individual cooperative owners.

In addition to being able to deduct the interest on their cooperative-share loans, co-op owners can also deduct the portion of their monthly fee that represents their share of the property taxes and the blanket mortgage on the building. The balance of the cooperative monthly fee, however, which covers maintenance and other common expenses, can't be deducted.

SECOND MORTGAGES AND EQUITY LINES

As I've said, interest on a first mortgage used to purchase a first or second home is fully deductible up to $1 million. Interest may also be deducted in full on a second mortgage (or on a home-equity line of credit) obtained on a first or second home, up to a maximum loan of $100,000.

For second mortgages or home-equity lines greater than $100,000, though, the interest is deductible only if the funds are used for "substantial" home improvements. What qualifies as a "substantial improvement" is, naturally, not defined in the law. You must assume that the IRS will define the term as restrictively as it can.

If you've always wondered what the difference was between an equity line of credit and a second mortgage, here it is:

A *second mortgage* is a loan for a specified amount, written for a specified term and targeted for a specific purpose. When the loan is approved, the borrower receives it in a lump sum.

An *equity line of credit*, on the other hand, is a preapproved credit line. Like the second mortgage, it's secured by the home, but it operates more like a revolving charge account.

If you obtain a second mortgage for $50,000, you begin paying interest on the full amount immediately, and you must repay the entire amount by the end of the loan term. With an equity line, on the other hand, you might receive approval for a $50,000 account but leave it untouched for a year. And in that case you would incur no interest charges.

To give an example: if you borrow $10,000 from the $50,000 equity account and repay $2,000 of the principal plus the interest owed the next month, you'll have $42,000 available on your credit line — that is, the $40,000 remaining after your initial loan, plus the $2,000 you repaid.

This illustrates the other important feature of the equity line: the principal that you repay becomes available to be borrowed again, with no further approvals required by the lender. On a second mortgage, your repayments reduce the loan principal but don't enable you to borrow additional funds. To borrow the money repaid on a second mortgage, you have to apply for another loan.

IMPROVEMENTS AND REPAIRS

You may be surprised and disappointed to discover that you can't deduct the cost of *improving* or *repairing* your new residence. Many new owners are. To them, bless their souls, it stands to reason that money invested in the *great American home* should be protected from the taxman as well as from the foreign tyrant.

The fact is, however, the system isn't set up that way. The first point is that *improvements* and *repairs* are different in the eyes of the IRS. The second point is that for a primary residence, the distinction doesn't matter, because neither repairs nor improvements are deductible.

A repair is anything you do to keep your property in good condition, such as repainting it inside or out, fixing its leaks, replacing its broken windows, or mending its fences. All such measures qualify as repairs and may endear you to your neighbors, but none of them improves your tax situation. Repair costs are deductible on rental property under certain conditions (see "Vacation and Rental Property," below), but not on a residence.

An improvement, unlike a repair, adds to the value of your property or prolongs its life. Adding a new room, finishing a basement, putting up a new fence (as opposed to mending an existing one), replacing the roof, installing a driveway — these are all definite, unambiguous home improvements. You can't deduct them, either.

You *can*, however, add the cost of any home improvements to your home's "basis" — that is, its value, which will be the financial starting point for calculating the "gain" you must tally for tax purposes when you ultimately sell it. Keeping accurate records of the improvements you make over the years is absolutely essential to ensure the most favorable tax treatment possible when you do sell.

So don't throw those old bills away. File them if you can, stuff them in a drawer, or stick them in a book. But hold on to them. Later on, you'll be glad you did.

GAINS AND LOSSES

The American Dream consists not just of owning a home but of moving up the housing ladder, trading less expensive homes for larger, more costly ones until you finally achieve the home of your dreams. The tax laws collaborate in the Dream in that they allow homeowners to defer the payment of taxes on any gain they realize when they sell one home in order to buy another one.

The rule is that you can defer, but not necessarily avoid, all of the gain (or profit) on the sale of your primary residence as long as you meet two conditions. First, you must buy a replacement residence that costs at least as much as the one you sold. And second, you must complete the purchase of the new home within a period that begins two years before and ends two years after the date of your sale.

When the time comes to calculate your gain on the sale of your first residence, the key factor is the home's starting "basis," as it's called in the trade. This, put simply, is the amount you paid for your home, a figure made up of the amount you bought it for in the first place (total purchase price — down payment plus mortgage) plus the value of any improvements you may have made (see above). You can also include any attorney's fees you paid in connection with the purchase of the home.

The difference between the *basis* of your home and the amount you *net* from the sale is the *taxable gain*, which you may defer by purchasing a replacement residence. Clear?

Try it this way: your *basis* may be the same when you're ready to sell the house as it was when you purchased it. Chances are good, though, that it will have increased or decreased over the period of your ownership. Improvements to the property are added to the basis; casualty losses, as from a fire or flood, are subtracted from the basis even as you claim them as tax deductions.

Now you can see how it works: the higher your *basis* at the time of the sale, the smaller your *gain* on the sale, and therefore the lower your *tax liability*.

Say you first bought your home for $50,000 and then over the years put in $25,000 in improvements. Your adjusted basis, then, would be $75,000. Say the sale of your home netted you $115,000 (after allowable deductions for expenses related to the sale), producing a net gain of $40,000. (Without the improvements, your gain would have been $65,000.) If you purchased a new residence within the replacement period (and if your new house cost at least as much as your old one), you would pay no capital-gains tax. If you failed to meet those requirements, you would have to pay the tax. Moreover, the preferential treatment for capital gains has been eliminated, so that for any sale occurring after 1987, the gain is taxed at the seller's marginal tax rate, which, depending on level of income, could be as high as 33 percent.

So it's crucial to document the improvements you make over the years. If you lose your original records, the IRS will accept other forms of proof, such as canceled checks, building permits, and before-and-after photos. But you'll avoid a lot of hassle later if you train yourself from the minute you move into your new home to keep your records organized and complete.

CALCULATING GAIN

If you sell your home, you'll probably want to defer any gain on the sale rather than pay taxes on it. Circumstances do sometimes arise in which it would make good financial sense to recognize the gain and pay taxes on it right away (for example, if you have a lot of tax-deductible losses that could wipe out the gain in a given year). If you find yourself in such a situation, you should delay the purchase of your new home until the replacement period (two years before and two years after the sale) has expired. If you buy a new primary residence within the replacement period, the IRS makes you defer the gain whether you want to or not.

Even if you defer the gain through the purchase of a replacement residence, you'll still have to calculate it, report it, and eventually pay taxes on it. Remember, you're only *deferring* your gain. The IRS has not forgiven it and certainly has not forgotten it. Any gain you realize on the sale of your home will ultimately have to be taxed; for now, though, it's just a bookkeeping operation.

Calculating the taxable gain that results from the sale of your home is a three-part procedure.

The first step is to determine exactly how much gain you actually realized on the sale. To do that, you must first establish your home's *basis* (again, its original cost plus the cost of any subsequent improvements and minus the cost of any casualty losses you've claimed), then subtract this basis from the *adjusted sale price* at which you're now selling it.

What do I mean by "adjusted" sale price? There are a number of sale-related expenses that you can legitimately deduct from your sale price. These include any fees you pay attorneys or real-estate brokers, recording fees, advertising fees, and the like.* You can also count as a sale-related expense anything you may have spent to have the place made presentable to the market. To illustrate: say you sold your home for $125,000 but it cost you $9,000 in fees for your broker and your attorney, and another $1,000 in sale-related fix-up expenses. Your *adjusted* sale price, therefore, is $115,000.

Next subtract the adjusted basis from the adjusted sale price. To use our earlier example: to the initial basis of $50,000, you added $25,000 in improvements, which makes $75,000 your new basis. Subtracting this new basis from your adjusted sale price of $115,000 gives you a gain of $40,000. The key question then is, how much of this gain, if any, is taxable now, and how much of it can be deferred? The answer depends on the purchase price of the new home you're buying. How much *equity* you have in your house (the difference between the sale proceeds and what you still owe on your mortgage) has nothing to do

---

* You cannot deduct any fees for attorneys, brokers, recording expenses, and so on that you pay in connection with the *purchase* rather than the sale of a home, but in most cases they can be added to your new basis.

with the gain you'll realize. The gain calculation centers strictly on the purchase price of your new home and the sale price of your old one.

Third and finally, compare the cost of your new home with the adjusted sale price of your old home. If the purchase price of the home you're buying equals or exceeds the sale price of the home you're selling, then all of the tax is deferred. If the new one costs less than the old, then only a part of the gain can be deferred. You must recognize and pay taxes on the balance in the year in which you sell the property. To turn to our example again: you realized $115,000 on the sale of your home. You bought a new home for $175,000. Since that exceeds your sale price, the entire $40,000 gain is deferred and subtracted from the basis of your new home. The basis of your new home, therefore, will be $135,000.

But what if your new or replacement residence costs only $100,000, say, or $15,000 less than the adjusted sale price of your old home? In such a case you have to recognize that amount of gain — $15,000 — immediately and pay taxes on it. The remainder of the $40,000 gain in the example — $25,000 — can be deferred and subtracted from the basis of your new home. In this instance your starting basis would be $75,000.

EXCLUSION OF GAIN

Under the existing tax laws, you can cheerfully scale the housing ladder, buying ever more expensive homes and deferring the taxes due on the gains from those you sell until you finally decide to stick with what you've got and not buy a replacement. At that point, the taxes on all the previous gains that you've deferred will come due.

The only relief from this requirement cuts in when you turn fifty-five. At that age you become eligible to exclude a specified amount of your realized gains. The tax laws currently allow couples to exclude up to $125,000 of gains realized on the sale of a primary residence (the limit is $62,500 for a single person or a married person filing separately), but three conditions must first be met: (1) at least one spouse must be fifty-five or older when the home is sold; (2) the individual or couple claiming the exclusion must have owned and occupied the home as a primary residence for three of the five years preceding the sale; and (3) neither spouse can have claimed an exclusion previously. The exclusion of gain is a one-time benefit. If either spouse has used it before, both are ineligible to claim it. If you claim the exclusion and then remarry, you cannot claim another exclusion, even if your new spouse has never taken advantage of that tax benefit.

LOSSES

What if you sell your residence for less than you paid for it? That's not a pleasant thought or a common occurrence, but it can happen. Just ask some of the homeowners of Texas, who saw values dip so steeply that many of them were compelled to decide that it made more economic sense to default on their mortgages than to try to sell their homes and use the proceeds to repay their lenders.

Perhaps the worst of it is that if you suffer a loss on the sale of your residence, the tax laws offer no compensation at all. Unlike a business loss, a loss incurred on the sale of a residence cannot be deducted. (The news isn't all bad, however — selling at a loss has no impact on the basis of your old home, and since you have no gain to worry about, it doesn't matter if the cost of your replacement residence is less than the selling price of your old residence.)

VACATION AND RENTAL PROPERTY

The tax laws governing rental property are much more complicated than those governing homes, more so now than ever since the tax reform act of 1986 set out to simplify them. Here I can only provide the most general kind of guide. If you need detailed practical information, you should consult an accountant or a tax attorney. You could call the IRS and ask, but, amazingly, their phone-in service experts can't be held responsible for the accuracy of their answers. And imagine it, the IRS's own hired bank of experts has been found to give wrong advice more than half the time!

The thrust of the 1986 tax reform was to close perceived tax loopholes, many of which involved real-estate investments. Under previous laws, owners of rental property were allowed to use any losses they incurred to reduce the income on which they had to pay taxes. So a doctor, say, who happened to own a few rental units on the side could deduct his rental losses from the income earned through his practice, thereby significantly reducing his owed income taxes.

The new tax law changed that. It created a distinction between investment activities that are *active* and those that are *passive*. Rental real-estate is among those activities classified as passive. Essentially the new law says that losses incurred from passive investment activities can only be used to offset income from other passive investments.

The one exception to this — and it's a provisional one, at that — is that investors who are actively involved in the management of rental property can still offset up to $25,000 in losses against their active income (that is, wages and dividends). The provision is that their active income cannot exceed $150,000. (The $25,000 maximum deduction is reduced for people earning more than $100,000 and is eliminated entirely for people earning more than $150,000.)

For individuals earning $150,000 or less, the tax benefits of rental-property ownership can still be attractive. As a rental-property owner, you can deduct the cost of repairs (which are not deductible for your primary residence) as well as any operating expenses you incur, such as advertising, maintenance, utilities, and insurance costs. Your mortgage-interest payments on your rental property can also be deducted, but they count toward the $25,000 ceiling on the losses you can claim. (Remember, $25,000 is the maximum loss you can claim if you're earning $100,000 or less. The allowable deductions are phased out between $100,000 and $150,000 and disappear entirely for those earning more than $150,000.)

If you occupy a portion of the property and rent a portion of it, you must do the bookkeeping as if you actually owned two separate properties. For example, if half the property is your personal residence and the other half is rented out, you can deduct half of the total expenses as rental expenses.

The tax laws also allow you to claim a deduction for the "depreciation" of your rental property each year. But under the new rules, rental property now depreciates over twenty-seven and a half years instead of nineteen, as formerly, reducing the depreciation benefit. The depreciation you claim also reduces your "basis" for calculating the gain when you sell your rental property.

To calculate your tax benefits or liabilities, total the income derived from your rental property and then subtract all your deductible expenses, including your annual depreciation allowance. Suppose you claim rental income of $15,000 and deductions of $25,000, for a net loss of $10,000. Under the new rules, if your annual income is $100,000 or less, you'll be able to deduct the entire $10,000 loss.

VACATION PROPERTY

For tax purposes, vacation property falls somewhere between property owned entirely for personal use and investment property. It can qualify as either of these or a little of both, and the new tax laws make the decision of how to classify it a lot trickier than it used to be.

The problem begins with the fact that the law allows you to deduct mortgage interest on a first and second home in full, up to a maximum combined mortgage amount of $1 million. Mortgage-interest payments on an investment property, however, are now limited by the passive-loss rules. So here's the rub: If you classify your property as being for "personal use" rather than "rental," meaning that you rent it to others for no more than fourteen days a year, then you'll preserve your mortgage-interest deduction, all right, but you'll be unable to claim deductions for depreciation or operating expenses, or any of the other deductions that are still allowed (with severe limitations) for rental property.

On the other hand, treating your home as an investment rather than as a personal-use property will entitle you to the rental deductions (if your income is less than $150,000) but may threaten your mortgage-interest deduction. That's because your deductions for rental property, including mortgage-interest payments, can't exceed the property income if you make more than $150,000, and are capped at $25,000 if you earn no more than $100,000. Generally speaking, the higher your income and the more limited the deductions you can claim, the more likely that it will be to your benefit to preserve your mortgage deduction by keeping the property in the personal-use category.

The determination of whether a property is a vacation home or an investment is based on the number of days you allocate for your own and your family's personal use of it. As long as your personal use doesn't exceed fourteen days or 10 percent of the time the property is rented at fair market value, then it qualifies as an investment property. If you exceed that "de minimis" personal-use limit, however, the home qualifies as a residence, and you're subject to a slew of complicated special rules limiting the rental expenses you can deduct. You'll have to determine first what portion of the use is personal and what portion is rental. You can deduct mortgage-interest payments only for the personal-use portion. So if you use the house half the time as a vacation home, you can deduct half the mortgage-interest payments, as you would for your primary residence. However, your rental expenses, including the mortgage interest allocated for rental use, can be deducted only up to the amount of rental income the property produces.

Calculating the tax impact of classifying a property as being for rental or personal use can be complicated, to say the least. This is definitely an area where you'd benefit from the assistance of a tax expert (and maybe a headache specialist as well).

HOME-OFFICE DEDUCTION

It's more difficult than it used to be under existing tax laws to claim a deduction for a home office, but it's still possible under two conditions:

1. You're self-employed (full- or part-time), and you operate your trade or business from the home office.

2. You're required by your employer to work at home. In this case the tax rules say that the home office must be for your employer's convenience, not for yours.

Further, to qualify for the deduction, your home office must be used "regularly and exclusively" in connection with your business. A combination study and family room won't pass muster with the IRS.

If you do operate a legitimate office at home, you can deduct a proportionate share of your overall house expenses. If the office represents one fifth of the house, you can deduct one fifth of the utility costs, the home insurance, and so on. If you repair the hot-water heater or the furnace, you can deduct a share of those costs as well.

One thing you cannot do, however, is use the home-office deduction to create a loss in your business. The home-office deduction you claim cannot exceed the gross income you report for your home-based business.

If you're thinking about claiming the home-office deduction, bear in mind that it will increase your tax liability if and when you sell the home. The tax laws allow you to defer your capital gain only on the portion of the sale attributable to the nonoffice portion of your residence. If you've been claiming one sixth of your home as an office, you'll also have to recognize one sixth of the gain immediately and pay taxes on that amount in the year in which you sell the home.

MOVING EXPENSES

The IRS will allow you to deduct some of the expenses involved in moving from one home to another, but only if the move is "job-related." And the IRS's definition of the term is quite specific.

First, moving-related expenses are allowed only if you're moving from one principal residence to another. The move from a college dorm or from a parent's residence to a new location to accept a new job doesn't qualify, even if you meet all the other conditions.

Second, you must meet the IRS's distance test. The distance between your new job and your former residence must be at least thirty-five miles greater than the distance between that residence and your old job. If your old job was ten miles from your old home, for example, then your new job must be at least forty-five miles away. If you're starting work for the first time, or reentering the job market after a long absence, your new job must be at least thirty-five miles from your former residence.

Third, the IRS applies a time test. To be able to deduct your moving expenses, you must work in the general area to which you relocate for at least thirty-nine weeks out of the first twelve months following your move.

If you meet all three of these conditions, you may deduct the cost of moving your household goods and traveling to your new residence. There's no limit to the deduction allowed for these expenses, and in fact, you're also allowed to deduct the cost of house-hunting trips and temporary living expenses incurred before you move into your new residence.* The maximum deduction currently allowed for moving expenses beyond relocating yourself and moving your belongings is $3,000. Of that amount, no more than $1,500 can be deducted for house-hunting and temporary living expenses combined.

Again, taxes are complex. Especially for second-time buyers, taxes may be an area in which professional advice would be so helpful as to be mandatory.

You'll live and learn, and perhaps you'll even write me a letter to suggest new bits of advice for the first-time buyers who will come after you. But here's a start to it, the process of owning and developing a home. I've tried to help you be clear-minded

---

* Under the new tax laws, however, you can deduct only 80 percent of the cost of meals incurred in connection with house-hunting trips, traveling to your new location, or interim living arrangements.

about what it will entail, and I haven't been shy about naming the difficulties.

On the other side of this caution is my solid belief that the great American dream is valid, and that home ownership is one of the most enriching and satisfying experiences we humans can have. The problems are real, but the rewards are hard to beat.

Appendix:
The Most Common House Styles

This appendix is made up of drawings of the chief house styles that you may encounter. There are many others, of course, and there are many variations of these styles, but these are the classics.

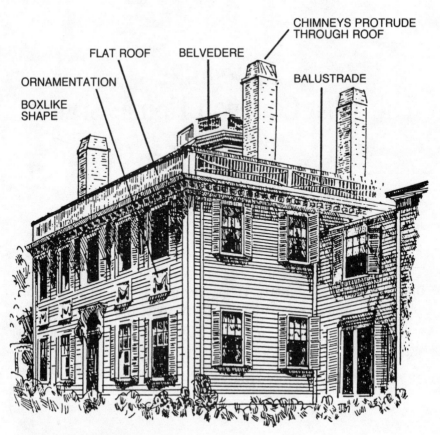

CHIMNEYS PROTRUDE
THROUGH ROOF

FLAT ROOF   BELVEDERE

BALUSTRADE

ORNAMENTATION

BOXLIKE
SHAPE

Colonial American

FEDERAL

Key Distinguishing Characteristics

The Federal is a multistory, symmetrical, box-shaped house with a flat roof.

Other Distinguishing Characteristics

Clapboard or brick exterior walls
One or more chimneys protruding through roof
Windows with small glass panes
Beautiful ornamentation
Belvedere
Balustrade

History

Prevalent throughout the cities in the East in the 1700s, this style takes on many forms. Some consider this and the Adams style to be the same.

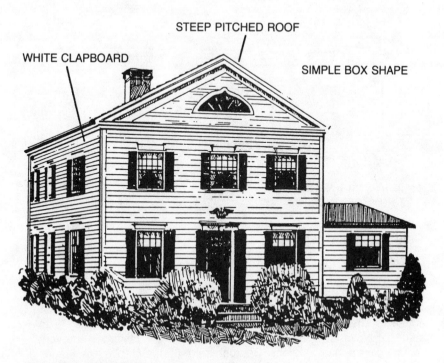

STEEP PITCHED ROOF

WHITE CLAPBOARD

SIMPLE BOX SHAPE

Colonial American

NEW ENGLAND FARMHOUSE

Key Distinguishing Characteristics

This is a simple, box-shaped house. The traditional material for the exterior siding is white clapboard. A steep pitched roof is used to shed heavy snow.

Other Distinguishing Characteristics

Central chimney used to support frame
Two square rooms on each floor is typical layout
Interior layout poor by today's standards

History

These simple houses were built in the 1700s and 1800s throughout the New England countryside. They were the favorite style among the farmers who could not afford the more elaborate styles of the times. Simple to construct and maintain, they were designed to use the building materials and techniques of the period.

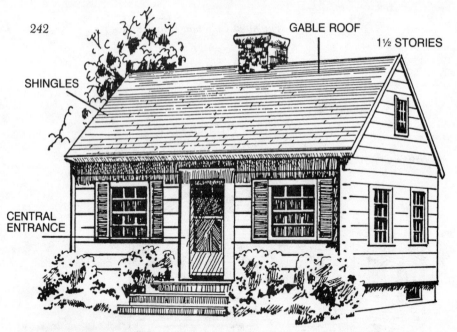

SHINGLES

GABLE ROOF

1½ STORIES

CENTRAL
ENTRANCE

Colonial American

CAPE COD COLONIAL

Key Distinguishing Characteristics

This is a small, symmetrical, 1½-story, compact house with a central entrance. The roof is the steep gable type covered with shingles. The authentic types have low central chimneys, but end chimneys are very common in the new versions. Bedrooms are on the first floor. The attic may be finished into additional bedrooms and a bath. A vine-covered picket fence is traditional.

Other Distinguishing Characteristics

Traditionally, exterior walls were white clapboard, natural shingles, or brick; modern versions have exterior walls of a wide variety of materials

Simple double-hung windows

Shutters same length as windows

Simple cornice with gutters immediately above first-floor windows

Easy to build, maintain, and heat

Inherent in the design is the necessity to walk through one room to reach another

History

The Cape Cod Colonial is the earliest dwelling type built by the American colonists that is still popular today. The early Cape Cods were very crude. They usually had one room on the first floor and a sleeping loft above. The modern version was the most popular house style in the US from the 1920s through the 1950s.

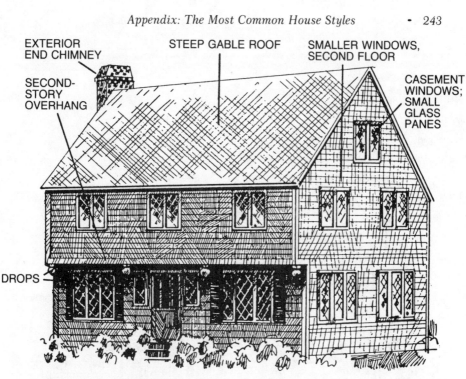

EXTERIOR END CHIMNEY

STEEP GABLE ROOF

SMALLER WINDOWS, SECOND FLOOR

SECOND-STORY OVERHANG

CASEMENT WINDOWS; SMALL GLASS PANES

DROPS

Colonial American

GARRISON COLONIAL

Key Distinguishing Characteristics

This is a 2½-story, symmetrical house with a second-story overhang in the front. The traditional ornamentation is four carved drops (pineapple or acorn shape) below the overhang.

Other Distinguishing Characteristics

Exterior chimney at end
Older versions have casement windows with small panes of glass
Later versions have double-hung windows
Second-story windows often smaller than those on first floor
Steep gable roof covered with shingles
Dormers often break through the cornice line

History

The Garrison Colonial is reputed to be patterned after Colonial block-houses used to fend off Indians, but it is probably an outgrowth of the overhang style of the Elizabethan townhouse. The style probably has been perpetuated because of its pleasant appearance. The carved drops were the ends of the framing beams on early versions of the house. Later they were added on for decoration. Examples of this style built in the 1600s are still standing today.

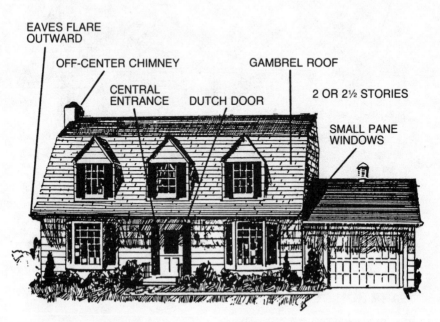

EAVES FLARE OUTWARD

OFF-CENTER CHIMNEY

CENTRAL ENTRANCE

DUTCH DOOR

GAMBREL ROOF

2 OR 2½ STORIES

SMALL PANE WINDOWS

Colonial American

DUTCH COLONIAL

Key Distinguishing Characteristics

The Dutch Colonial is a moderate-sized, 2- to 2½-story house with a gambrel roof and eaves that flare outward.

Other Distinguishing Characteristics

Central entrance
Dutch entrance door
Double-hung windows with small panes of glass
Exterior may be made of a wide variety of material such as clapboard, shingles, cut stone, brick, or stucco
Second-story dormers through roof are common
Chimney rarely in the center

History

This is an indigenous American style that did not originate in Holland, as is commonly believed. The Dutch settlers built them in Pennsylvania starting in the 1600s and soon after in New York.

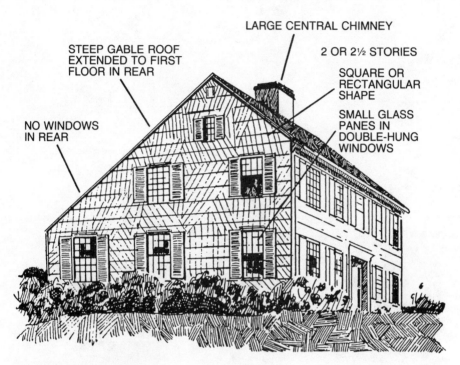

STEEP GABLE ROOF
EXTENDED TO FIRST
FLOOR IN REAR

LARGE CENTRAL CHIMNEY

2 OR 2½ STORIES

SQUARE OR
RECTANGULAR
SHAPE

NO WINDOWS
IN REAR

SMALL GLASS
PANES IN
DOUBLE-HUNG
WINDOWS

Colonial American

SALT BOX COLONIAL OR CATSLIDE (IN SOUTH)

Key Distinguishing Characteristics

This is a 2- or 2½-story, square or rectangular house with steep gable roof that extends down to the first floor in the rear.

Other Distinguishing Characteristics

Exterior walls usually clapboard or shingles
Large central chimney
Large double-hung windows with small panes of glass
No windows in rear
Shutters the same size as windows
In order to obtain traditional lean-to look, headroom in the rear must be
    sacrificed

History

The Salt Box is a Colonial New England farmhouse that grew in the form of a lean-to shed or room added to the rear of the house. The rear was oriented to the north to ward off cold winter winds. Its name comes from the resemblance to the salt box found in old country stores.

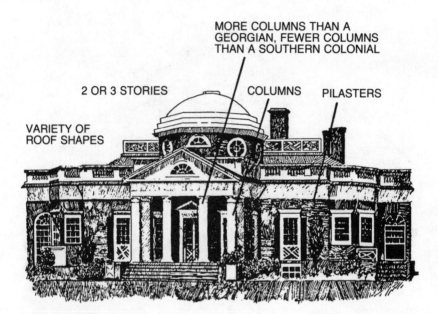

MORE COLUMNS THAN A
GEORGIAN, FEWER COLUMNS
THAN A SOUTHERN COLONIAL

2 OR 3 STORIES   COLUMNS   PILASTERS

VARIETY OF
ROOF SHAPES

Colonial American

CLASSIC COLONIAL

Key Distinguishing Characteristics

A large, impressive showplace, the Classic Colonial is a 2- or 3-story house with a columned exterior. It has more columns than a Georgian Colonial and fewer columns than a Southern Colonial.

Other Distinguishing Characteristics

Columns have Doric, Ionic, or Corinthian capitals
Pilasters in the walls are common
Porticos at vehicular entrance with roof supported by columns
Variety of roof shapes on same house

History

Based on classic Greek architecture, the style was introduced by Thomas Jefferson, who built Monticello in 1772 and remodeled it several times up to 1803. There is very little difference between a Classic Colonial and a Greek Revival, and many architectural historians use the terms synonymously.

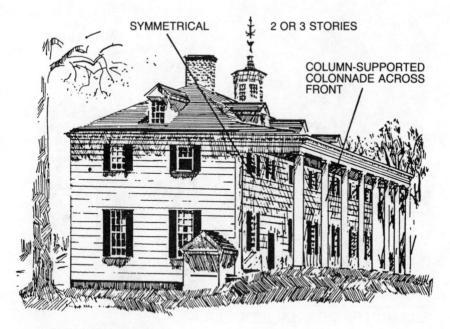

SYMMETRICAL   2 OR 3 STORIES

COLUMN-SUPPORTED
COLONNADE ACROSS
FRONT

Colonial American

SOUTHERN COLONIAL

Key Distinguishing Characteristics

The Southern Colonial is a large 2- or 3-story frame house with a characteristic colonnade extending across the front. The roof extends over the colonnade.

Other Distinguishing Characteristics

Hip or gable roof covered with shingles
Symmetrical
Second-story balcony
Balustrade
Belvedere
Double-hung windows with small panes of glass
Shutters same size as windows
Cornices with dentils

History

The style is a southern conception of the New England Colonial and Georgian Colonial modified to suit the warmer climate. The classic example pictured here is Mount Vernon, built in the 1700s.

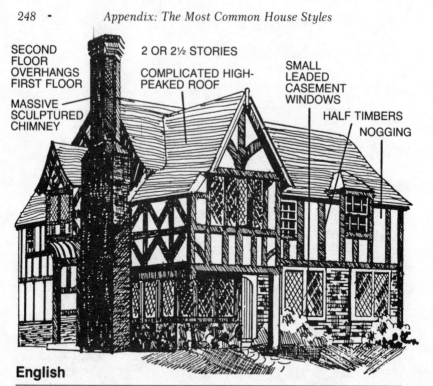

SECOND FLOOR OVERHANGS FIRST FLOOR

MASSIVE SCULPTURED CHIMNEY

2 OR 2½ STORIES

COMPLICATED HIGH-PEAKED ROOF

SMALL LEADED CASEMENT WINDOWS

HALF TIMBERS
NOGGING

English

ELIZABETHAN OR HALF TIMBER

Key Distinguishing Characteristics

This is a 2- or 2½-story house, often with part of the second story overhanging the first. It has less stonework and is less fortlike than the Tudor. Stone and stucco walls with half timbers are most common.

Other Distinguishing Characteristics

Massive sculptured chimneys
Used brick between half timbers is called "nogging"; when not covered with stucco it is "exposed nogging"
Complicated high peaked roofs, which are expensive to install and subject to leaks because of complex valleys
Small leaded-glass casement widows
Interior often has large halls and a spacious living room with a large fireplace and beamed ceilings
Bedrooms are on second floor

History

These houses were erected in England throughout the prosperous reign of Queen Elizabeth (1558–1603), particularly in the London area. The characteristic protruding second story supported by wooden brackets is a carryover from narrow London lots where extra space could be obtained by overhanging the street.

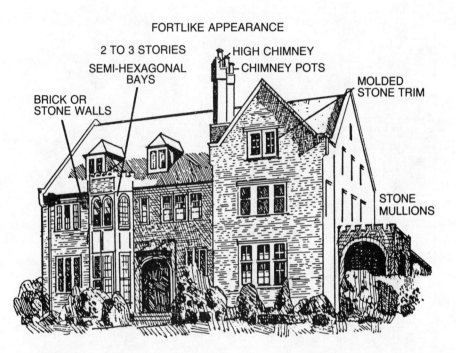

FORTLIKE APPEARANCE

2 TO 3 STORIES — HIGH CHIMNEY

SEMI-HEXAGONAL BAYS — CHIMNEY POTS

BRICK OR STONE WALLS

MOLDED STONE TRIM

STONE MULLIONS

English

TUDOR

Key Distinguishing Characteristics

The Tudor is an imposing-looking house with fortresslike lines. Siding is chiefly stone and brick with some stucco and half timbers. Windows and doors have molded cement or stone trim around them.

Other Distinguishing Characteristics

Usually 2½ stories
Stone or cement window mullions and transoms
Casement windows with leaded glass (often diamond-shaped)
High, prominent chimneys with protruding chimney pots
Semi-hexagonal bays and turrets
Interior often laid out with odd-shaped rooms full of nooks and crannies, large fireplaces, beamed ceilings, and rough plaster walls

History

The style started in England in the late fifteenth century, during the reign of the House of Tudor. It did not become popular in the US until the late 1800s.

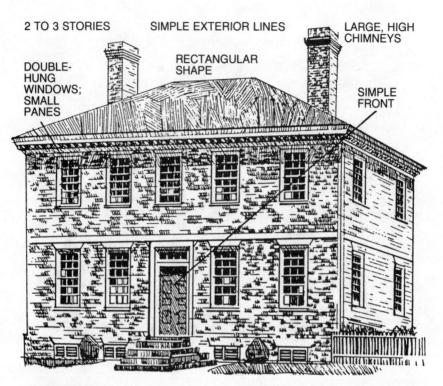

2 TO 3 STORIES   SIMPLE EXTERIOR LINES   LARGE, HIGH CHIMNEYS

DOUBLE-HUNG WINDOWS; SMALL PANES   RECTANGULAR SHAPE   SIMPLE FRONT

English

WILLIAMSBURG GEORGIAN OR EARLY GEORGIAN

Key Distinguishing Characteristics

The houses built in Williamsburg were representative of the early Georgian houses built in America throughout the early 1700s. They had simple exterior lines and generally fewer of the decorative devices characteristic of the later Georgian houses. Most were 2- or 3-story rectangular houses with two large chimneys rising high above the roof at each end.

Other Distinguishing Characteristics

Sliding double-hung windows with small panes
Simple front entrances

History

Williamsburg, Virginia, was the cultural and political capital of the Colonies during most of the 1700s. The houses here were based on the styles developed in England during the reign of the four King Georges. The Williamsburg houses were built in the early 1700s. With gifts of about $40 million, John D. Rockefeller, Jr., restored the community.

SIMPLE, INFORMAL STYLE

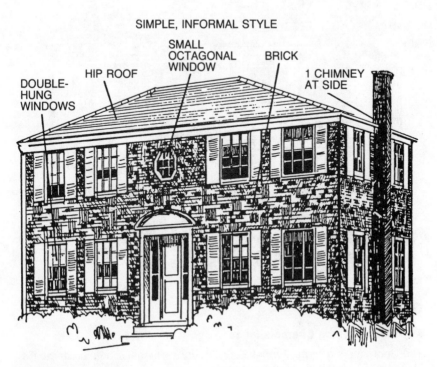

DOUBLE-HUNG WINDOWS
HIP ROOF
SMALL OCTAGONAL WINDOW
BRICK
1 CHIMNEY AT SIDE

English

REGENCY

Key Distinguishing Characteristics

This is a 2- or 3-story symmetrical house with a hip roof. A small octagonal window over the front door is traditional.

Other Distinguishing Characteristics

Almost always brick, often painted white
One chimney on side
Double-hung windows
Shutters same size as windows
A simple informal style without the classic lines of the Georgian

History

The style reached its peak of popularity in England between 1810 and 1820. Many of these houses were built in the US in the late 1800s and throughout the 1900s, and are still being built today.

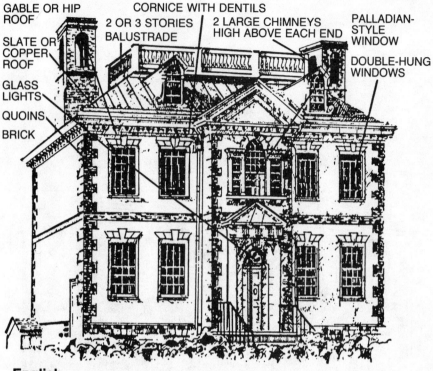

GABLE OR HIP ROOF

SLATE OR COPPER ROOF

GLASS LIGHTS

QUOINS

BRICK

CORNICE WITH DENTILS

2 OR 3 STORIES
BALUSTRADE

2 LARGE CHIMNEYS
HIGH ABOVE EACH END

PALLADIAN-STYLE WINDOW

DOUBLE-HUNG WINDOWS

English

GEORGIAN

Key Distinguishing Characteristics

The Georgian is a large, formal 2- or 3-story rectangular house characterized by its classic lines and ornamentation.

Other Distinguishing Characteristics

Traditional material is brick
Some made of masonry, clapboard, or shingles
Gable or hip roof
Slate shingles or copper roofing
Two large chimneys rising high above the roof at each end
A Palladian-style set of three windows on the second floor over the front entrance or at each end
Front entrance with Greek Columns
Glass lights on side and above front entrance door

History

The style became popular in England during the reign of the four King Georges. They were built in large numbers here in the 1700s and 1800s. The house pictured is Mount Pleasant, built in 1750 in Philadelphia. It contained a large number of the features that would traditionally be included in the Georgian style.

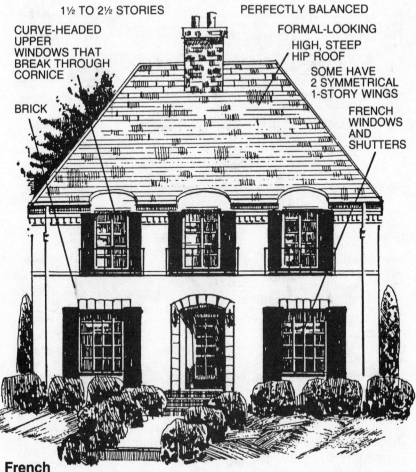

1½ TO 2½ STORIES

PERFECTLY BALANCED

CURVE-HEADED UPPER WINDOWS THAT BREAK THROUGH CORNICE

FORMAL-LOOKING

HIGH, STEEP HIP ROOF

SOME HAVE 2 SYMMETRICAL 1-STORY WINGS

BRICK

FRENCH WINDOWS AND SHUTTERS

French

FRENCH PROVINCIAL

Key Distinguishing Characteristics

The French Provincial is a perfectly balanced, formal 1½- to 2½-story house with a high, steep hip roof and curve-headed upper windows that break through the cornice.

Other Distinguishing Characteristics

French windows or shutters on first floor
Two symmetrical 1-story wings
Usually made of brick

History

The style originated in France during the reign of Louis XIV (1643–1715) by the rich who wanted showplace homes.

STOOP UP TO
FIRST FLOOR

BROWNSTONE
TRIM

4 OR 5
STORIES

COMMON WALLS   BRICK   FLAT ROOF

SIMPLE
DOUBLE-
HUNG
WINDOWS

Nineteenth-Century American

BROWNSTONE OR BRICK ROW HOUSE
OR EASTERN TOWNHOUSE

Key Distinguishing Characteristics

These houses usually cover an entire city block. Most are 4 or 5 stories with a stoop leading up to the first floor. They have common side walls with the house on either side.

Other Distinguishing Characteristics

Built of brick
Often faced or trimmed with chocolate sandstone called brownstone
Flat roof
Simple double-hung windows

History

Brownstones became popular in the late 1800s in New York and other large eastern cities. They tend to develop individual characteristics in each different city.

2 OR 3 STORIES

PITCHED ROOF   COMMON SIDE WALLS

BAY
WINDOWS   HEAVILY DECORATED,
PAINTED

Nineteenth-Century American

WESTERN ROW HOUSE OR WESTERN TOWNHOUSE

Key Distinguishing Characteristics

Like the eastern version of the townhouse, these houses are usually built to cover an entire street or block. They have common side walls with the house on either side.

Other Distinguishing Characteristics

2 or 3 stories
Exterior walls may be wood, stucco, or brick
Bay windows
Heavily decorated and painted exteriors
Pitched roof

History

This style is the West's answer to the eastern row house. The main difference is that each unit has its own individual, unique design. They were built starting in the late 1800s and are still popular today. Thousands of these units have been built in San Francisco and other large western cities.

BALCONY ACROSS FRONT AT SECOND FLOOR

SHINGLE
ROOF

2 STORIES

RAIL SIMPLE
IRON OR WOOD

Nineteenth-Century American

MONTEREY

Key Distinguishing Characteristics

A 2-story house with a balcony across the front at the second-floor level.

Other Distinguishing Characteristics

Asymmetrical shape
Balcony rail is simple ironwork or wood as contrasted with lacy ironwork
of Creole style

History

Thomas Larkin, a Boston merchant, moved to Monterey, California, and in 1835 built his version of a New England Colonial out of adobe brick. Most of the other houses in Monterey at that time were one story. In addition to the second story, his house also introduced to the area the second-floor porch, roof shingles, and the fireplace. The house was widely copied throughout the West and became known as the Monterey style.

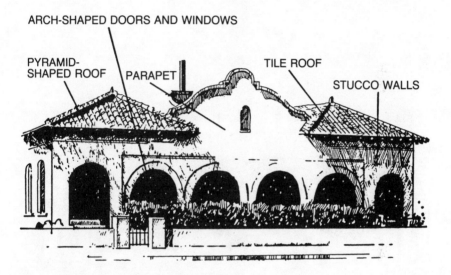

LOOKS LIKE OLD MISSION CHURCH

ARCH-SHAPED DOORS AND WINDOWS

PYRAMID-SHAPED ROOF   PARAPET

TILE ROOF

STUCCO WALLS

Nineteenth-Century American

MISSION

Key Distinguishing Characteristics

These houses look like the old mission churches and houses of southern California. The doors and windows are arch-shaped.

Other Distinguishing Characteristics

No sculptural ornamentation
Roof often hidden by the parapets
Towers and turrets with pyramid-shaped roofs
Exterior walls made of stucco

History

This is the style developed in the West in the 1800s when the people became aware of their architectural past. It was popularized as a reaction against the conventional eastern styles that were being built in the West at the time.

SMALL, COMPACT SHAPE   1 STORY

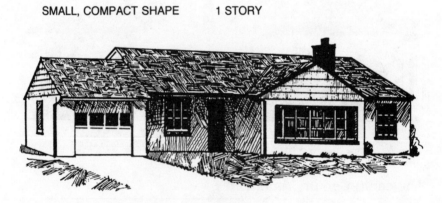

Early-Twentieth-Century American

CALIFORNIA BUNGALOW

Key Distinguishing Characteristics

A 1-story, small, compact house.

Other Distinguishing Characteristics

Usually made of wood
Traces of South Seas, Spanish, and Japanese influences on many

History

At the peak of the bungalow's popularity, from 1900 to 1920, the names bungalow and California bungalow were often used synonymously, although one writer of the time classified bungalows into nine different types. The name comes from the Indian word *bangla* — of Bengal.

Post–World War II American

CALIFORNIA RANCH

Key Distinguishing Characteristics

A California Ranch is a 1-story, ground-hugging house with a low pitched roof.

Other Distinguishing Characteristics

Large double-hung, sliding, and picture windows
Sliding glass doors leading onto patios

History

The ranch house of the West has spread in popularity throughout the US. Today the term is commonly used to describe a wide variety of 1-story houses, including many smaller ones that used to be called bungalows.

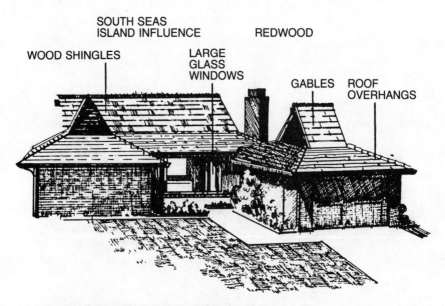

Post–World War II American

NORTHWESTERN OR PUGET SOUND

Key Distinguishing Characteristics

This is a low ranch-type house with generous overhangs at eaves and gables. The exterior walls are often redwood.

Other Distinguishing Characteristics

Roof shape reflects South Sea island influence
Large glass windows
Wood shingle roof covering

History

The style was first developed in 1908 by Ellsworth Storey, a young architect who designed a group of these cottages. The style did not really become popular until after World War II.

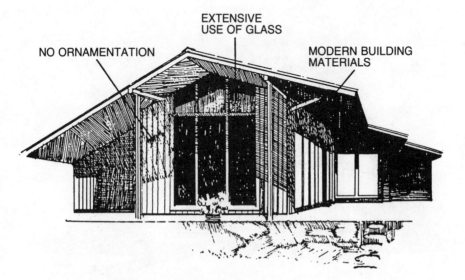

EXTENSIVE
USE OF GLASS

NO ORNAMENTATION

MODERN BUILDING
MATERIALS

Post–World War II American

FUNCTIONAL MODERN OR CONTEMPORARY

Key Distinguishing Characteristics

The exterior style of a contemporary house is an integral part of the overall design. Its function is to enclose some living areas with modern materials yet integrate the indoor and outdoor space into one unit.

Other Distinguishing Characteristics

Modern building materials
Extensive use of glass
Lack of ornamentation

History

The contemporary is today's version of the revolution in house styles started by the great American architects Frank Lloyd Wright and Henry Hobson Richardson, the German architects of the Bauhaus, and other architects around the world in the past 100 years.

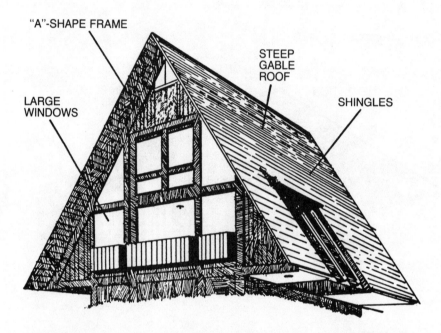

"A"-SHAPE FRAME

STEEP GABLE ROOF

LARGE WINDOWS

SHINGLES

Post–World War II American

"A" FRAME

Key Distinguishing Characteristics

In this style, the frame is the shape of one or more A's.

Other Distinguishing Characteristics

    Steep gable roof covered with shingles
    Front and rear have large glass windows
    Interior often only roughly finished
    Sleeping area often is semi-enclosed or sometimes is a loft area

History

With the explosive growth in vacation homes since World War II, millions of families now own second homes that are used primarily for recreational purposes. The simple "A"-frame style has been popular in the mountains and near lakes and oceans for this purpose.

Glossary

Adjustable-rate mortgage (ARM). A mortgage on which the interest rate moves up or down periodically in accordance with changes in a specified financial index.

Adjusted basis. The starting point for determining the gain or loss realized on the sale of a home. See *Basis.*

Adjusted sale price. The sale price of a home less allowable selling expenses. Important for determining the amount of gain or loss on the sale.

Amortization. Reduction of the principal amount of a loan through periodic payments made according to an agreed-upon schedule.

Annual percentage rate (APR). The "true" cost of money borrowed, reflecting the stated interest rate plus points and fees charged for the loan. Lenders are required to disclose the APR as well as the stated interest rate.

Application fee. The amount, usually nonrefundable, that a lender charges for processing a borrower's application for a loan.

Appraisal. An estimate of the market value of a property, usually based upon the sale prices of other properties in the same neighborhood. Lenders will base the size of the mortgage they are willing to approve in part on the appraised value as determined by a professional appraiser.

Appreciation. Increase in a property's value over time. The opposite of depreciation.

Asbestos. At one time a popular insulating material, now recognized as a cancer-causing agent. The presence of asbestos in a home may be a concern for prospective buyers.

Assessment. The value of a property as established by local officials for purposes of calculating the property taxes owed. The assessed value of a property may be, but isn't always, equal to its appraised value (see *Appraisal*).

Assumable mortgage. A loan issued to the owner of a property, which can be taken over by the new owner of that property, who then accepts the responsibility for making the payments. Fixed-rate mortgages typically are not assumable; VA, FHA, and adjustable-rate mortgages usually are.

"Bare-walls" coverage. Master insurance policy for a condominium or a cooperative, covering the building's shell and common areas only. See *"Single-entity" coverage.*

Basis. The original purchase price of a property plus allowable purchase expenses (such as legal fees and recording costs) and improvements, and less any casualty losses. The basis is the key factor in the equation used to determine the capital gain or loss on the sale of real estate.

Binder. A "good-faith" deposit, usually between $500 and $1,000, accompanying a buyer's offer to demonstrate serious interest in purchasing the property. In insurance, an agreement confirming temporary coverage pending the issuance of a formal policy.

Biweekly mortgage. A mortgage on which payments are made every two weeks instead of monthly. The effect is to spread the repayment of the loan, thereby reducing the total amount of interest paid.

Blanket mortgage. In a cooperative, the mortgage covering the building as a whole, as distinguished from the "share loans" that buyers must obtain to finance the purchase of their individual units.

Broker. An agent licensed to receive a commission for negotiating the sale or lease of property.

Buy-down. A mechanism for temporarily reducing the interest rate on a mortgage loan.

Buyer's broker. A broker retained to represent the buyer's interests in a real-estate transaction, paid by the buyer and responsible for negotiating on the buyer's behalf. This differs from the typical arrangement, in which the broker acts as the agent of the seller and is paid a commission by the seller from the proceeds of the sale.

Call. The lender's right to demand immediate payment of the outstanding balance on a loan, either if the borrower violates the terms of the loan agreement, or if the note is payable "on demand."

Capital gains. The taxable "profit" on the sale of real estate, which must either be recognized (and paid) or deferred.

Cesspool. A cavity dug in the land outside a home to receive and retain drainage and sewage.

Closing. The legal occasion during which the deed to a property is transferred from the seller to the buyer.

Closing agent. The individual (generally either the lender's attorney or an escrow agent) who serves as "master of ceremonies" at the closing.

Closing costs. The final fees that must be paid to complete the property transfer. The borrower typically is responsible for paying these fees, but sometimes the seller contributes all or part of the cash required.

Commitment. The lender's notice to the borrower that the mortgage has been approved. The notice, usually presented in letter form, should also include an explanation of the terms and conditions under which the loan will be granted.

Common areas. In a condominium or cooperative, the portions of the property owned jointly by all unit owners.

Condo association. The governing body of a condominium, in which all unit owners have voting rights.

Condo conversion. The legal process of transforming an apartment building (or any other structure) into a condominium.

Condo documents. The legal papers establishing a condominium and detailing the ownership terms and rules and regulations governing it.

Condo fee. The monthly maintenance fee that condo unit owners are required to pay as their share of the common-area expenses. The monthly fee is not tax-deductible on a condominium, but a portion of it may be on a cooperative.

Condo master policy. The insurance policy covering the common areas in a condominium.

Condominium. A form of ownership in which some portions of a property are owned separately while others are owned in common by all of the condominium owners.

Contingency. A condition or conditions specified in the real-estate purchase contract, which must be met before the transaction can be consummated. Also, a provision or provisions specified in a loan commitment upon which the commitment is conditional.

Convertible option. A provision in some adjustable-rate mortgages, giving the borrower the right to convert to a fixed rate under specified conditions and terms.

Cooperative. A form of joint property ownership, similar to a condominium except that unlike condo owners, who actually own their individual units, cooperative buyers own shares in the corporation that owns the cooperative building and have long-term leases on their units.

Cooperative-share loan. A loan for the purchase of a cooperative unit. See *Blanket mortgage.*

Counteroffer. A response to proposed contract terms. If the buyer offers to pay $200,000 for a property priced at $250,000, for example, the seller might "counter" by proposing to accept $225,000 instead. Any change in the terms of the original offer constitutes a counteroffer.

Credit check. A review of the borrower's record of paying off past loans, credit cards, and charge accounts, undertaken by the lender before it will approve a mortgage.

Credit life insurance. Insurance that will repay the outstanding loan balance to the bank should the borrower die.

Credit report. Information detailing the credit history of the borrower, which the lender obtains prior to approving the loan.

Deed. A legal instrument conveying title to real property.

Deed restrictions. Any provisions in a deed restricting ownership or use of the property — for example, limitations on rights-of-way, or easements granted to other parties.

Default. The failure to adhere to the terms of an agreement. A borrower who does not make mortgage payments or does not make them on time is in "default" of the mortgage and thus subject to the penalties specified in the loan agreement.

Deferral of gain. A legal means of delaying the payment of taxes due on the profit realized from the sale of a primary residence, which takes effect when the replacement residence is purchased for at least as much as the selling price of the original property.

Deposit. A percentage of the purchase price, paid by the buyer when the Purchase and Sale agreement is signed and typically held in escrow until the transaction is completed.

Depreciation. A decrease in property value over time. Owners of investment property are allowed to claim a deduction for depreciation, but no such deduction is allowed for depreciation of a primary residence.

Down payment. A portion of the purchase price, which the borrower is required to pay in cash and which may not be borrowed from the mortgage lender.

Dual agency. An arrangement in which the broker in a real-estate transaction represents both the buyer and the seller. Illegal in most jurisdictions unless disclosed to and accepted by both parties.

Earnest money. In some jurisdictions, synonymous with *binder* — a small sum offered by a prospective buyer to demonstrate serious interest in a property. In other jurisdictions, "earnest money" refers to the much larger sum paid as a deposit by the buyer when the Purchase and Sale agreement is signed.

Easement. The legal right to use another person's land for limited purposes — one example would be an easement to use a portion of a neighbor's drive-way. Similarly, a utility easement would give a utility company the right to run wires or lay pipes across a property.

Encumbrance. A claim levied against a property, inhibiting the owner's ability to transfer the title. Liens and attachments are the most common forms of encumbrances.

Equity. The owner's "stake" in a property — equal to the down payment plus any principal repaid on the mortgage loan, plus any increase in value due to appreciation or improvements the owner has made, less the value of any outstanding mortgages, liens, or other encumbrances.

Equity line of credit. A home-equity loan (see below) that operates like a revolving line of credit. The borrower pays interest only on the amount of credit tapped, and as the borrowed principal is repaid, it becomes available to be borrowed again.

Escrow. The placing of money (or documents) in the control of a custodian until the conditions of a contract are met. In a real-estate transaction, the buyer's deposit typically is held in escrow (in a segregated bank account, separate from the assets of the escrow agent) until the closing.

Exclusion of gain. Under federal tax laws, the one-time right, available to homeowners age fifty-five or older, to eliminate their tax liability on a portion of the gain (up to $125,000) realized on the sale of a primary residence.

Exclusive agency. An agreement between a homeowner and a real-estate broker, giving the broker the exclusive right to sell a property but specifying that he or she is not entitled to a commission if the owner sells the property on his or her own while the agreement is in effect.

Exclusive right to sell. Similar to exclusive agency, except that the broker is entitled to a commission during the period covered by the listing agreement even if the owner finds the buyer on his or her own.

Fannie Mae (FNMA). An acronym for the Federal National Mortgage Association. One of the two major players in the secondary mortgage market (also see *Freddie Mac*), Fannie Mae purchases mortgage loans originated by local lenders and establishes the guidelines that most lenders use in qualifying prospective borrowers.

Fair market value. What a willing buyer will pay a willing seller for a property.

Federal Housing Administration (FHA) mortgage. A loan insured by the Federal Housing Administration. The fact that down payments of less than 5 percent are acceptable makes FHA loans attractive, but purchase-price limitations can be a problem in areas where home prices are high.

Fixed-rate mortgage (FRM). A loan on which the interest rate remains the same throughout the loan term, unlike the rate on an adjustable-rate mortgage (see above), which is adjusted periodically.

Foreclosure. A legal process whereby a lender exercises its right to take possession of a property owned by a borrower who has defaulted on a loan secured by the property.

Freddie Mac (FHLMC). An acronym for the Federal Home Loan Mortgage Corporation. With Fannie Mae (see above), one of the major purchasers of residential mortgages in the secondary mortgage market.

"Free-of-all-tenants" clause. Legal language inserted in many agreements for the sale of multifamily or rental properties, requiring the owner, essentially, to evict all existing tenants before the property is sold.

General-warranty deed. Standard deed conveying property in most jurisdictions, in which the seller warrants that he or she owns the property, that it is free of all encumbrances, and that the seller will defend the title against all claims, regardless of when the defect may arise. This definition may vary in different jurisdictions.

"Good-faith estimate." An approximation of closing costs, which a lender is required to give to a prospective mortgage borrower within three days of the time an application for a loan is submitted.

Graduated-payment mortgage (GPM). A mortgage loan on which the interest and principal payments start off below market level but increase yearly, possibly eventually rising above the payments on a conventional mortgage.

Growing-equity mortgage (GEM). Similar to a graduated-payment mortgage (see above) except that the interest rate remains fixed while monthly payments increase at specified intervals, thus accelerating the repayment of the loan and reducing the amount of interest paid over the loan term.

Hazard insurance. A homeowner's policy typically required by mortgage lenders, insuring the property against damage or loss.

Home-equity loan. Equivalent of a second mortgage (see below), where the owner borrows against the equity in a home. Also see *Equity line of credit.*

Home inspection. The professional scrutiny of a home to assess its overall condition and identify existing or potential structural and/or mechanical problems.

HUD-1 form. Another name for the RESPA statement (see below), detailing all the loan closing costs and itemizing all payments made by and due from both the buyer and the seller.

Hydronic heating systems. A system that transmits heat through hot water or steam.

Improvement. For real-estate tax purposes, any change that adds to a property's value, increases its useful life, or adapts it to a new use. Improvements can be added to the basis of a property, but they cannot be deducted. (See *Repair.*)

Income-to-debt ratio. A lender's calculation of the percentage of income represented by a borrower's housing payments plus all other revolving debt payments.

Index. The guide used by lenders to determine periodic adjustments in adjustable-rate mortgages.

Index rate. The rate on the market index used to determine changes in an adjustable-rate mortgage (see *Index*). If the borrower's starting rate is *below* the index rate, it is said to be "discounted."

Inspection contingency. A clause in a purchase agreement making the sale contingent on the outcome of a structural and/or pest inspection of the premises. (See also *Home inspection; Pest inspection.*)

Interest. The cost of borrowing money.

Joint tenancy. A form of ownership in which two or more individuals have an equal interest in a property, which passes to the surviving owner or owners if one dies.

Leaching field. A large area into which the liquid that flows through a septic system is discharged. See *Septic system.*

Lien. Any legal claim against a property, filed to ensure payment of a debt or discharge of an obligation.

Listing. A real-estate broker's description of property available for sale.

Listing agreement. A contract between a real-estate broker and a property owner, specifying the terms under which the broker is authorized to sell or lease the owner's property and the terms under which a commission is due the broker.

Listing broker. The broker in a real-estate transaction who is retained by the owner to sell a property. See *Selling broker.*

Loan-to-value ratio. The relationship between the mortgage on a property and its value. If the mortgage is $80,000 and the property is worth $100,000, the loan-to-value ratio is 80 percent.

Loss payee. On an insurance policy, the designated recipient of the funds should a claim for loss or damage be paid.

Maintenance fee. Another term for the common-area fee, paid monthly by condominium and cooperative owners. See *Condo fee.*

Margin. On an adjustable-rate mortgage, the amount the lender will add to the index (usually 2 or 3 percent) to determine the adjusted rate.

Mechanics' lien. A claim against a property filed by someone who has furnished labor or materials to the owner for which he or she has not been paid.

Metes and bounds. Common terminology for describing the boundaries of a property.

Mortgage. A legal document in which the owner of a property pledges it as security to guarantee repayment of a loan.

Mortgagee. The lender in a mortgage transaction.

Mortgage banker. A lender who originates loans and sells them. See *Portfolio lender.*

Mortgage insurance. A insurance policy protecting the lender should a mortgage borrower default on a loan.

Mortgage broker. Someone who, for a fee, brings together a borrower in search of a mortgage loan and a lender willing to approve it.

Mortgagor. The borrower in a mortgage transaction.

Multiple Listing Service (MLS). A system for disseminating, to participating members, information on properties for sale.

Negative amortization. A process whereby the principal amount on an adjustable-rate or graduated-payment mortgage may increase over time. This occurs when payment increases are fixed or limited while there are no restrictions (or fewer restrictions) on the interest-rate adjustments allowed over time.

No-documentation loan. A program offered by some lenders, requiring less extensive verifications than a standard loan-approval process. Typically available only to borrowers able to make relatively large down payments.

Note. A legal document in which the borrower agrees to the repayment of a loan according to the terms specified.

Odd days' interest. The interest due on a loan from the closing date until the first day of the following month.

Offer to purchase. A formal document through which a prospective buyer proposes to purchase a property for a specified amount and under specified terms and conditions. Acceptance of the offer by the owner creates a contract binding on both parties, subject to any contingencies specified.

Open listing. A listing agreement under which any broker who sells the property is entitled to a commission. See *Exclusive agency; Exclusive right to sell.*

Origination fee. A fee charged by the lender for processing a borrower's loan application. Typically calculated in "points," as a percentage of the loan, and due to be paid at the closing.

Owner-occupied property. Property occupied by the purchaser, as opposed to investor-owned property rented to someone else.

Payment cap. A limit on the increase allowed on the monthly payments required for an adjustable-rate mortgage. If payment increases are limited but interest-rate adjustments are not, negative amortization (see above) could result.

Percentage interest. A condo or cooperative owner's proportionate share of common-area ownership, reflected in the weight of the owner's vote in the condominium or cooperative association.

Personal-use property. Vacation property that does not qualify or qualifies only partially for investment deductions allowed for rental property.

Pest inspection. A professional assessment of past or present infestations by pests, often included as one of the contingencies in a Purchase and Sale agreement.

PITI. Lender's shorthand for the key components of the monthly mortgage payment: principal, interest, taxes, and insurance.

Plot plan. A sketch showing property boundaries and the approximate location of structures on a parcel of land, required by mortgage lenders and included in the collection of documents needed before closing.

Points. The fee mortgage lenders charge for processing a loan, usually due at the closing. Each point represents one percent of the mortgage amount. As a form of prepaid interest, points charged for loans on a primary residence generally are tax deductible.

Portfolio lender. A lender who originates and retains mortgage loans rather than selling them on the secondary market.

Preapproval. The process of obtaining preliminary approval for a mortgage before the application is complete. May or may not constitute a formal commitment by the lender to make the loan. Not to be confused with prequalifying (see below).

Prepayment penalty. A fee that some lenders charge borrowers who repay their loan before the end of the designated term.

Prequalification. An informal estimate of the maximum mortgage a borrower could obtain, based on a calculation of available income and existing debt.

Principal. The original amount borrowed, on which interest is calculated.

Private mortgage insurance (PMI). An insurance policy that protects the lender should the borrower default on the mortgage. Usually required for borrowers whose down payment represents less than 20 percent of the purchase price.

Purchase and Sale agreement (P&S). A legal document requiring the purchaser to buy and the owner to sell a property under the terms and conditions specified.

Quitclaim deed. In most jurisdictions, a "what-you-see-is-what-you-get" deed. The seller relinquishes whatever interest he has in the property but makes no assurances about how good his claim to the property might be.

Radon. An odorless, colorless gas that exists naturally in the soil but can pose an environmental hazard if it becomes trapped inside a dwelling.

Rate cap. The maxium increase allowed — both annually and over the term of the loan — in the rate on an adjustable-rate mortgage.

Rate lock. The lender's agreement, usually offered for a fee, to stand by the interest rate in effect at the time the loan commitment is made, even if rates rise (or fall) between the commitment and the closing.

Real Estate Settlement Procedures Act (RESPA). A federal law that requires lenders to specify in detail all the costs involved in a real-estate closing.

Realtor. A real-estate broker who belongs to the local or state affiliate of the industry's professional trade assocation, the National Association of Realtors (NAR).

Recording fees. In a real-estate transaction, the charges for filing the documents effecting the transfer of ownership and clearing the title.

Refinancing. The process of obtaining a new mortgage, typically at a lower rate, to repay and replace an existing loan.

Rent-loss insurance. An insurance policy assuring that a landlord's rental income won't be interrupted if an existing tenant leaves or if damage to a unit prevents its rental for a period of time.

Repair. Under the tax laws, anything that maintains a property or keeps it in good working order. The cost of repairs is an allowable deduction for rental property, but not for a personal-use residence. See *Improvement.*

Replacement period. The time frame for buying another primary residence, in order to defer the gain realized on the sale of the former residence.

Reserve fund. Money that should be set aside regularly by a condominium or cooperative association to finance large capital expenditures for replacements or repairs.

Rider. A clause added to an agreement specifying additional conditions or terms.

Right of first refusal. An owner's promise to allow an individual or entity to make the first offer when a property becomes available for sale, or to match an offer submitted by another prospective buyer. First-refusal clauses are often found in cooperative documents, less frequently in condominiums.

Sales agent. In most areas, an agent licensed to sell real estate, but only when working under the supervision of a licensed broker. A broker can be the owner of a real-estate firm; a sales agent can be affiliated with a firm but cannot own it.

Secondary market. The individual and institutional investors that purchase the mortgages lenders originate.

Second mortgage. An additional loan behind the first mortgage, also secured by a property. Usually written with a higher interest rate and for a shorter term than the first mortgage.

Selling broker. In a real-estate transaction, the broker who actually finds the buyer. See *Listing broker.*

Septic system. The system that disposes of waste materials in homes without access to municipal sewer service.

Setback requirements. The local rules specifying the distances required between homes, between structures and rear lot lines, and between homes and streets.

Settlement. Another term for the real-estate closing.

"Single-entity" coverage. A master insurance policy for a condominium or cooperative, protecting all fixed parts of the building, including those located within individual units as well as those in the common areas. (See *"Bare-walls" coverage.*)

Sole ownership. Possession by a single person or entity, as distinguished from forms of joint property ownership. See *Tenancy by the entirety* and *Tenancy in common.*

Special-warranty deed. In most jurisdictions, a limited warranty of title, in which the seller promises not to file any claim and to defend the title against any claims filed by or through the seller or the seller's heirs. See *General-warranty deed; Quitclaim deed.*

Survey. A drawing that shows the legal boundaries of a property and the location of the house and other buildings on a lot. Similar to a plot plan (see above) but sometimes more precise.

Sump pump. An apparatus used to keep basements prone to wetness dry.

Tenancy by the entirety. A form of joint ownership available only to married couples, in which the ownership interest of a deceased spouse passes automatically to the surviving spouse. The arrangement normally cannot be severed during the marriage without the consent of both spouses.

Tenancy in common. A form of joint ownership by which a deceased owner's interest in the property goes to his or her heirs rather than to the other owner or owners.

Title. The legal evidence of ownership, a document containing basic evidence upon which ownership is based.

Title flaw. Any encumbrance (see above) on a title that interferes with the owner's ability to transfer ownership.

Title insurance. A form of insurance available for mortgage lenders and buyers of real property, assuring payment of legal costs for defending a claim against the title, and reimbursing for losses incurred if a competing title claim prevails.

Title search. A detailed examination of the ownership documents, undertaken to ensure that there are no liens or other encumbrances (see above) on the property and no questions about the seller's ownership claim.

Transfer fees. The fees charged by some states and some local governments whenever real property is sold. The amount is usually calculated as a percentage of the purchase price.

"Truth-in-lending" disclosure statement. A form required by federal law to be presented to the borrower, providing detailed information about the terms and costs of the loan.

UFFI (urea formaldehyde foam insulation). A once-popular home-insulation product that fell into disfavor after the discovery that improper installation could result in the potentially toxic release of formaldehyde fumes.

Underwriting guidelines. The rules and standards lenders use to determine a borrower's eligibility for a loan.

VA (Veterans Administration) loan. Mortgages issued by lenders but guaranteed by the Veterans Administration and available only to eligible veterans and their spouses and dependents.

Vacation property. A second home devoted entirely or partially to the personal use of the owner.

Variance. A limited exemption from local zoning requirements.

Ventilation. The flow of air inside a building.

Warm-air heating system. A system that uses fans or blowers to circulate warm air from the furnace throughout the house.

Warranty. A written or implied guarantee that property (including mechanical systems or appliances) is in the condition described and will perform as promised.

Index